H|8|71

Britain in
a divided Europe
1945–1970

Elisabeth Barker

Weidenfeld and Nicolson
5 Winsley Street London W1

ISBN 0 297 00401 8

Printed in Great Britain by Cox and Wyman Ltd,
London, Reading and Fakenham

Contents

PART I

Britain's European role after 1945: Its frame in place and time

1   Britain's role in Europe, 1945–70: Missing the bus?

'Great Britain has lost an empire and has not yet found a role.' This was said by Dean Acheson, former United States Secretary of State, at the American Military Academy at West Point on 5 December 1962. It has been repeated time and again, until it has almost become a meaningless jingle. It came to be widely accepted, both inside and outside Britain, as a fair summing-up of British policy, or lack of policy, towards Europe in the quarter-century following the second world war. Dean Acheson explained what he meant: 'the attempt to play a separate power role – that is, a role apart from Europe, a role based on a "special relationship" with the United States, a role based on being the head of a "commonwealth" which has no political structure, or unity, or strength . . . this role is about played out.' At the time, the British Institute of Directors called this statement a 'calculated insult to the British nation'; the Conservative Prime Minister, Harold Macmillan, said it was a mistake to underestimate the British, a mistake made by Napoleon, the Kaiser and Hitler, among others. This seemed hardly fair on Acheson, who had often proved his friendship for Britain. Many people in Britain, in the self-critical mood of the 1960s, were inclined to accept his verdict as just.

Another American politician, George Ball, a former Assistant Under-Secretary of State, took up the theme in his book, *The Discipline of Power*, published in 1968. 'The "victory" of 1945,' he wrote, 'reinforced the illusion that Britain was still a great power.' 'In 1945 the Empire still seemed more powerful than all of Western Europe – and the British believed that it was. Thus when Britain could have had the leadership of Europe for the asking, she saw no reason to ask.' George Ball, a passionate believer in the vision of a tightly integrated, ultimately federal Western Europe, then charged Britain with a whole series of errors, as he saw them. 1947: resistance to the French argument for giving a supranational structure to the Organisation for European Economic Cooperation, created to administer American aid to war-devastated Europe; 1949: veto of an ambitious plan of Jean Monnet, the French economic planner and chief prophet of 'supranationality', for a merger of the French and British economies; 1950: refusal to take part in the Schuman Plan – the plan inspired by Monnet and sponsored by the French Foreign Minister, Robert Schuman, for a European Coal and Steel Community; early 1950s: steering clear of the European Army scheme which Churchill himself had first mooted. Then, George Ball went on, came the British refusal to take part in the creation of the Common Market – the European Economic Community – through the Rome Treaty of 1957. This, in spite of the fact that, as George Ball commented, the Suez affair of 1956 had made Britain look less and less like an independent 'great power'. 'The "special relationship" with America turned out to be not so special after all: and the Commonwealth came close to fragmentation after the strain.'

It is easy to interpret the history of Britain's relationship with the rest of Europe, between 1945 and 1970, as a short-sighted and arrogant failure to see that Britain's future lay in pooling its resources, and merging some part of its national independence, with other West European states, in particular, the Common Market Six. British politicians, on this interpretation, clung far too long to an unreal dream of world-wide empire and an equally unreal dream of a privileged and influential friendship with the strongest world power, the United States.

It is true that those British politicians who had held responsible office during the 1939–45 war – in which Britain played a world-wide role and was, at least in theory, one of the victors – found it difficult to adjust to a much narrower role on a much more limited stage. This applied to Churchill, Eden and Macmillan among the Conservatives; Attlee, Bevin and Morrison among the Labour leaders. In spite of party differences there was a great deal of common ground between them: in particular, the theory of the three interlocking or overlapping circles – Britain's link with Europe, its link with the Commonwealth and its link with the United States. Yet all were prepared to throw over the traditional British policy of trying to maintain a balance of power in Europe without making any permanent commitments to any side. Two devastating wars had proved its feebleness. They were willing and eager to make long-term binding commitments in Europe. But all instinctively shied away from merging Britain in a federal or supranational European structure – except for the youngest of them, Macmillan, who, in 1961, took the revolutionary decision to negotiate for membership of the supranational Common Market. But even Macmillan had very little enthusiasm for its supranational aspect.

Ten years earlier, Herbert Morrison, during his brief spell as Foreign Secretary in the Labour Government, had resisted the pleas of the West German Chancellor, Dr Adenauer, that Britain should feel itself 'to be a part of Europe, not merely a neighbour', by saying that although Britain was now fully committed to the defence of Western Europe, 'it was a fact that Britain was an island and that was not the fault of the British; that was the way God had arranged things and the British had to make the best of it.' Morrison added that there were also certain constitutional traditions in Britain that were not always understood on the continent; the position of parliament was stronger than in other European countries.[1]

In January 1952, Eden, speaking at Columbia University in the United States, explained his resistance to 'the frequent suggestions that the United Kingdom should join a federation on the continent of Europe.' 'This,' he said, 'is something which we know in our bones we cannot do.' Eden went on: 'our thoughts move across the seas to the many communities in which our people play their part, in every corner of the world. These are our family ties. That is our life. . . .'[2] In May 1953, Churchill, explaining why Britain would not join the proposed European Defence Community nor a federal European system, said: 'we feel that we have a special relation with both. This can be expressed by the preposition "with" but not "of". We are with them but not of them.'

The war generation of politicians therefore believed that although in the post-war world Britain should and must, in its own interest, play an active role *in* Europe, it should also play a role *outside* it, and must remain free to play this extra-European role.

It could fairly be argued that until the early 1960s, and perhaps even later, British politicians of whatever party exaggerated the extra-European role which Britain was capable of playing. Some of them sometimes had nostalgic dreams of British importance which amused or irritated critical Americans or continental Europeans. But they were not the only West European politicians to indulge in such dreams. De Gaulle also had his dreams at a time when the British were drastically cutting down their ideas of their own importance.

The particular charge made against British political leaders of the period 1945–70 was that until 1961 they failed to 'enter Europe' or to join in 'making Europe', and that after 1961 they tried to 'enter Europe' in a half-hearted or insincere way. This was clearly what Acheson had in mind when he delivered his verdict on Britain.

'Europe' in this context was used in a very special and somewhat misleading sense. It meant the six continental countries which created the European Coal and Steel Community, the European Economic Community and Euratom, and which in the early 1950s made an abortive effort to form a European Defence Community. If Russia is left out of account, the Six included the three biggest and strongest European countries except Britain – France, West Germany and Italy. Nevertheless, the Six formed only one part of Europe. Of the non-Communist states of post-1945 Europe, twice as many were outside the community of the Six as inside it, with a total population only a little less than the total population of the Six (around 160 million in 1950).

There were also the Communist-ruled countries of Eastern Europe – the six states which came to be allied with the Soviet Union in the Warsaw Pact, and Yugoslavia and Albania which broke with Moscow. Their total population was around 100 million. They still regarded themselves as Europeans, as they showed in the 1960s when they pressed for a European security conference. They were certainly part of 'Europe' in the ordinary sense of the word. The Soviet Union, too, claimed to be not only a world superpower but also a European power with special rights in Eastern Europe. It was in any case clearly a major factor in European affairs.

The 'Europe' of the Six which Britain failed to 'enter' was therefore a good deal less than half of 'Europe' as most Europeans understood the word. Some of its creators saw in it the kernel of a much wider European community which would embrace first the other non-communist countries and later the East Europeans. But though the Six developed into a powerful and thriving economic group, they failed to achieve political unity among themselves or to open their community to wider European membership. In 1970 they still formed 'Europe' only in a specialised and narrow sense.

Britain's policies in Europe between 1945 and 1970 cannot therefore be seen purely in the context of its relations with the six Common Market countries. They have to be set in the much wider context of the whole of Europe, both West and East, and the enormous changes which came about in Europe as a result of the 1939–45 war.

One of these was the European countries' loss of economic and military power in relation to the outside world. Europe's leading role in the world, unquestioned before the 1914–18 war, already slipping during the inter-war years, was destroyed by the 1939–45 war. It was not only Britain which lost an empire; several other European countries also lost theirs. Both economically and militarily, the European countries found themselves overshadowed by the superpowers, the United States and the Soviet Union; by 1970 they were also dazzled by Japan's economic achievements and watchful of Communist China's huge economic and military potential. In the quarter-century after the second world war all European countries had, in one way or another and in varying degrees, to make big adjustments in their attitudes towards the outside world.

The other far-reaching change brought about by the second world war was the division of Europe. This, unlike the decline in Europe's world role, was not part of a continuing and probably inevitable process. It was a direct result of the military operations leading to Hitler's defeat, which brought Soviet armed forces into the heart of Europe. It was not even the line marking the extreme western limit of Soviet military conquest in Europe; except in Austria, Soviet forces did not advance so far west.

In central Europe, the post-war dividing line resulted from pro-posals drawn up in 1943 by a committee of British planners, known as the Attlee Committee, which provided for the joint occupation of Germany by Britain, the United States and the Soviet Union, each with its own zone. The Attlee Committee's proposals on occupation zones were accepted first by President Roosevelt and later, at the Yalta three-power conference, by Stalin. After the defeat of Hitler, the Western allies dutifully withdrew from their military positions to the agreed border between the Soviet occupation zone and the western occupation zones: this later became the frontier between the German Federal Republic (West Germany) and the German Democratic Republic (East Germany). To the south and south-east, the dividing line between West and East ran roughly along the line to which the Soviet armies had advanced in pursuit of the Germans; this was adjusted in favour of the Soviet Union in Czechoslovakia, and in favour of the Western allies in Austria, which was freed from all foreign troops ten years later.

7

Britain in a divided Europe

The East–West dividing line, drawn by the accident or make-shift arrangements of war, soon became an impassible frontier which split Europe in an entirely new and entirely unnatural way. However disastrous the European wars of the preceding century or more, peacetime intercourse between European countries had been relatively free and open. The post-1945 East–West frontier interrupted normal relations in almost every field: political, economic, cultural, and above all freedom of movement and communication. This dangerous unnatural condition affected all Europeans in varying degrees, but most painfully the 100 million or so East Europeans who found themselves under Soviet overlordship.

British political leaders, during the period 1945–70, tried in various ways, with small success, to grapple with the problem of lowering or piercing the East–West barrier, either by standing up to Moscow or by conciliating Moscow. In the early post-war years, their first aim was to stop any further advance westwards of Soviet power; but even at that stage they tried to keep open East–West communications. As the period 1945–70 closed, this was still the most difficult problem facing Europe – far more difficult than the problem of West European economic integration. The Soviet invasion of Czechoslovakia in 1968 showed that the Soviet Union was determined to keep the barrier impassible. The strategic arms limitation talks (SALT) between the Soviet Union and the United States led in 1970 to some fear among Europeans that Washington might be willing to give a tacit pledge of permanent non-interference and disinterest in Soviet-dominated Eastern Europe, in return for a reliable understanding with Moscow over nuclear armaments.

In 1945, Britain was still counted as one of the 'big three' – the war victors in Europe. By 1970, Britain had no special status in the problem of East–West relations in Europe, except for two things. It was a second-class nuclear power (for what that was worth in terms of political influence, which was uncertain), and, under wartime agreements, it was one of the four powers with special responsibilities for Germany as a whole and for Berlin. Neither was a strong card. In any case by 1970 it was obvious that, among the West European countries, it was West Germany which had to take the lead in lowering East–West barriers in Europe. Yet Britain still had a part to play.

The framework of Britain's European policies between 1945 and 1970 was therefore the *whole* of Europe. And an important yardstick for measuring the worth of these policies is whether they were directed only to making Western Europe safe, strong and prosperous, or whether they also looked beyond the East–West dividing line to the future of a wider Europe. This too is the fair measure of Britain's European role – or failure to find one.

2 Britain in Europe: Traditional attitudes

When General de Gaulle was discussing a Franco–Soviet treaty with Stalin in December 1944, he said that history showed that Britain was incapable of acting decisively or quickly. This was partly because of its geographical position and partly because of the need to consult the Dominions, which were far away and had diverging interests. In 1914, de Gaulle said, Britain had hesitated before coming into the war, and acted only because Belgium was invaded. If Britain decided to go to war in September 1939, it was after a series of capitulations. For these reasons, de Gaulle preferred to conclude a treaty with the Soviet Union before concluding one with Britain.[3]

Seven years later, Herbert Morrison, as Labour Foreign Secretary, tried to defend British policy against criticism from Dr Adenauer by explaining its historical background. He said that in the nineteenth century Britain did not feel itself a part of Europe. It had pursued a policy of the European balance of power, but had reserved the right to keep out of military conflicts or to intervene on either of two sides in a war that broke out in Europe, guided by the British interest and not that of the well-being of Europe. It was one of the consequences of this policy that in 1914 the German Kaiser did not know until the last moment how Britain would behave in a conflict.[4]

Morrison presented pre-1945 British policy in this light because he wanted to show the strong contrast with the post-1945 policy, by which Britain had entered into binding defence commitments towards European countries and had established economic partnership with them. This, he said, represented an enormous step forward compared with the past, perhaps as great as that taken by the United States in its post-war cooperation with other countries and continents.

Morrison was making a valid point. In the wars against Napoleon Britain had come to play a leading part in alliance with other European states. In 1815 it emerged from these wars as one of the four victorious powers (the others being Austria, Russia and Prussia). These four powers concluded a twenty-year treaty of friendship and said they aimed to keep the peace settlement intact and to maintain the Concert of Europe through 'government by conferences'. But within seven years Britain had drawn apart from the other three because it did not want to join with them in interfering in the internal affairs of other countries in order to suppress political upheavals. In its foreign policy, it resumed an independent course. In Europe, Britain soon found itself more in sympathy with its former enemy, France, than with its former allies.

At the same time, British interest was increasingly focused on the world outside Europe. Britain's world-wide naval supremacy, following the Napoleonic wars, could be used to protect and foster overseas trade. Other assets were a far-stretching colonial empire, which was a useful source of raw materials, a very big merchant marine and the fact that by the end of the Napoleonic wars London had replaced Amsterdam as the banking centre of Europe. In 1819 the Bank of England's notes were the only ones that circulated throughout Europe at their face value in gold.[5]

In these circumstances, it was not surprising that during the nineteenth century the British looked out towards remoter continents rather than into Europe. From the second half of the century onwards, however, they showed great sensitivity to events in south-east Europe, where the decay of the Turkish Ottoman Empire and Russia's urge to expand south-westwards towards the Mediterranean combined to produce an unstable and sometimes explosive situation. The British, fearing that a Russian irruption into the Eastern Mediterranean would threaten their imperial interests, tended to back the decaying Ottoman Empire against Russia – for instance in the ill-conceived and ill-executed Crimean war of 1854–6. But a policy of propping up a highly reactionary Empire did not fit well with the other British tendency to support liberal movements, or what would later have been called 'national liberation movements', in Europe. So from time to time the British Government publicly reproached the Ottoman Empire for its behaviour towards its European subjects and urged it to reform its methods. Yet the fear of Russian expansion in the Balkans and the Eastern Mediterranean persisted and, after lying dormant for many years, it re-awoke in the second world war when Stalin revealed his aims.

In the early years of the twentieth century, however, it was overlaid by fear of Austria–Hungary's expansionist policy in south-east Europe. This new British fear would have been much less sharp if

Austria had not been supported and pushed along by Germany. It was around the turn of the century that Britain had become aware of the threat from the young, united, prosperous, dynamic, militarily strong Germany, determined to outbid Britain in naval power, seeking a dominant role to play both inside and outside Europe. The British were uncertain in their reactions to this new phenomenon in Europe; they were seriously worried; they were admiring; they were reluctant to regard war against Germany as necessary or inevitable. So, in spite of the Entente Cordiale with France from 1904 onwards, Britain hesitated to take a clear-cut stand when, in the summer of 1914, Germany decided to back Austria–Hungary's expansionist policy in south-east Europe with armed force.

How much blame Britain should therefore bear for the outbreak of the first world war is still an open question. Morrison's remarks to Adenauer in 1951 suggested that at least in his generation, a sense of Britain's guilt, or share of guilt, still lingered on.

There was a far more clear-cut reason for a British feeling of guilt about the circumstances which led up to the second world war. After 1918 the British soon found it difficult to keep up vengeful feelings towards the Germans, or to give whole-hearted sympathy to French demands for retribution and repression of the German people and for cast-iron security against renewed German aggression.

The rise of the two European dictators, first Mussolini and then Hitler, produced confused and ambiguous reactions in Britain. Some politicians advocated conciliation because they thought Britain needed time to rearm. This was a defensible policy, if not necessarily a wise one; and it was the defence most often put forward for Chamberlain's appeasement policy and for the 1938 Munich Agreement which led quickly to the destruction of Czechoslovakia. Yet it is clear that Chamberlain, at least up to March 1939, believed, with curious naïve vanity, that he could reach a fair and satisfactory settlement with Hitler by means of personal contact, sweet reasonableness and persuasion. (Chamberlain was the first British politician to practise 'summitry' – a practice in which he was followed, in varying circumstances, by Churchill, Eden, Macmillan and Wilson.)

Chamberlain's summit meetings with Hitler failed – except in one respect. At Munich Chamberlain deprived Hitler of the war he wanted to wage against Czechoslovakia, and forced him to obtain the Sudeten German territories by diplomatic means instead of the military means which he would have preferred. He thereby postponed the outbreak of war in Europe for a year – though whether or not this benefited Britain and the Western powers long remained in dispute. But in achieving this, Chamberlain convinced Hitler that he had nothing to fear from the West. It was true that at the height of the crisis, Chamberlain did deliver a clear warning to Hitler. He sent him a formal message that if Germany attacked Czechoslovakia, and France, in pursuance of its treaty obligations to Czechoslovakia, became engaged in a conflict with Germany, then Britain would feel obliged to support France. (Britain had no treaty with Czechoslovakia.) This message, however, seemed to have very little effect on Hitler except to make him angry. In any case, its impact was almost cancelled out by the fact that Chamberlain simultaneously exerted heavy pressure on Czechoslovakia to give up the territories Hitler wanted, without resistance.

In the circumstances, it was not surprising that when, in the following March, Chamberlain joined the French Government in guaranteeing Poland immediate support if attacked, this checked Hitler only briefly. He probably did not take it very seriously. The subsequent Anglo–French guarantees to Rumania and Greece against aggression had still less effect. The Munich agreement had badly damaged the credibility of British warnings to Hitler and thus it was that, undeterred by Chamberlain, in the end Hitler had his war.

In fairness to Chamberlain – and to Britain – it should be said that very probably Chamberlain could not have stopped him, once Germany had been allowed to rearm. Moreover, responsibility for repeated failures to check Hitler, during the 1930s, must be shared by Britain and France – even though de Gaulle, in his *Memoirs*, laid the blame for French passivity on the fact that Britain did not 'take the initiative'.[6] Nevertheless the whole Munich business left many people in Britain with a sense of guilt, or at the very least, a feeling that the kind of diplomacy which Britain practised in the 1930s was feeble and inadequate. Something firmer and clearer would be needed in the future. This feeling had its influence on British policy in Europe in the post-1945 period.

There remained the question whether Britain's hesitations and ambiguities, before the two world wars which did such grave harm to Europe, stemmed from a lack of interest in Europe or a sense that Britain did not belong to Europe. It was true before the 1914–18 war that Britain did not want to get involved in quarrels between continental European states unless it felt that its own national (or imperial) interests were threatened. It was also true that in the 1920s and 1930s the British – ignoring the fact that the 1914–18 war had been sparked off in a south-east European town, Sarajevo – showed remarkably little interest in Eastern Europe. The countries of this vast area were generally regarded as pleasingly exotic but painfully backward, both economically and politically; as incapable of Western-type democracy, allowing themselves to be ruled by dicta-torially-inclined Kings or Generals or Admirals. Czechoslovakia was admitted to be an exception. There seemed to be little understanding in Britain that the various peasant parties of Eastern Europe – the natural political representatives of the majority of the people – had little chance of exercising power unless they could show some hope of curing economic evils; and that needed outside help. France maintained political links with the three Little Entente countries, Czechoslovakia, Rumania and Yugoslavia, but allowed them to melt away when serious trouble came. Britain had no commitments until 1939. Both Britain and France allowed Hitler to carry out the economic and political penetration of Eastern Europe unhindered during the 1930s, and thereby to prepare the ground for war. They also made it possible for Stalin to claim that, in imposing Communist rule after the war, he was sweeping away reactionary, unrepresentative regimes.

However, it cannot be said that Britain stood aloof from Europe before either war: in fact, before both, British diplomacy had been very active in Europe. The real charge against Britain was not 'un-Europeanness' so much as a mistaken belief that skilful diplomacy could be an efficient substitute for solid military alliances or for forward-looking economic policies.

Another difficulty was that the traditional style of British dip-lomacy was often misunderstood in other countries. Lord Strang, who served in the Foreign Office for over thirty years and was Permanent Under-Secretary in the post-war years, described it in his book, *Britain in World Affairs*: 'it is a policy that usually prefers compromise to victory; that seeks by mutual concession to reach durable understandings; that will prefer not to allow questions of prestige to interfere unduly with practical diplomacy for concrete ends. . . . It is this conciliatory quality in British foreign policy which is often a cause of concern to foreign governments, and indeed of unjust suspicion.'[7] From 1914 onwards, the dangers of the British method were obvious. International relations seemed to have moved into a phase in which conciliatory diplomacy was often interpreted as an act of submission, and that occasional 'aggressive displays', or at least displays of preparedness for war, were necessary in order to prevent real aggression.

In the post-1945 period, British political leaders thought that they had learned from the mistakes and disasters of the past and were launching new policies and methods, especially in Europe: permanent involvement in European affairs, binding long-term commitments, full-scale military alliances going as far as military integration in peacetime, economic cooperation. Some continental leaders recognised that the British were trying to strike out along new paths. Others, such as de Gaulle, continued to see Britain as the country which, throughout the history of Europe, had always refused both to allow 'the Continent' to unite or to merge itself with it.[8]

3 Britain in Europe: The heritage of the second world war

British policies towards Europe after 1945 had their roots in the war years. In spite of the change of government in 1945, there was a great degree of continuity in foreign policy. This was partly because the Labour leaders had served with Churchill and Eden in the War Cabinet from 1940 on, and partly because the biggest political issues of the post-war years were already present, in some form or other, during the war. One was Britain's relationship with its wartime European allies. Another was Britain's confrontation with Soviet expansionist aims in Europe. There was of course also the problem of Germany; but in this case there was very little continuity between the Roosevelt–Churchill 'unconditional surrender' policy of the war years, or the various allied plans for the dismemberment or 'pastoralization' of Germany, and the policy which the United States and Britain actually followed towards Germany after 1945. Post-war economic realities destroyed the assumptions behind the wartime planning for Germany.

Since Britain's so-called 'special relationship' with the United States was later thought to debar it from 'entry into Europe', it is relevant that this had its roots in the war years, even in the period before the United States was actually at war.

Britain and the European Allies
As Hitler over-ran one European country after another, in 1940 and 1941, European leaders, sometimes also Kings and Queens, sought refuge in London. In most cases, they set up governments in exile, inevitably working closely with the British Foreign Office, and, in so far as they were able to carry on the fight, with the British armed services and merchant marine. The communications between the exiled leaders and their own countries, whether by broadcasts or by secret means, passed through British channels; where it was possible to organise resistance in the occupied countries, this normally required close cooperation between the exiled governments or authorities and the British Special Operations Executive. All these

16

activities meant that there had to be a network of everyday contacts between the British and the exiled Europeans; because Britain, as the host country and the undefeated ally, had the upper hand, there was inevitably some friction.

Nevertheless, these working relations of the war years brought a wide range of British men and women into much closer touch with people from European countries from Norway to Albania, and with their outlook, way of life and problems. These working relations went beyond purely political or military matters. For instance, there was a conference of Allied Ministers of Education which met in London from 1943 to 1945, mainly to plan for post-war needs in education and scholarship. At a purely personal level, as men and women escaped from the occupied countries and came to Britain, many acquaintances – and some marriages – were made. This was also true of German and Italian prisoners-of-war who did agricultural and other work in the latter part of the war. A good many of the wartime exiles, whether from necessity or choice, settled in Britain after the war (especially the Poles). In all, the wartime experience made the British more conscious of their fellow-Europeans and European affairs.

In one sense, this wartime period was stimulating and pleasing. From the time of the fall of France in mid-1940, London became the capital of Europe – that is, of anti-Hitler Europe. For the people of the occupied countries, Churchill was the acknowledged European leader. London was the centre of the war effort in Europe, as well as sheltering the exiled politicians and monarchs. The BBC broadcasts to Europe had very great prestige, in both occupied and enemy countries. The BBC also made it possible for the exiles to speak directly to their own people. With the over-running of Yugoslavia and Greece in April 1941, exiled politicians and Kings from south-east Europe accepted British hospitality and political leadership.

The sensation of being at the very heart of European affairs, and of a widely-spread European alliance, was new and flattering for the British, at many levels. But it was very often linked with a totally contrary sensation, which in its own way was equally flattering to the British ego. It was summed up in an anecdote of Eden's. In his memoirs, Eden wrote about his 'mood of exultation' during May and June 1940: 'it was about this time that Churchill told me that he had seen the King, who said that I had seemed in wonderful spirits. When His Majesty asked me why, I had said: "Now we are all alone, Sir.

Britain in a divided Europe

We haven't an ally left." ' This feeling was a very general one, and was perhaps less arrogant than it appeared. It was part of the odd, totally illogical feeling of euphoria which came over people in Britain in the summer of 1940 and enabled them to face the Battle of Britain and the threat of invasion almost in holiday mood. It revealed more about the British psychological reaction to great stress than about the British attitude towards the European allies. The fact that Polish and Czechoslovak pilots took part in the Battle of Britain alongside British pilots, for instance, was good for British morale and was appreciated.

Although some of the allies – notably the French, the Poles, the Greeks and the Yugoslavs – faced Britain with a series of appallingly difficult political problems as the war went on, and although the British were no doubt at times over-bearing or impatient, Churchill and Eden took these problems extremely seriously and did not under-estimate their importance. Nor, however sharp their clashes with de Gaulle, as leader of the Free French, did they ever doubt that France was the closest and most important of the European allies, in the long-term post-war context, as well as for war purposes.

That was why, when the fall of France seemed very close, Churchill impulsively blessed the plan for a union of Britain and France in a single State, with a common parliament and common citizenship. This had been inspired by Jean Monnet (who was then in London in the French economic mission, together with his colleague, René Pleven (later a French Prime Minister)) and had been backed by de Gaulle. The immediate aim of the plan was to strengthen the hand of those members of the French Government who wanted to carry on the war, if not on the soil of France, then outside it. But the long-term aim also appealed to Churchill and his government. Attlee later described how Churchill brought the draft plan to the Cabinet. They studied it silently. 'The difficulties were apparent, but the need for a gesture of high drama even more so. As they read, the imaginations of all the members of the War Cabinet were caught by the possibili-ties inherent in a proposal that went much further than anything before in the history of wartime alliances. . . . Unanimously, after only a brief discussion, the War Cabinet approved.'[9]

The plan was abortive because it came too late to hold the French Government together. Yet even if it had an urgent operational purpose, and even if, at that agonising moment, the British were for once in a mood for high drama, the members of the Cabinet, of all

18

three political parties, must surely have taken some serious account of its long-term political implications, both for Britain and for the Commonwealth. They would hardly have accepted without hesitation the idea of full union with any country except France.

Throughout all the difficulties and bitter quarrels with de Gaulle which followed, both over questions of military operations and over the political status of de Gaulle's National Committee, the idea of France as Britain's natural and inevitable partner persisted. Over the immediate wartime problems Eden was often at loggerheads with Churchill who, he thought, gave way too easily to Roosevelt's views, especially his dislike of de Gaulle.

Already in March 1943, Eden, during a visit to Washington, found that his policies were at odds with those of the United States. The Americans did not want to see a sole French authority established, preferring to deal with individuals, and content to see de Gaulle and his rival, General Giraud, 'fall apart'. This, Eden wrote in his memoirs, was contrary to his own doctrine; the British Government would much prefer to deal with a single French authority. Nor did he like an American proposal that Allied forces landing in France should administer liberated French territory. In Eden's words, 'it seemed to me that Roosevelt wanted to hold the strings of France's future in his own hands so that he could decide that country's fate'. (Eden did not however take seriously a remark which Roosevelt made at a private dinner, that after the war, armaments in Europe should be held by Britain, the United States and Russia; the smaller powers should have nothing more dangerous than rifles.)[10]

In July 1943, Eden set out his ideas on paper for Churchill's benefit. He said there were grounds for believing that some at any rate of the governing authorities in Washington had little belief in France's future and did not wish to see France restored as a great imperial power. British policy must be different, Eden argued. Britain's main problem after the war would be to contain Germany. Britain's treaty with the Soviet Union would therefore need to be balanced by an understanding with a powerful France in the West. 'These arrangements,' Eden wrote, 'will be indispensable for our security whether or not the United States collaborate in the maintenance of peace on this side of the Atlantic.' 'In dealing with European problems of the future,' Eden went on, 'we are likely to have to work more closely with France even than with the United States. . . . Europe expects us to have a European policy of our own, and to state it. That policy must aim at the restoration of the independence of the smaller European allies and of the greatness of France.'[11]

Churchill oscillated between a real love for France and extreme reluctance to quarrel with Roosevelt. On various occasions he tried to persuade Roosevelt to look on the French, and de Gaulle in particular, more kindly. He seemed to have little success. In June 1944, when the Allied forces landed in France, Eden, Attlee and Bevin combined to urge Churchill to recognise the Provisional Government which de Gaulle had formed. Churchill, who had himself often been infuriated by the General, stuck to Roosevelt's anti-de Gaulle line. In the end he came round to the view of his Cabinet colleagues and tried tactfully to change Roosevelt's opposition to recognition. In the end Roosevelt jumped in and recognised the French Provisional Government first, leaving Churchill lagging behind.

Once this hurdle was cleared, there was the problem of securing the agreement of the Americans and Russians to a French share in the task of occupying Germany. At the three-power Yalta conference in February 1945 (de Gaulle never forgot nor forgave the exclusion of France), Roosevelt made what Churchill called 'a momentous announcement': the United States would take all reasonable steps to preserve peace, but not at the expense of keeping a large army in Europe, 3000 miles from home; the American occupation would therefore be limited to two years. Churchill saw that in this case Britain would have to occupy the entire western part of Germany single-handed. He therefore pressed for French help in the task. 'To give France a zone of occupation was by no means the end of the matter. Germany would surely rise again, and while the Americans could always go home, the French had to live next door to her. A strong France was vital not only to Europe but to Great Britain. . . .'[12] In the end the French occupation zone was agreed, but too late to avoid leaving France with a sense of resentment. In the post-war period, de Gaulle remembered the occasions when Churchill had – as he saw it – let him down, rather than the occasions when the British had shown their friendship and loyalty to France.

Planning for Western Europe

In the latter part of the war, a certain amount of post-war planning for Western Europe went on in London, in a very tentative way. In July 1944 Eden threw cold water on a plan for a closely integrated 'Western Union', primarily economic, to be formed by Britain and the West European allies, which had been suggested in a dispatch from the British Representative with the French National Committee in Algeria, Duff Cooper. Eden was worried about it because the American Government was suspicious of any proposal tending to divide up the world into blocs and feared that their formation would encourage isolationism in the United States. Eden also seemed to think that a 'Western Union' might conflict with the Anglo-Soviet alliance, which – whatever his suspicions of Stalin's expansionist aims – he expected to be a vital element in British policy in Europe in the post-war world.

Four months later, however, the Foreign Office and the Chiefs of Staff were discussing a possible West European defence organisation. Churchill was sceptical about it, arguing that all the West European countries were hopelessly weak and asking how Britain could possibly afford to defend them until a strong French army had been re-created. Eden agreed that it would be absurd for Britain to enter into any commitments for the defence of Norway, Denmark, Belgium or Holland, except in conjunction with the French. But he argued that the lesson of the disasters of 1940 was the need to build up a common defence association in Western Europe, which would prevent another Hitler, 'whensoever he might come', from pursuing a policy of 'one by one'. The best way of creating such an association, Eden said, would obviously be to build up France. This could lead to a system whereby France in the first place and the smaller West European allies in the second place agreed to organise their defences together with Britain according to some common plan. Eden concluded: 'I think we should have to reconcile ourselves to making a rather larger land contribution than the famous two divisions which was all we had to offer last time. . . .'

Churchill, who had little time for post-war planning, remained un-enthusiastic. He was worried about the possible impact on the Soviet Union and the Soviet war effort. In the same month, November 1944, he sent a message to Stalin playing down 'talk in the press about a Western bloc,' and stressing the value he attached to the Anglo-Soviet Treaty.[13]

However, in December 1944, when de Gaulle visited Moscow, Stalin questioned him about 'the Western bloc'. De Gaulle, apparently with deliberate vagueness, spoke of possible 'arrangements' with the Benelux countries and Italy, and eventually with Britain. But he made quite clear his existing differences with Britain; he rejected firmly a suggestion of Churchill's for an Anglo-Soviet-French Pact which Stalin transmitted to him; he concluded the French-Soviet Treaty, and took no action on a treaty with Britain, mainly because of the bitter Anglo-French quarrel over Syria and Lebanon.

The discussions of the British planners in London in 1944 foreshadowed the post-war Western Union, later expanded into Western European Union, in which Britain promised to keep rather more than the 'two divisions' of 1939 permanently stationed on the mainland of Europe.

The Allies in Eastern and South-Eastern Europe
Britain's problems with its Polish, Yugoslav and Greek allies were in varying degrees a part of the wider problem of relations with the Soviet Union. Towards Poland, the British felt they had a special obligation. It was in fulfilment of their guarantee to Poland that they had declared war (even if, from the Polish point of view, this was at the time a purely platonic gesture). They felt committed to the restoration of an independent Poland with a representative government, in which members of the exiled Polish Government in London should have a fair part; they did not feel the same obligation to restore the pre-1939 frontiers of Poland. As the war progressed, the fate of Poland became the main bone of contention between Britain and the Soviet Union.

Towards Greece, the British felt they had obligations of traditional sentiment and of admiration and gratitude for Greek resistance to the Italians and Germans in 1940 and 1941; moreover, Britain had suffered 40,000 casualties fighting in Greece in 1941 and considered that it therefore had a stake in the country's future. Britain's strategic interest in the Eastern Mediterranean and memories of past Russian efforts to penetrate the area may also have played a part. The immediate British aim was the restoration of Greece with guaranteed freedom to form a Western-style democratic government. The preponderant role played in the resistance movement in occupied Greece by the Communist-run organisation EAM/ELAS (the National Liberation Movement and its guerrilla units), and its determination to swallow up or destroy rival non-Communist organisations and to monopolise British supplies of arms and money, presented a very unpleasant problem to the British Government and to the British officers sent into Greece to maintain contact with the resistance. Churchill complicated matters still more by his sense of personal loyalty to the exiled King George II of Greece, who was unpopular. The Greek Communists, by presenting themselves as patriotic anti-monarchists, could win support from non-Communists. So, within weeks of the liberation of Greece in 1944, the country was plunged into civil war with a small British force trying to prevent a complete takeover by EAM/ELAS, while the Soviet Union remained passive and neutral. After a dramatic Christmas visit by Churchill and Eden, a settlement was reached; EAM/ELAS temporarily gave up the struggle, though they resumed it three years later. British intervention was condemned in the American press as old-fashioned imperialism and strongly criticised by a large section of the British Labour Party. But Churchill stood firm and in effect kept Greece within the Western sphere of influence.

Yugoslavia presented Britain with a very special problem. When, on 27 March 1941, the Yugoslav General Simović and a group of officers deposed the Prince Regent Paul, who had signed a pact with Hitler, Churchill welcomed the event in ringing terms. Yugoslavia, he said, had found its soul. Four days later, a British general and a British diplomat arrived secretly in Belgrade and had an elaborately concealed meeting with Simović and his colleagues, with the aim of concerting military action if and when Yugoslavia was attacked by the Germans. This was followed by an equally secret meeting between Eden (who was in Greece), the Greek General Papagos and a Yugoslav General on the Yugoslav-Greek frontier. But on purely practical grounds, it proved impossible to draw up a joint military plan. So when the Germans attacked Yugoslavia early in April, Britain was unable to give any help to the Yugoslavs, though British troops were fighting alongside the Greeks on the mainland and in Crete.

On the basis of this very flimsy form of alliance, Britain found itself providing hospitality to Simović, the young King Peter, and a group of disunited Yugoslav politicians: the Serbs and Croats were particularly at loggerheads, as they had been in peacetime Yugoslavia. There was also a group of fire-eating young officers of extreme Serb nationalist views, who had considerable influence with Simović and infuriated the Croats.

The British aimed to encourage resistance in Yugoslavia to the German and Italian occupying forces, and to work with the exiled group (or groups) in London for this purpose. They soon made contact with the Serbian Colonel Mihailović, who was strongly backed by the young officers in London. However, the Colonel did very little and seemed more hostile to the Croats (with some reason, given the wartime atrocities against the Serbs of the Croat Ustaši, a pseudo-fascist organisation) than he was to the Germans. During 1942 broadcasts were heard in London from a station called Radio Free Yugoslavia praising the resistance achievements of Tito and the Partisans. Since the station could be located in the Soviet Union, it was clear that they were communists. In the spring of 1943 Britain sent in officers who made contact with the Partisans and reported that they were indeed carrying out effective resistance to the Germans and Italians, even if they were also fighting from time to time against Serbian bands vaguely owing allegiance to Mihailović. All the elements were present for a civil war between the Communist-led Partisans and Mihailović's Serbian nationalist movement.

Since, however, Tito's Partisans were really causing trouble to the Germans (and, until the Italian surrender, the Italians), Churchill followed a different policy from the one he followed in Greece. Britain backed Tito with arms, medical supplies and above all with good publicity. It tried to bring about a reconciliation between Tito and Mihailović, but this was a total failure. There was also the problem of King Peter and the Yugoslav Government in London. Churchill, at a personal meeting in the Mediterranean, managed to persuade Tito to agree to a face-saving coalition government under a non-Communist Prime Minister acceptable to Tito. King Peter was put into political cold storage. This arrangement was acceptable to the Soviet Union. It lasted only briefly and in practice, once Yugoslavia was free of the Germans, Tito's forces were in control of the country. (There were also Soviet forces in Yugoslavia at that moment, but Tito seemed to keep political authority effectively in his own hands.) There was no civil war. Yugoslavia simply became a communist-governed State, practising communism according to the strictest tenets of the faith, in a way which the Soviet Union found first slightly ridiculous, then irritating and finally something of a menace.

Of Italy, Churchill had a very low opinion, even after the removal of Mussolini in 1943 and the armistice which followed. However, when he visited Italy in August 1944, he changed his mind; according to his own later account, he had always had a great regard for the Italian people, except when Britain was actually fighting them! From then on he took up a friendly and protective attitude towards Italy, determined to safeguard it against Soviet trouble-making and

Yugoslav territorial claims. Since Britain was playing the chief military role in Italy in the long struggle against the Germans, he considered Italy, for wartime purposes at least, as firmly within the British sphere of interest.

Anglo-Soviet Relations in the War Years

Relations between Britain and the Soviet Union, during the war, were conducted on two levels. Churchill, although he had favoured British intervention in Russia after the Bolshevik Revolution of 1917, was determined to establish the closest possible military partnership with the Soviet Union and, for this purpose, to establish good personal relations with Stalin. This was at the top level. At a slightly lower level, there was a political confrontation between Britain and the Soviet Union throughout the war years. At both levels, relations were always uneasy.

In June and July 1939 Britain had negotiated with the Soviet Union for a treaty of alliance, in the hope that a clear alignment of Britain, France and the Soviet Union would stop Hitler from starting war. Because, in late August 1939, the Soviet Union signed a treaty with Germany instead, there were doubts whether the Soviet leaders were ever sincere in their negotiations with the British and the French. William Strang (later Lord Strang) who, as a senior Foreign Office official, conducted the negotiations for Britain, wrote later that there was little doubt that the Russians thought it would be in their interest to reach agreement with Britain, and that the negotiations were seriously intended.[14] The trouble was that the Russians would not sign a treaty unless it were accompanied by a detailed military convention on the methods by which the Western powers would help Russia against both direct and indirect aggression. In particular the Soviet Union demanded the right to send troops into and through Poland. Poland refused to agree to this, fearing that if Soviet troops once entered the areas ceded by Moscow to Poland in 1921, they would never leave. This was the immediate cause of the breakdown, though other Soviet demands for precise military commitments might also have caused trouble.

Even if the Soviet Union had been sincere in entering negotiations with Britain, the British people as a whole were nevertheless painfully shocked by the Soviet-German Pact of August 1939 – the public perhaps more than the Government. Then came the carve-up of conquered Poland, with the Soviet Union taking the Eastern half with Hitler's blessing. At the end of November 1939 came the Soviet attack on Finland, which provoked an outcry in Britain and at one moment brought Britain to the verge of war with the Soviet Union. (This folly was luckily prevented by the refusal of Sweden and Norway to allow the passage of British troops through their territory.)[15]

When Hitler attacked an unprepared Soviet Union in June 1941 (Stalin had refused to listen to British warnings about Hitler's intentions), there were mixed feelings in Britain. Churchill, however, saw the enormous strategic advantage of having the Soviet Union as an ally and immediately proclaimed a most friendly welcome. Most people in Britain followed his lead, buried the past and felt sincere friendship for the Russians. They even came to think of Stalin as 'Uncle Jo'.

However, although Churchill was willing to sink the political quarrels of the past for the sake of a common war effort, political differences soon reared their head again. The British wanted an Anglo-Soviet Treaty of a simple straightforward kind. The Soviet Union immediately raised questions of post-war frontiers. Eden visited Moscow in December 1941, and saw Stalin. Stalin said he wanted the Curzon line as the future frontier with Poland – which meant that the Soviet Union would regain most of the territory that it had had to cede to Poland in 1921. He also wanted the frontiers with Finland and Rumania established in 1941, when the Soviet Union had annexed territory from both countries which it had then lost again as a result of the German invasion. He wanted the right to maintain bases in Finland and Rumania, together with a guarantee for the exits from the Baltic. To show good will, Stalin kindly suggested that Britain might like bases in Denmark and Norway. Eden said he could agree to nothing without consulting his Cabinet colleagues. He also told Stalin that even before the attack on Russia, President Roosevelt had asked Britain not to enter into any secret arrangements on the post-war reorganisation of Europe without consulting him. Molotov told Eden: 'in the absence of a settlement of the frontier question, no sound basis would be created for relations between Great Britain and the Soviet Union.'[16]

Eden left Moscow without agreement on a treaty, clearly shaken. (In fact the claims which Stalin had presented were rather more modest than those which he presented to Hitler in November 1940.) In January 1942 Eden wrote a memorandum for his colleagues: 'on the assumption that Germany is defeated ... and that France remains, for a long time, at least, a weak power, there will be no counterweight to Russia in Europe ... Russia's position on the European continent will be unassailable. Russian prestige will be so great that the establishment of Communist governments in the majority of European countries will be greatly facilitated, and the Soviet government will naturally be tempted to work for this.'[17]

The conclusion which Eden drew from this was that Britain – if possible in conjunction with the United States – should tie the Soviet Union down as soon as possible to fixed post-war frontiers. However Roosevelt seemed to take a much rosier view of Soviet intentions and strongly disliked advance territorial commitments. Roosevelt – much to Eden's annoyance – decided to intervene personally in the Anglo-Soviet discussion; according to Eden, he told the Soviet Ambassador in Washington that he could not support any treaty which dealt with frontiers, until the war had been won; but he promised that after the war the United States would support Russian efforts to achieve 'legitimate' security.[18]

Eden then offered the Soviet Union a new draft treaty, establishing a post-war alliance against German aggression, without any mention of frontiers. When Molotov arrived in London on 20 May 1942, he continued to insist on frontier guarantees; on 25 May he suddenly said he had received authority to sign. Obviously Stalin had changed his mind – possibly because of Roosevelt's intervention.

Not many problems were solved, however, by the conclusion of the Anglo-Soviet treaty. Differences over Poland remained a running sore in relations between Britain and the Soviet Union throughout the war, in spite of British efforts to find common ground between the London Poles and the Russians. The future frontiers of Poland were only one of the problems. In the end the London Poles accepted, in the East, the Curzon Line, and the cession of Lwow, as inescapable. The British on their side went on worrying about the large area of German territory which Moscow wanted to give Poland in the West, fearing (wrongly, as it turned out) that this would saddle the Poles with insoluble problems. More serious than the frontiers was the increasingly obvious determination of the Soviet Union to put in power a Polish Government formed exclusively by men guaranteed to be totally 'friendly' to the Soviet Union; this would automatically debar all the London Poles, who were constantly and bitterly attacked by Moscow.

Britain in a divided Europe

The crisis over this problem, between the West and the Soviet Union, was at its height in the closing weeks of the war in Europe, with Churchill urging the Americans to stand firm and resist Stalin's demand. It was not until the month after the end of the war in Europe that Churchill persuaded the former Polish Prime Minister in London, the Peasant Party leader, Mikolajczyk, to go to Moscow and join forces there with the Soviet-created Polish Provisional Government (see below p. 50).

The problems of Yugoslavia and Greece became involved in a wider British attempt, in 1944, to reach some sort of understanding with the Soviet Union which would set a limit to its political expansion in Europe. The other south-east European countries, Rumania, Bulgaria and Hungary, also came into the picture. The non-communist, anti-German political leaders in these countries had turned to Britain as their main hope. This was natural. British military, naval and air strength in the Eastern Mediterranean was an important strategic and political factor. Secret contacts were established between the British and the Rumanian Peasant Party leader, Iuliu Maniu, and his associates; the Bulgarian Agrarian Party leader, G. M. Dimitrov (to be distinguished from the Bulgarian Communist leader, Georgi Dimitrov), was working with the British authorities in the Middle East; Hungarian opposition politicians made secret approaches to the British. The British Government was most scrupulous in telling the Soviet Union what was going on and in refraining from using these contacts for anti-Soviet purposes. As the Germans retreated, pursued by the Soviet armies, all three countries changed sides; Rumania, which had suffered heavy losses fighting alongside the Germans against the Russians, now suffered fresh losses fighting alongside the Russians against the Germans. Soviet propaganda soon created the legend that the change of sides, in all three countries, had been the achievement of local communists. In fact, it was mainly the work of non-communist pro-Western politicians (in Rumania, King Michael personally), who still hoped that Britain and other Western Powers would have some influence in the future of their countries.

Oddly enough, the first tentative move for an understanding over Eastern Europe came from the Soviet side. In August 1943 the Soviet Ambassador, Maisky, before leaving his London post, told Eden that he was interested in possible operations in the Balkans. Eden proposed a coordination of policies. Maisky said that after the

28

war 'we could each have a sphere of influence in Europe, the Soviet Union in the East and Britain and America in the West'. By this means the West could exclude the Russians from French affairs and the Mediterranean and the Russians could claim the same freedom in the East. But, Maisky said, it would be better for each side to admit the other's right to an interest in all parts of the continent. Eden said he preferred the second choice.[19]

By March 1944, however, Eden was telling Foreign Office officials of his growing fear that Russia had vast aims which might include the domination of Eastern Europe and even the Mediterranean.[20] He then (on 5 May) suggested to the Soviet Ambassador in London that Britain and the Soviet Union should agree that during the war Britain would take the lead in Greece and the Soviet Union in Rumania.[21] A few days later the Ambassador said his government was willing to accept this but first wanted to know if Britain had consulted the United States. There followed a sour Anglo-American exchange of messages, both at the Churchill–Roosevelt level and at the level of Foreign Secretaries, in which the American objection in principle to 'spheres of influence' was reaffirmed. The Americans seemed to want three-power consultation on everything, which Churchill said would never work in a fast-moving war. Churchill also had to deny that he had any concern with post-war political developments and to say that he was thinking purely of a short-term wartime operational arrangement. If this was Churchill's real view, it was certainly not Eden's. Eventually Roosevelt agreed to a three-month trial period for the proposed arrangement; but by this time Stalin was obviously enjoying playing off the British against the Americans and delayed still further. It was not until Churchill saw Stalin in Moscow in October 1944 (by which time the Soviet armies were in control in Rumania and Bulgaria) that the extraordinarily casual 'percentage agreement' on Eastern Europe was reached. Rumania was to be 90 per cent under Soviet predominance; Greece 90 per cent British; Yugoslavia 50–50; Hungary 50–50 (Hungary was not yet under Soviet military control); Bulgaria 75–25. Churchill had written down these percentages on a half-sheet of paper and passed it to Stalin, who had ticked it with blue pencil. Churchill then said: 'might it not be thought rather cynical if it seemed we had disposed of these issues, so fateful to millions of people, in such an off-hand manner?' Stalin was quite unworried.

Churchill continued to maintain that this 'percentage agreement' had nothing to do with spheres of interest; if he had not, he would have shocked the Americans and some of his own colleagues at home. Nevertheless, it seems clear that by this time he was consciously trying to get Stalin to accept certain limits to the Soviet Union's future 'predominance' in Eastern Europe; he certainly feared that wherever Soviet troops arrived, an effort to impose a strictly-controlled pro-Soviet regime would be made. This was shown by what had already happened in Rumania and Bulgaria. Churchill's attempt to stem the advance of Soviet power had only very limited success. The Soviet Union quickly established 100 per cent control in Rumania and Bulgaria and, after a certain transition period, in Hungary (for which Molotov had in any case obtained a revision to 80–20 in favour of the Soviet Union). The Yugoslav Communists, when they got to hear of it, were furious at the thought that they should have been the object of a 50–50 deal; they thought they should be free to be just as communist as they wished, without any limitations imposed by Stalin. The main – almost the only – achievement of the agreement was that in Greece, in the crucial period of upheaval around Christmas 1944, the Russians refrained from backing EAM/ELAS.

Churchill was correct in his belief that the course of military operations, in the closing phase of the war, would shape the future political pattern of Europe. That was why, at least from September 1944, he was, in his own words, 'very anxious to forestall the Russians in certain areas of central Europe.'[22] To achieve this – and also for what he believed to be sound military reasons – he pressed for a strategy which would allow the British Commander in Italy, Field-Marshal Alexander, to make a thrust across the Adriatic, seize the Istrian peninsula, strike through the Ljubljana Gap, and try to reach Vienna before the Russians. He had mentioned this project at the three-power conference in Teheran in November 1943; it became the subject of sharp disagreement between the American and British military planners in the summer of 1944, accompanied by a most unhappy exchange of messages between Churchill and Roosevelt. The Americans over-ruled Churchill partly on strategic grounds, partly because Roosevelt was afraid of upsetting Stalin. In any case, Alexander's forces were so weakened to supply needs elsewhere that it became impossible for him to act.

Churchill, undaunted, went on trying to persuade Roosevelt – and after his death in April 1944, President Truman – to see the importance of the actual lines which Soviet and Western armies would hold in Europe at the moment of Hitler's defeat. Churchill held that this was a different matter from the occupation zones in Germany agreed by Britain, the United States and the Soviet Union at Yalta in February 1945. (The borders between the occupation zones in Austria were not finally settled until after the fighting had stopped.) In the closing phase of the war, Churchill urged that this three-power agreement should not inhibit nor limit the advance eastwards of the Western armies. The rejection of his plan for a thrust through Trieste into south-eastern Europe had left Vienna to the Russians; but it was still militarily possible for the Western allies to capture Berlin and Prague. Churchill tried hard to persuade the Americans to see the great political importance which Western conquest (or liberation) of these two European capitals could have. However Eisenhower, as Supreme Commander in Europe, with the President's backing, decided to concentrate his main final drive against the Germans in a south-easterly direction, leaving Berlin to fall to the Soviet armies. And the Americans, though they entered western Czechoslovakia, reaching Pilsen and Budejowice, turned a deaf ear to the appeals of the people of Prague who had risen against the Germans; they wished to avoid any friction with the Soviet armies advancing on Prague from the East.

Nevertheless, at the moment of German surrender, Western troops had advanced up to 100 miles beyond the agreed border-line between the Soviet and Western occupation zones. Churchill doggedly continued his struggle. He wrote to Eden on 4 May 1945: 'the allies ought not to retreat from their present positions to the occupational line until we are satisfied about Poland . . . and the conditions to be established in the Russianized or Russian-controlled countries in the Danube Valley, particularly Austria and Czechoslovakia, and the Balkans.'[23] Churchill urged Truman, in a message of 11 May, that it should not be left to the military commanders to decide on withdrawal westwards: this should only be decided by governments, in the light of the wider problems dividing the West and the Soviet Union. The next day he sent another message, urging him not to pull American troops out of Europe too quickly. 'What is to happen about Russia?' he asked. '. . . An iron curtain is drawn down upon their front. We do not know what is going on behind. There seems little doubt that the whole of the regions east of the line Lübeck–

Trieste–Corfu will soon be completely in their hands. To this must be added the further enormous area conquered by the American armies between Eisenach and the Elbe, which will, I suppose, in a few weeks be occupied, when the Americans retreat, by Russian power. . . .'[24]

Churchill was successful over his first request: the question of withdrawal to the line of the occupation zones was dealt with by governments, not by military commanders. But he failed over the central issue, of using the question of withdrawal as a bargaining counter at a meeting of the 'big three' in order to compel Stalin to live up to the provisions of the Yalta agreement about democratic freedoms for Poland and other East European countries. It was in fact a fairly strong bargaining counter. The area involved, according to Churchill, was 400 miles long and 120 miles wide at its greatest depth, and contained many millions of Germans and Czechs.[25] On the other hand, Stalin also had important bargaining counters in the possession of Berlin, Prague, Vienna and considerable areas of Austria, which the Western Powers expected to form part of their occupation zones.

Truman was sensitive to demands in the United States that American troops should be brought home by Christmas, and to the suspicions of some of his advisers of British 'imperialist' aims in Europe. He decided that the withdrawal to the occupation lines must take place in advance of any 'big three' meeting to discuss longer-term political problems and he accepted the date proposed by Stalin, 1 July. The Western troops started withdrawing on that day, followed by millions of refugees. Churchill commented later: 'Soviet Russia was established in the heart of Europe. This was a fateful milestone for mankind.'

In one case, in which the United States used the tough bargaining tactics advocated by Churchill, they had a certain success. There was an 'informal understanding' between the Americans and the Beneš coalition government in Prague that American troops would not leave Czechoslovakia so long as Soviet troops stayed there. The American Government proposed to Stalin that there should be simultaneous withdrawal, to which Stalin agreed. Early in December 1945 Beneš told the United States that he believed that the Soviet Government had kept its promise to withdraw by 1 December. Soviet troops did not re-enter Czechoslovakia, except for military manoeuvres, until 1968.[26]

Britain in Europe: The heritage of the second world war

The 'Special Relationship': the Roots in the War Years
The British motive for seeking a 'special relationship' with the United
States must have been the clear knowledge – at least from the spring
of 1940 onwards – that without large-scale economic and material
aid from America, Britain, even with the Commonwealth virtually
united behind it, could not hope to win the war. Britain had not the
manpower or resources to reconquer occupied Europe. It was therefore necessary to get as close as possible to the United States.
President Roosevelt responded with very valuable aid through Lend-
Lease, while in return the British Government informed and consulted
Washington on its war effort – and was prepared to accept friendly
advice in return – even during the period of American neutrality.
Three months before the United States was brought into the war by
the Japanese attack on Pearl Harbour, Roosevelt and Churchill,
rather remarkably, joined in issuing the eight-point Atlantic Charter,
which was virtually a statement of general war aims – a demonstration
of the closeness of neutral America and belligerent Britain.

After the United States came into the war, the two leaders ordered
very close cooperation at every level and in every activity. This
pooling of resources extended to such fields as economic warfare,
intelligence and the development of nuclear weapons. The British
felt (rightly or wrongly) that they were superior in experience and
know-how in almost all fields, while the Americans were superior in
manpower and money; the partnership seemed a fair bargain and the
British hoped to retain equal status with the Americans. This however did not happen; and as the scale of the American contribution
to the war soared, Britain's influence on the Americans quickly
dwindled. When the allied troops landed in Normandy on D-Day in
June 1944, there was rough equality between American troops and
British and Canadian troops; in the following February there were
over twice as many Americans.

Long before then, however, Churchill had allowed himself to be
over-ruled by Roosevelt on important issues at times when his
Cabinet colleagues thought he should have stood out. Given the
toughness and obstinacy of Churchill's character, this seemed odd.
The reason was perhaps to be found in the unusual personal relationship between Churchill and Roosevelt which developed during
the war years. The two men had met extremely briefly soon after the
1914–18 war. When Churchill entered the Chamberlain government
in September 1939, as Secretary of State for the Navy, Roosevelt

telegraphed inviting him to correspond with him direct on naval or other matters. With Chamberlain's permission, Churchill, in his own words, 'furnished him with a stream of information about our naval affairs'.[27] After Churchill became Prime Minister he exchanged frequent long personal messages with Roosevelt – over 1700. There were also nine meetings between them, at which they had long intimate talks.

Churchill set enormous store by this personal relationship and developed a strong feeling of affection and loyalty for Roosevelt, which became even stronger in the final months of Roosevelt's life when he was obviously seriously ill. This meant that although Churchill had long and tough arguments with Roosevelt he disliked quarrelling with him and was willing to be over-ruled.

Churchill also seems to have had a higher opinion of Roosevelt's wisdom than some of his Cabinet colleagues. Eden, in his memoirs, was politely sarcastic about Roosevelt's ideas on Europe – for instance, that there should be a state called 'Wallonia' to be formed by the Walloon parts of Belgium and Luxemburg, Alsace-Lorraine and part of Northern France, or that Yugoslavia should be broken up by separating Serbia from Croatia and Slovenia. Eden wrote: 'Roosevelt was familiar with the history and geography of Europe. Perhaps his hobby of stamp-collecting has helped to this knowledge, but the academic yet sweeping opinions which he built upon it were alarming in their fecklessness.'[28]

Attlee also took a critical view. 'I don't think Roosevelt really understood European politics. I don't think any American did,' he said later. Whenever the British advocated anything in the East of Europe, the Americans thought 'we were following some strange imperial design of our own.' 'They thought that we were just an obsolete old imperialist colonial power and that they understood Russia much better than we did. That was Roosevelt's line at Yalta.' Attlee added that in consequence the British had to agree to many things they ought not to have agreed to, in particular, giving Russia far too great a predominance in Eastern Europe.[29]

The 'special relationship', during the war years, turned out to be an unequal relationship. If the British had been willing to 'turn nasty', perhaps they could have achieved something nearer to equality. But Churchill would never have allowed it; in any case, to exert black-mail from a position of weakness would have been contrary to British habits in international relations. In spite of the inequality, the

Britain in Europe: The heritage of the second world war

British believed that the 'special relationship' had been essential for winning the war. They expected it to continue in the post-war years, as essential for keeping the peace; at the same time they were haunted by fear of an American return to isolationism, such as happened after the 1914–18 war.

PART II

Britain in Europe:
The post-war years, 1945–50

4   The British mood and the Soviet challenge

People in Britain reacted to victory in Europe, in May 1945, with cheerfulness and a brief outburst of collective gaiety. Debarred by national selfconsciousness from the sin of pride, they indulged in the permitted substitute of half-humorous, self-deprecating satisfaction. Churchill was as usual uninhibited by British reserve. There was a moment of emotion when the House of Commons met on 8 May 1945. *Punch*'s 'Impressions of Parliament' gave a vivid picture:

> Over all hung that curious brand of excited jollity found only in the Commons ... which takes the form of facetious questions. ... In the middle of a pause of complete silence the door opened and the entire House ... turned like a Wimbledon Centre Court to look at the man who walked slowly in. ... Members rose, jumped on the benches, waved their order-papers, opened their lungs and just yelled long and loud. ... For the new arrival was the Prime Minister, blushing and grinning ... and then, quite unaffectedly, taking out a crumpled handkerchief and flicking away a tear that began to trickle down his cheek.

Churchill then told the House that 'all Europe had been freed from the yoke of the tyrant'. There was a roar of cheers. 'Raising his voice, Mr Churchill cried with proud challenge: "Advance, Britannia! Long live the cause of Freedom! God Save the King!" '

Only from Churchill would such rhetoric have been tolerated. He had been accepted as a national leader – and also as a sort of national mascot – above party politics. When, a few weeks later, he stepped down to lead the Conservative Party in the election campaign, a majority voted against him. During the war there had been remarkable national unity, from the three-party War Cabinet downwards. Because of wartime difficulties and disciplines, through service in the armed forces or auxiliary services, rationing, billeting and the black-out, the complex British class system had become softened and blurred. It was no longer so easy to tell a person's class origins; nor was it popular to try to do so. There was something much nearer social and economic equality than ever before. Many people found this a novel and stimulating experience. Interest in social reform had been deliberately stimulated by the Government – partly to keep up spirits when the war seemed unending – in particular, through the Beveridge Plan, the first blueprint for the Welfare State.

The general mood in 1945 was one neither of exhaustion nor of exultation; there was an urge to build a new life at home. Most people were uninterested in world roles or European roles, though some thought that if Britain could build a new kind of society, neither capitalist nor communist, this might provide a model and a hope for other countries which did not wish to imitate either the Soviet system or the American way of life.

It was in this mood that British voters turned out Churchill and the Conservative Party and gave Labour a big majority. They had, at that moment, very little idea of the scale of the problems and difficulties which faced Britain. Ordinary voters did not know how much of Britain's economic and financial strength had been drained away by the six years of war, nor how dependent the country was on continued American support. Nor did they know how bad relations with the Soviet Union had already become. For the sake of allied unity and general morale, the Government had kept Anglo-Soviet differences as quiet as possible. In February 1945, in the foreign affairs debate after the Yalta conference, Churchill said he believed that the Soviet leaders wished 'to live in honourable friendship and equality with the Western Democracies. I feel also,' Churchill went on, 'that their word is their bond . . . I decline absolutely to embark on a discussion about Russian good faith.' Not surprisingly, most people assumed that Anglo-Soviet relations would shake down into some kind of peacetime cooperation. The last thing they wanted was to face the possibility of a new war, or even of a cold war.

Even Churchill himself, with all his fears for the future, still had hope of bringing Stalin to realise that he could not browbeat the West, and to accept political partnership. Just before the war in Europe ended, he thought it worth while to send a long emotional message to Stalin: 'there is not much comfort in looking into a future where you and the countries you dominate, plus the Communist Parties in many other states, are all drawn up on one side, and those who rally to the English-speaking nations are on the other. It is quite obvious that their quarrel would tear the world to pieces. . . . Even embarking on a long period of suspicions, of abuse and counter-abuse, and of opposing policies would be a disaster hampering the great developments of world prosperity . . .'. Churchill went on to a direct appeal: 'do not, I beg you, my friend Stalin, underrate the divergences which are opening . . . .' Stalin's reply was harsh.

When the Labour Party took office at the end of July 1945, its leaders had to plunge into the middle of the Potsdam Conference at which the confrontation with Stalin was continuing. Throughout the next five years, the main problem dominating the Labour Government was how to stand up to the Soviet Union in Europe, and help other West Europeans to do the same, while at the same time grappling with Britain's grave economic difficulties.

The two men who carried the chief responsibility for shaping policy, Attlee as Prime Minister and Bevin as Foreign Secretary, were very different, but formed an excellent partnership. Attlee was modest, quiet, sensible, practical and level-headed. Bevin has been called a lovable egotist. He was sometimes explosive, fertile in ideas, far-seeing except for odd blind spots. A country boy, he got a job as a dray-man in Bristol; he became involved in trade union organisation and, after establishing the giant Transport and General Workers Union, became the dominant figure in the whole trade union movement. The technique which he learnt in this part of his career was hard and tough bargaining aimed at eventual agreement based on mutual interest. This was the technique which he set out to apply as Foreign Secretary, in dealings with the Soviet Union. As a member of the War Cabinet (as Minister of Labour) Bevin had taken a special interest in foreign affairs and had been very friendly with Eden. He was well able to carry on from the point where Churchill and Eden left off.

This was not what many Labour supporters and members of parliament wanted. They believed in the idea of a new, specifically socialist foreign policy. Friendship with the Soviet Union, rather than the United States, seemed to them the main goal in foreign affairs; they believed that by removing all causes for Soviet fears or suspicions, all difficulties could be removed. Many pinned excessive hopes on the new United Nations Organisation (as they had on the League of Nations in the 1920s and 1930s) and very much disliked the idea of military expenditure on the scale which a long-term policy of standing up to the Soviet Union required. Bevin therefore needed courage and strength to face a great deal of criticism from inside the Labour Party. He had both, though he bitterly resented being 'stabbed in the back' by people who, he thought, ought to have been giving him support he badly needed.

Britain in a divided Europe

The Soviet problem was many-headed. Soviet policy towards Europe
had fluctuated, from 1941 on, in relation to the extent of Soviet
military achievement and political bargaining power at any given
moment. In late 1941, when German armies were deep inside Soviet
territory, Stalin's aims had been relatively modest. By July 1945,
when the victorious Soviet advance, together with the withdrawal of
Western troops to the occupation line, had placed Soviet armed
forces in control of all Eastern Europe and one-third of Germany,
including Berlin, Soviet claims were far greater – to extend Soviet
power, though not the state frontiers, to the heart of Europe. In the
last eight months of the war, the Soviet authorities on the spot had
done their best to exclude the British and Americans from any say in
Bulgaria, Rumania, Poland, Hungary and even, at first, in Austria,
where they made it as difficult as they could for British or American
missions to gain access or to operate efficiently. This was what
Churchill meant when he wrote to Truman: 'an iron curtain is drawn
down upon their front.'

The first Soviet aim in 1945 was obviously to consolidate control
over the whole of this vast area of Europe, through the presence of
Soviet troops, the establishment of governments in which local
Communists (if possible, trained in Moscow) held key positions and
above all direct Soviet control of internal security in the countries
concerned. This last objective was quickly achieved. In this field,
Yugoslavia was the one exception; Tito's resistance to Soviet efforts
to penetrate his security services was to become one of the causes –
perhaps a very important one – of the Soviet-Yugoslav quarrel of
1948; it also enabled him to survive Soviet attempts to remove him.

It was as a direct consequence of this determination to consolidate
Eastern Europe that the Soviet Union also aimed to exclude all
Western influences and contacts. Everyone from the West, whether
soldier, diplomat or journalist, was seen as a potential spy. Western
sympathy for the struggling non-communist political parties, before
they were completely crushed, was seen as subversive activity.

Once Stalin had determined to exclude the West (which in 1945
meant the United States and Britain) from Eastern Europe, it might
have seemed logical for him to seek a full-scale agreement with the
West on spheres of influence, by which in return for a Western pledge
of non-interference in Eastern Europe, he would have given a Soviet
pledge of non-intervention in Western Europe. This would have been
an expanded and extended form of the 'percentage agreement' with

Churchill. It seems to have been what Maisky was hinting at when he talked to Eden in August 1943.

By 1945, however, Stalin had a bigger aim. He wanted to have things both ways. He wanted to shut the West out of Eastern Europe, but at the same time to keep the right to intervene in Western Europe. The chaos and devastation caused by war could provide good economic and social ground for revolutionary action; the Italian and French Communist parties were powerful and had both won prestige by their part in the wartime resistance. In Germany, the wartime agreements on occupation gave the Soviet Union the right to a share in the overall control of the whole country.

It was not until ten years later that the Soviet Union at last gave up the policy of having things both ways – trying to intervene in Western Europe as well as shutting off Eastern Europe – and settled for the more modest aim of a European settlement based on a permanent, universally recognised and accepted East–West division.

It was the Soviet policy of having things both ways that Attlee and Bevin had to deal with. They tried to do two things: to fight a rear-guard action over Eastern Europe, and to strengthen Western Europe, politically, militarily and economically.

5   Britain and Eastern Europe: The rear-guard action, 1945–50

Under the armistice terms with the three East European countries which had fought with Germany – Rumania, Bulgaria and Hungary – three-power control commissions were set up for the period until peace treaties were signed. From the start the British and American elements in these commissions (the military missions) found themselves left out in the cold; they were rarely consulted by the Soviet element, and their views counted for very little. On the other hand, they could keep themselves reasonably well-informed on local political developments. The Soviet Union therefore wanted to get rid of the three-power commissions as soon as possible; and this could only be done by the conclusion of peace treaties with governments accepted by the Western Powers.

At the Yalta conference in February 1945 it was agreed that the big three would jointly assist any European liberated state or former Hitler satellite 'to form interim governmental authorities broadly representative of all democratic elements in the population and pledged to the earliest possible establishment through free elections of governments responsive to the will of the people.' The big three were to consult together and discharge their responsibilities jointly.

This gave the two Western Powers some ground from which to put up a struggle about the nature of the East European governments and the kind of elections held in the East European countries. But if Yalta gave the West a vague general right of intervention, it soon proved remarkably ineffective. This was the situation when Attlee and Bevin arrived in the middle of the Potsdam conference, replacing Churchill and Eden.

Bevin, according to Attlee, had at one time said that the Russians might be more friendly to a Labour government than a Conservative government. Given his realism, his own prolonged struggle against communists inside the British trade union movement and the deep-rooted Soviet dislike of all forms of democratic socialism, it was surprising that he should ever really have thought this. Certainly Attlee and Bevin got no welcome from Stalin at Potsdam. The conference was cancelled for a day because of an 'indisposition' of Stalin's. Attlee said later that, relying on information from the British Communist Party, Stalin had expected a Conservative majority of about eighty seats in the election, and did not conceal his disappointment, nor his dislike of the Labour Party.[1]

At Potsdam, therefore, the Labour leaders could do little except stand firm and give away as little as possible. The West even got a little out of Stalin: it was spelt out in the Potsdam Declaration that peace treaties with Bulgaria, Finland, Hungary and Rumania would have to be signed with 'recognised democratic governments', and that each of the three big powers would separately decide whether or when to establish diplomatic relations with them. In his first major speech as Foreign Secretary, in the House of Commons on 20 August 1945, Bevin said that the governments set up in Bulgaria, Rumania and Hungary did not, in the British view, represent the majority of the people; one kind of totalitarianism was being replaced by another. 'The governments . . . do not impress us as being sufficiently representative to meet the requirements of diplomatic relations.' Nor did he accept the electoral law under which elections were about to be held in Bulgaria.

British and American pressures secured a temporary easing of political conditions in the three ex-enemy countries. For a time, opposition political parties, including peasant parties, with their own newspapers, were allowed to function, though always under threat. After the Moscow conference of the three Foreign Ministers in December 1945, a further step was taken which cost the Soviet Union very little but looked well at the time. Members of opposition parties (two in each case) were to enter the Rumanian and Bulgarian Governments. After three-power consultations in Bucharest, the Rumanian Government was duly expanded; the opposition representatives were powerless, but the Western Powers recognised it in February 1946. After that, American and British protests about the Rumanian election of November 1946 carried little weight. In Bulgaria things moved more slowly. The opposition leaders – Nikola Petkov for the Agrarians, Kosta Lulchev for the small Socialist Party – took a tough line over their conditions for entering the Government and the negotiations got nowhere. In spite of this, elections were held in October 1946 in which the Opposition won 101 out of 465 seats, even though electoral irregularities provoked American and British complaints. Georgi Dimitrov, the Communist leader, kept the situation fluid by going on talking about a working agreement with the Opposition.

On 10 February 1947 the treaties of peace with Bulgaria, Rumania, Hungary and Finland were signed by all the powers. At this moment Britain and America had still not recognised the Bulgarian Government. Britian took this step a few days later, though America continued to hold out. Britain sent a note to the Bulgarian Government drawing attention to the obligation to maintain basic freedoms contained in Article 2 of the peace treaty; Britain had decided to give recognition 'in the hope that it is the intention of the Bulgarian Government henceforth ... to secure to all persons under their jurisdiction the fundamental freedoms'.

This was no more than a pious hope. Six months later the Agrarian leader, Petkov, a man of great courage who had worked with the Communists in the small Bulgarian resistance movement during the war, was charged with military conspiracy, tried and sentenced to death. After the sentence had been passed Britain and the United States asked Bulgaria to delay the execution and proposed three-power consultations with the Soviet Union to review the sentence. The Soviet Union said it had full confidence in Bulgarian justice. The day after Petkov was hanged, Britain sent a note to Bulgaria about the 'judicial murder'. It said that the British Government considered it had not only the right but also the duty to record its dismay and condemnation. It cited Article 2 of the peace treaty, which had come into effect one week earlier, and said Petkov had died for the right of men to hold and express their own political opinions according to their personal consciences.

It was said by the Bulgarian Communists that if the British and Americans had not intervened, Petkov would not have been executed, but that Bulgaria had been forced to demonstrate its independence. Seeing how readily the Communist Government executed fellow-Communists such as Traicho Kostov not long afterwards, it seems unlikely that Petkov would have been spared. However, when in November 1947 the Rumanian Peasant Party leaders, Maniu and Mihalache, were sentenced to solitary confinement for life, also on charges of conspiracy with the Americans and the British, the British reaction was less prompt and forthright, possibly in part out of consideration for the condemned men.

In Hungary the course of events was rather different – at least for three years after the war. The Provisional National Government formed in December 1944, when fighting against the Germans was still going on in the country, appeared to result from an attempt to give representation to genuine political forces. In September 1945, the Soviet Union established diplomatic relations with Hungary. Three days later the United States followed suit, having obtained assurances from the Hungarian Government about carrying out free and unfettered elections. In August, Bevin had classed the Hungarian Government along with the Rumanian and Bulgarian Governments as unrepresentative of the majority of the people. However, after elections held in November 1945, giving the decidedly non-Communist Smallholders' Party 245 out of 409 seats, Britain recognised the resulting government. Hungary promptly demonstrated its independence by liquidating a joint trading company set up under a far-reaching Soviet-Hungarian economic pact concluded before the election. Britain and the United States had protested against this pact on the grounds that it was designed to give the Soviet Union an unshakeable grip on the Hungarian economy. The Soviet Union had replied that it did not consider that legitimate British interests were affected.

For a short time it seemed as though Hungary might manage to preserve the same sort of internal political independence as Finland had so remarkably achieved and maintained. But during 1947 the familiar process of Soviet-backed pressure and intimidation took place. The honeymoon period of cooperation between non-Communists and Communists ended and the Communists took over. By 1948, in spite of the varying course of events, all three ex-enemy East European countries had reached the same point: complete elimination of any political forces other than the communist parties, except for small splinter groups which were either front organisations for the communists or under full communist control. The era of the purge of communists – some of them genuinely independent-minded and with real national loyalties, some the unfortunate victims of chance denunciation – had opened. Soviet aims had been achieved; Britain and the United States had been effectively shut out.

In theory, the two Western Powers could have held out longer: they could have refused to recognise governments or sign peace treaties until some real guarantees of political freedom had been given. But in the three countries, Britain and America had virtually no local power; they were incapable of safeguarding anything so fragile, requiring such constant vigilance, as political freedom. They also hoped that after the treaties were signed the political atmosphere would be lightened by Soviet troop withdrawals; however, the Soviet Union was not obliged to withdraw until a treaty with Austria had been concluded, and it was able to delay this until 1955.

Most important of all, Britain and America were anxious to conclude a peace treaty with Italy so that the process of stabilisation of a democratic system and economic recovery could go ahead; and it was quite clear that the Soviet Union would not sign the Italian treaty until the Western Powers signed the East European treaties. So the Western bargaining position was weak.

The parting shots in the Western rear-guard action were fired in the United Nations. The ex-allied East European states became members of the UN as of right. But when, in August 1947, Bulgaria, Rumania and Hungary applied for membership, the Security Council rejected them; America and Britain played the leading role and easily obtained the necessary majority. In retaliation, the Soviet Union vetoed Austria and Italy, among others. In October a Soviet spokesman said that Moscow would veto Finland and Italy until the West gave way over Hungary, Rumania and Bulgaria.

Britain and America held on. Taking their stand on their right to intervene under the provisions in the treaties for maintaining basic freedoms, they sent similar notes to Bulgaria, Rumania and Hungary in April 1949, accusing them of violating Article 2 of the treaties. The British notes spoke of 'the arbitrary exercise of police powers and the perversion of the judicial process for political ends', and of the establishment of 'a network of police and other agents who observe, report on, penetrate and interfere with the private opinions . . . and activities of citizens'. The Western notes were rejected by all three governments in unpleasant terms.

In October 1949 Britain and America tried a new ploy. They asked the UN Assembly to request a ruling from the International Court of Justice on their right of intervention in Hungary, Rumania and Bulgaria, together with other related questions. The Assembly agreed; the International Court met in the spring of 1950 and at first gave a favourable ruling; but then, faced with the refusal of the three governments to comply with the procedures proposed, the Court said it could do no more. In November 1950 the Assembly condemned the 'wilful refusal' of the three governments to fulfil their treaty obligations, but without visible effect. It was not until 1955 that the UN, as a result of a behind-the-scenes package deal, admitted a batch of sixteen new members, including Hungary, Rumania and Bulgaria. The United States, still registering displeasure, abstained on the vote; Britain voted in favour.

In the three 'allied' East European countries – Poland, Yugoslavia and Czechoslovakia – Britain was in an even weaker position than in the 'ex-enemy' countries. The withholding of recognition was not an appropriate weapon and peace treaties were not needed. The Czechoslovak leader, Beneš, and his Foreign Minister, Jan Masaryk, had spent the war years in London. They negotiated a treaty with the Soviet Union in December 1943 on their own initiative. On Christmas Eve 1944 Beneš had forecast that he would form a new government of representatives of all political shades, except those 'who have collaborated with the enemy, are guilty of Fascism, or do not grasp the meaning of the new times'. This last phrase was obviously meant to exclude those who did not realise the need for very close alliance with the Soviet Union in the post-war world, because of Czecho-slovakia's geographical position and as protection against Germany. As Masaryk said in a broadcast a few days later: 'our foreign policy will be based on the solid, unalterable and mighty foundation of our treaty with the Soviet Union; . . . our relations with our other neigh-bours will be determined in the light of our Soviet treaty.' Beneš, on leaving London with his government in February 1945, broadcast a farewell message of thanks to the British people, and said: 'you trusted us enough to let us plan our political liberation in our own way.' The British could only wish him well in his optimistic belief that he could achieve a satisfactory partnership with the Soviet Union and with his own Communists. Perhaps the British themselves were over-optimistic about the outlook for a relatively free and democratic Czechoslovakia; otherwise they would hardly have been so painfully shocked by the communist take-over, with open Soviet support, in March 1948. There was nothing Britain could do, except speed up plans for the defence of Western Europe.

In Yugoslavia, the British had themselves sponsored the transition-al political arrangements which, as things turned out, paved the way for a Government of National Unity under Tito himself in March 1945. After a short period under a Regency Council, the monarchy was abolished and Yugoslavia became a federal republic. King Peter never returned to Yugoslavia from London.

Before then, relations between Britain and Yugoslavia had been very badly strained when Tito's forces occupied the Italian port of Trieste at the head of the Adriatic. The Slovene-speaking population of the Istrian peninsula and the hinterland of Trieste was put forward as justification for a claim to incorporate all the area, including Trieste itself, into Yugoslavia. Churchill was determined that forces under Field-Marshal Alexander should hold Trieste; he did not want to allow Tito to pre-judge the terms of the peace treaty with Italy, and he wished to protect Italian interests. A head-on clash was narrowly avoided; Trieste came under Anglo-American occupation though Yugoslav troops remained in the hinterland and in most of the Istrian peninsula. Local tension continued and mounted during the 1946 negotiations for an Italian peace treaty. The treaty put forward the compromise solution of a Free City of Trieste but it was not put into effect because of the violent emotions in Italy and Yugoslavia.

For this and many other reasons British influence in Yugoslavia was very small in the early post-war years. The Yugoslav Communist leaders felt the greatest mistrust for Britain. Milovan Djilas, at that time prominent among them, wrote later: 'we were suspicious of the British. . . . Our fears were made especially great because of our naïve notions about their espionage – the British Intelligence Service. Our attitudes were compounded of doctrinaire clichés, sensational literature. . . .'[2] Suspicion and even hostility towards Britain was shown by accusations made in political trials. The 50–50 agreement had vanished without trace; already in June 1945 Churchill was complaining to Stalin: 'in fact it is at present more like 90–10, and even in that poor 10 we have been subjected to violent pressure by Marshal Tito.'[3] Before long Stalin also found out the difficulty of dealing with Tito and his colleagues. After the Tito–Stalin break in 1948, there was a gradual change to a friendlier Yugoslav attitude towards Britain; economic aid and trade were welcomed; wartime contacts were revived; Tito visited London. When the Trieste problem was finally settled by agreement between Yugoslavia and Italy in 1954, the essential private negotiations took place at the Foreign Office in London, with Britain and the United States giving benevolent help from the side-lines.

In Poland, Britain had a bigger right to intervene. Moreover British opinion, inside and outside Parliament, had been badly shocked by Soviet failure to help the Warsaw rising against the Germans and Soviet blocking of American and British offers of help; there were strong feelings that the Government must do something effective about Poland. After victory in Europe, it seemed urgent, particularly to Truman, to get some sort of settlement with the Soviet Union. In June 1945, three-power talks took place in Moscow resulting in an agreement on the steps to be taken to set up a representative government. Political representatives from inside Poland and from London (notably Mikolajczyk) were brought to Moscow for talks with the Soviet-sponsored Provisional Government there. Agreement was again reached, and a Government of National Unity was formed in Warsaw on 28 June, with Mikolajczyk as Second Deputy Prime Minister. He told a vast crowd in Warsaw: 'we Poles want to live as a free and independent people in closest alliance with our neighbour Russia.' Britain recognised the new government on 5 July – reminding it of the Yalta declaration calling for free and unfettered elections in liberated countries.

However, the elections were not held until January 1947. In the previous summer Britain, along with the United States, had formally protested about various forms of political intimidation, including arrests of Peasant Party supporters, and had urged that in the coming election there should be equal facilities for all democratic parties. As relations between the Communist-dominated party alliance and the Peasant Party got steadily worse during the autumn, Britain and the United States had sent further notes. But the elections gave the Communist alliance an enormous majority and the Peasant Party only twenty-eight seats. The United States said that it did not intend to break off diplomatic relations, though the election did not fulfil the Yalta and Potsdam agreements. Britain reacted by saying there was clear evidence of suppression and intimidation in the election; the undertakings given to Britain, the United States and the Soviet Union had not been fulfilled. There was no mention of the question of diplomatic relations. In effect, the two Western Powers admitted that they were helpless.

Finland was happily exempted from the Soviet drive to impose wholly subservient regimes throughout Eastern Europe, partly, perhaps, because during the Soviet-Finnish war Moscow had learned to respect Finnish toughness, but probably mainly because of Soviet interest in gaining favour with a potentially neutral Scandinavia. Whatever the reasons, the Finnish election of the summer of 1945 was apparently free from Soviet interference and produced a broadly-based government. Britain recognised this government and resumed trade and financial relations with Finland in August 1945.

Britain in a divided Europe

The whole British–American rear-guard action over Eastern Europe in the early post-war years could be seen as a futile and undignified waste of diplomatic energy. It certainly showed that diplomacy, when not backed up either by local strength (such as was used in the Berlin air lift) or by willingness to risk a nuclear war, was a very frail weapon against the Soviet Union. It also showed the folly of using ambiguous terms such as 'democracy' or 'freedom' in agreements with the Soviet Union. Backed by Moscow, the East European Communist governments increasingly ignored Western protests. The whole attempt to keep a foot in the East European door could be seen as a fiasco.

Yet on a long-term view it could be argued that it was right and necessary that Britain, not only as one of the big three but even more as a European power, should demonstrate as clearly as possible that it could not accept the Soviet interpretation of what constituted a 'friendly' government. Throughout the war and after, Britain had accepted the Soviet desire to have friendly governments on its western frontier. But – whatever the 'percentage agreement' may have meant – Britain could never have given its blessing to the Soviet doctrine that a 'friendly' government meant a government entirely subservient to Soviet interests and orders, so that even the smallest degree of political freedom or diversity was banned. This re-emerged after the 1968 invasion of Czechoslovakia as the Brezhnev doctrine, which shocked those with short memories. Just as it was a problem for Britain in the early post-war years, so then it was a problem for all Western Europe, to know how to deal with a doctrine which cut off 100 million East Europeans from the rest of Europe.

6 Britain's economic weakness and political strategy, 1945–50

The rear-guard action over Eastern Europe had one advantage: it cost little and made no demands on Britain's economic resources. It could be conducted on the basis of Britain's wartime status as one of the big three; this was a dwindling asset, but it was still a very real one, and was not disputed by the Soviet Union. In fact, at this time the Soviet Union directed its main propaganda attack against Britain. On the other hand, Britain's policies towards Germany, and towards the West European allies, demanded money, manpower and resources, at first, above all, coal. In the past Britain had exported coal; Western Europe badly needed coal but Britain could no longer supply it – in spite of Bevin's appeals to the miners.

Britain had liquidated its overseas investments to carry on the war; it had lost over one-quarter of its merchant shipping. Vast sterling balances had been accumulated by foreign countries, including the Arab states and India. On top of this President Truman – acting impulsively on domestic political grounds – cut off Lend-Lease aid suddenly, as soon as the war against Japan was over. Dean Acheson later described the decision as most harmful.[4] This left Britain in such straits that it had urgently to seek a large loan from the United States in order to carry on. The American Government at that time did not realise how grave the British position was and demanded as a condition of the loan a promise that Britain would make the pound sterling convertible by 1947. British experts knew that this was far too soon; convertibility could not in fact be maintained. The end result of the American loan, which was unrealistically small and had unrealistic conditions attached, was the British monetary crisis and the devaluation of sterling in 1949.

With its finances in such a precarious state, Britain was continuing to maintain armed forces not only in Germany but in a string of bases round the world. (The Commonwealth, with surprising unanimity, had made a very useful military contribution during the war, and had added weight to Britain's influence in war councils; but it represented a burden and a responsibility as well as a source of political strength and prestige. When the British, starting with Attlee's grant of independence to India, Burma and Ceylon, began the long process of 'de-colonisation', they hoped to shed most of the burden but keep the political strength and prestige. By the 1960s, this had proved unrealistic.) Keeping troops abroad meant a shortage of men in the factories at home, as well as unproductive expenditure. The Labour Government's ambitious programme for a steep increase in exports to solve the grave balance of payments problem could not be carried through. In short, Britain was in a poor position to give aid to others because it badly needed aid itself.

Attlee and Bevin believed that their foreign policies could not be cut to fit Britain's economic weakness; they were even ready to try to cover up this weakness as far as possible, so as to be able to play the role – particularly in Europe – which they thought vitally necessary in the post-war years. Francis Williams, who worked closely with Attlee and knew both Attlee and Bevin well, made this clear in his books on the two men. Bevin's approach was that even if Britain could not wholly disguise its weakness, it dare not allow it to be recognised to its full extent; it must draw reinforcement from all the resources of political skill possible. Bevin, from his trade union career, was experienced in 'building patiently from weakness and presenting to the world a massive self-confidence when little stood behind it but his own stubborn will'.[5]

The reason why Attlee and Bevin wanted Britain to appear strong was that they believed there would be a power vacuum in Europe if it did not. They did not think Stalin wanted a war but, as Attlee put it to Francis Williams, 'to leave nothingness might tempt the Soviet to strike out for domination over the whole of Europe and the Middle East and thus divide the world beyond hope of repair'.[6] So during the whole of the early post-war period Attlee and Bevin felt they were fighting a holding operation in order to gain time.

Quite soon after the Potsdam conference, Bevin came to the conclusion that Britain could not stand up to Soviet power in Europe without the United States. But the Americans were preoccupied with domestic politics; American public opinion was against getting entangled in Europe, mistrustful of Britain's supposed imperialist aims and slow to understand the reality of the danger from Soviet power in Europe. Bevin believed that in time the Americans would come to see the danger and accept that involvement in Europe was in their own interest. But the process might take time; any prodding from the

British might have exactly the wrong results. It was a question of waiting for the right moment. Bevin thought that Stalin might help by over-playing his hand and trying to take too much. In the meantime, Britain had to appear strong in Europe so as not to leave an empty void.

Bevin apparently realised that this policy of bringing in the Americans as a counterweight to Soviet power in Europe might for a time compel him to accept American demands which he did not like (West German rearmament was one instance). But he hoped that as West European strength grew, this would create the possibility of greater freedom of action.

Bevin therefore looked a long way ahead; he was flexible and open-minded, except when one of his prejudices was touched. He did not regard the creation of a Western defence alliance, for which he worked so hard, as an ultimate end in itself; it was rather a policy which was made urgently necessary by a special set of circumstances – the devastation of Europe caused by the 1939–45 war, the advance westwards of Soviet power, Britain's weakness, whether temporary or permanent, the need for American power to check the Soviet advance and provide a counterweight in Europe. If Bevin had not died in 1951, his ideas would not have remained static; they could well have developed with the developing strength of Britain and Western Europe as a whole, and the resulting possibilities for a new effort to find an understanding with Moscow. During the Attlee-Bevin partnership of 1945–50, however, the economic weakness of Britain – and the rest of Western Europe – was a determining factor in British policies towards Europe.

7 Britain and Germany, 1945–1950

Apart from the imposition of communist regimes in Eastern Europe, the central struggle between the Soviet Union and the Western Powers was over Germany. At Yalta the occupation zones had been agreed; Churchill had insisted that a fourth zone should be created for France. It was also agreed that there should be overall four-power control through an Allied Control Council, together with local four-power control of Berlin, which became an enclave inside the Soviet Zone. There were subsequent agreements, of a not very satisfactory kind, on rights of access to Berlin from the Western Zones.

In contrast with earlier plans of a very harsh kind, such as cutting up Germany or stripping it of virtually all heavy industry, the big three seemed agreed, by the end of the war, that Germany should remain united (though of course a large area in the East passed under Polish control) and that a single German Government should be formed with which a peace treaty could be concluded. It was also assumed that the peace treaty would be signed before long (Roosevelt had talked of keeping American troops in Germany not more than two years after the end of the war).

However, the Soviet Union set out to do the same thing in Germany as in Europe as a whole: that is, to exclude the West from the Soviet Zone while claiming the right to intervene and to derive economic profit from the Western Zones. In the early post-war years, the Soviet Union was probably working for a situation in which Germany could be united under a government formed by such methods that it could be brought under Soviet control. If this could have been achieved it would of course have meant a further vitally important advance westwards of Soviet power. In particular, the Soviet Union would have gained control of the great industrial complex of north-west Germany, which fell within the British occupation zone. However, by the end of the 1940s, Moscow was beginning to lose all hope of this. But until the mid-1950s, it continued to talk about German unity and a united German government in the hope of preventing the rearmament of West Germany as a member of NATO. When this failed the Soviet Union decided that its interest was to keep Germany divided and to secure Western recognition of the division of Germany, and of all Europe, as permanent.

Bevin's attitude to the German problem was strictly practical, based on economic necessity. He did not much like Germans, and as for the German Social Democrats, he apparently could not forgive them for the pro-war attitude they took in 1914. He got on rather better with the Christian Democrat leader, Dr Adenauer, than with the post-war Social Democrat leader, Dr Schumacher.[7] On the other hand, Bevin saw that a policy of economic punishment of Germany would be self-defeating. At the World Trade Union Conference in February 1945, when the Soviet delegates had been demanding passionately that the Germans should make full reparation for the suffering and destruction they had caused, Bevin was sympathetic but added: 'the Labour movement will have to be very careful in working out the methods of its approach to the problem: it would be only too easy to make 60 million people in the centre of Europe a submerged labour force which, if not handled correctly, can bring down the standards of all other countries.'

At the end of the war, Britain found itself occupying the heavily-populated, highly-industrialised but badly-bombed area of north-west Germany, including the key industrial area, the Ruhr. Roosevelt had wanted this zone for the United States but the British had stood firm. It was in fact a drain on British resources, not a source of strength. The population was swollen by millions of refugees. Food supplies and coal were badly needed; the traditional food-supplying area lay in the Soviet Zone and was cut off. The Russians were busily removing industrial plant and food from their own zone for their own needs; in addition, under the heading of reparations, they were demanding industrial plant from the West, in particular the British zone; they wanted a share in the control of the Ruhr; they also wanted reparations from 'current production'.

The most bitter quarrels between Britain and the Soviet Union, in the immediate post-war years, were over this economic problem. At the crucial Foreign Ministers' conference in Moscow in the spring of 1947, Bevin wrote a long personal letter to Attlee: 'the Russians clearly . . . want to create a situation in which everyone will forget what they have done in their zone, and that they shall be able to come in, disregarding all this, force the British and American tax-payer to stand it, rehabilitate their own zone at our expense and then on top of that get reparations from current production. The discussions have been very cold, frank and firm. The result is that it is impossible to reconcile the instructions given me by the Cabinet with the desires and determination of Russia to loot Germany at our expense.'[8]

It was this commonsense determination to protect the British tax-payer which brought Bevin to see that the programme laid down for dismantling certain sections of German industry, in order to remove its economic capacity to wage another war, was quite impracticable, for very much the same reason that made him oppose Soviet demands for industrial plant from West Germany. Germany needed industry on a scale which would enable it to export enough to buy the necessary imports, especially food. The Germans must be able to pay their own way, rather than be a drain on the Western tax-payer. (At a later stage a similar argument reconciled him – nearly – to the re-arming of West Germany: if Britain were to have fewer workers available for industry because British troops were defending Germany, while West Germany, unarmed, was free to devote all its manpower to industrial production, then Britain would soon lose its chance of competing with West Germany in world markets.)

In the series of conferences of Foreign Ministers, in one capital after another, in the early post-war years, it was the Soviet demand for reparations – which would indirectly have had to be paid by the Western Powers – which barred the way to any serious consideration of a German peace treaty. At one conference Bevin told Molotov that he was not prepared to face Parliament with the implication that he had bought a peace conference from the Soviet Union for so many hundred million dollars. The actual figure demanded by Molotov in 1946 from Germany as a whole was 10,000 million dollars.

The need to make West Germany economically self-supporting led directly to the first potentially dangerous confrontation with the Soviet Union. The United States, after starting with an extremely tough official policy towards Germany, had gradually changed its view. By September 1946, the Secretary of State, James Byrnes, said that Germany should not be turned into an economic poor-house; the United States therefore favoured economic unification. In December 1946 Bevin and Byrnes said they had decided on the economic union of the British and American zones. This came into effect at the end of May 1947 – after the failure of the Moscow

Foreign Ministers' conference. The French remained aloof for some months but then added their zone to 'Bizonia'.

In November 1947 the four Foreign Ministers met, this time in London, and the old arguments were rehearsed. Bevin put forward a plan for a federal constitution for the whole of Germany, based on the assumption that Germany would be treated as a single economic unit. The Soviet Foreign Minister, Molotov, replied with his demand for 10,000 million dollars' worth of reparations, four-power control of the Ruhr and the cancellation of the fusion of the Western zones. He coupled this with a plan for the immediate creation of a central German Government and in this context asked the Foreign Ministers to hear the proposals of a communist-sponsored 'German People's Congress' which had just met in Berlin with the aim of influencing the Foreign Ministers' conference. The Western Ministers said they did not think the People's Congress was representative. The London conference ended in disagreement on all points. There seemed a curious contradiction in the Soviet position: on the one hand Molotov wanted a central German Government, formed according to communist ideas; on the other hand he wanted Germany to remain economically split.

The economic unification of the three Western zones led on in the first few months of 1948 to plans to enable the West Germans to govern themselves. On Bevin's suggestion, Belgium, Holland and Luxemburg were drawn into the discussions. Simultaneously (in March) Britain, France and these three countries signed the Brussels Pact creating the Western Union. A fortnight later the Soviet authorities placed restrictions on Western allied land access to Berlin, though not on West German access. Early in June recommendations about the future political development of West Germany, drawn up by the three Western powers and the three Benelux countries, were announced in London.

Nine days later the Soviet representative left the four-power military command in Berlin. The Western Powers announced currency reform in West Germany. Five days later the Soviet Union announced currency reform for East Germany and Berlin, including the three Western sectors of the city. The Western powers then extended the new West German currency to West Berlin. Immediately, the Soviet Union imposed a ban on all traffic from the West to Berlin – except by air. It obviously thought that it could starve out West Berlin. However, the Western powers replied with the Berlin air-lift. The Americans played the major part in it, but the British contribution was important.

At one stage, the American military commander, General Clay, suggested sending through an armed convoy by road to Berlin, believing that the Soviet Union would not stop it by force. The American State Department, Britain and France opposed the idea and it was dropped. In May 1949, following a skilful piece of American diplomacy, the Soviet Union lifted the blockade; their only condition was that the four Foreign Ministers should meet yet again. They met in Paris, without result, so Western plans for West Germany went ahead. According to Sir Ivone Kirkpatrick, who was at the Paris conference, the Russians admitted privately that they had gambled and lost, and that the only thing to do had been to liquidate the adventure. This pattern of Soviet behaviour was seen again later in the second Berlin crisis, the Cuban missile crisis and on other occasions.

The next stage was for the West Germans to draw up a constitution which the three Western powers could approve and to reach agreement on the powers which the Western governments would need to retain. After this had been done, West German elections were held in August 1949. In September the West German parliament – the Bundestag – met in Bonn and elected Adenauer as Chancellor. The West German State – though with certain limitations on its freedom of action which lasted until the mid-1950s – had come into existence.

Bevin had fully backed these political developments in West Germany, though he had argued against the Americans' desire for a very loose form of federation; he thought they wanted to give too little power to the central government and too much to the governments of the Laender (the component states of the federation). But when it came to the question of rearming the West Germans, he had a very strong instinctive reaction against the idea, which was also most unpopular in the Labour Party. Moreover it could be argued that the Germans themselves did not want it; the Social Democrat leaders attacked it hotly, and there grew up a much wider 'Ohne Mich' ('Count me out') movement.

Adenauer himself was extremely cautious about rearmament, in the early stages. In November 1949 he told the American Secretary of State, Acheson, that he had no interest in it[9] and told an American newspaper that he was against it. At the very outside he would be willing to consider a German contingent in the framework of a

European federation. The following month, however, he told a Christian Democrat conference in Dusseldorf that he was worried about West Germany's security in view of the way the Russians were arming the People's Police in the Soviet zone. He would only agree to West German participation in European defence – which he thought the Western powers would want – on a basis of complete equality.[10]

No further move was made until June 1950. But things were on the move in the United States. At the beginning of June, Acheson said that the United States would continue the policy of German demilitarisation. The American defence chiefs thought differently. General Bradley said that from a strictly military point of view he believed the defence of Western Europe would be strengthened by the inclusion of Germany. American missions in Bonn, Paris and London urged the same thing.

The decisive factor was the outbreak of the Korean war on 25 June 1950. This produced panic in West Germany, where it was seen as a curtain-raiser to a Soviet war of aggression in Europe. Sir Ivone Kirkpatrick reported that many West Germans sought to re-insure with the Russians; there was hoarding of foodstuffs and some people prepared for flight. Only 4 weak British and American divisions and practically no air force were facing 22 Soviet divisions in East Germany.[11] Adenauer was giving much higher estimates, including 60,000 armed East German People's Police. He was personally convinced that the Russians were intending to attack and thought the West Germans would be neutral because the advancing troops would be (East) Germans and because American military reverses in Korea had taken away their confidence in American strength.[12]

To deal with this situation, Adenauer proposed to the three Western Powers the creation of a West German federal police force of 150,000 men, to be ready for service by the following spring. At the same time he demanded a demonstration of military strength by the three powers. It was at this moment that Churchill, by a speech at the Council of Europe at Strasbourg, threw a new stone into the pool – a proposal (which of course had no backing from the Labour Government) for a European Army, including West Germans. Adenauer, in reply to a question from the American High Commissioner, approved the Churchill plan; but he continued [to press his own proposal for a federal police force strong enough to stand up to the East German People's Police. In this, he was backed by the three parties represented in the Government and by the opposition Social Democrats.

When the three Western Foreign Ministers met in September 1950 in New York, Bevin backed the Adenauer plan, and fought hard for it against American opposition. In the meantime the French had come up with far-reaching though vague proposals for military, political and economic integration in NATO. The American defence chiefs were willing to consider military integration under an American commander and an increase in American troops in Europe, but only on condition that West German units were brought in. The result was that the American Government came up with a 'one package' plan containing all these three elements. They also argued that since Adenauer's plan for an armed federal police would require an amendment of the West German constitution, it would mean undue delay. In the end Bevin gave way to the Americans; the French who were very unhappy about the German part of the package, said neither yes nor no, and later produced the ill-fated plan for a European Defence Community which was eventually killed by the French Assembly in 1954. So this particular element in the American package was eliminated, and six or seven years passed before there were West German soldiers in NATO. The Americans however, fulfilled their side of the package promptly.

Acheson, in his memoirs, said that he was inclined to agree that the 'one package' plan had been a mistake (see p. 105); he had held out against it but gave way when convinced that it was the necessary price for acceptance by the American defence chiefs of a united NATO command.[13] Bevin presumably gave way for the same reason, even though it meant unpopularity in his own party: Labour, like the French Socialists, felt strongly about rearming Germans. American acceptance of much greater and more direct involvement in the defence of Western Europe must have seemed to Bevin an achievement of one of his most important aims.

The whole affair is however only understandable in the light of the extraordinary shock which the outbreak of the Korean war caused not only in West Germany but elsewhere in Western Europe, including Britain. It was universally seen as a Soviet-inspired act of aggression, probably linked with plans for further aggression elsewhere. Attlee, usually level-headed enough, sent Truman a message in July 1950 suggesting that fresh trouble might now be started in Greece. Later, such fears seemed exaggerated; but the Korean war came only a year after the end of the Berlin blockade and less than a year after the Greek government forces had defeated the Soviet-backed communist forces after a hard fought struggle. It was therefore not surprising that the Soviet Union should seem both violent and unaccountable – as it did again later, notably when it invaded Czechoslovakia in 1968. In 1950, the Soviet Union, by sponsoring the North Korean assault, also unintentionally sponsored West German rearmament.

8 Bevin and the defence of Western Europe, 1945–50

The wartime discussion within the British Government about the post-war defence of Western Europe had been largely a theoretical exercise. Churchill was too heavily involved in immediate problems and dangers to give much thought to post-war planning, except in so far as he was deeply worried about Soviet power in Europe. He felt his way forward instinctively or by intuitive leaps rather than by means of carefully drawn up political blueprints. He also feared that planning for Western defence would arouse Stalin's suspicions.

Bevin, when he became Foreign Secretary, presumably found what plans had been prepared in the Foreign Office during the war, and then made up his own mind. He had always been interested in Europe. At the TUC conference in 1927 he spoke passionately in favour of the project for a European Economic Union. 'Cast your eye over Europe, with its millions of underfed, with its millions of people with a wretchedly low standard of living,' he said, going on to attack the trade barriers in Europe which were keeping living standards low. He also felt warmly towards France. During the war, he joined Eden and Attlee in standing up for de Gaulle against Churchill. In August 1945, in his first big speech as Foreign Secretary in the House of Commons, he said he was most anxious that Britain should be on the best of terms with 'that great country', France, so that both together could contribute not only to the economy but also the stability of Europe as a whole. Certain matters however had to be cleared up first. (He meant mainly the quarrel with de Gaulle over Syria.) He pursued the aim of friendship with obvious sincerity and warmth, even though problems of the occupation of Germany often divided the British from the French who clung to the idea of detaching the Rhineland and the Ruhr, as well as the Saar, from Germany, long after the Labour Government had decided that this would do more harm than good. He had a good deal more fellow-feeling with the French over the dismantling of German industry and over West German rearmament than the Americans did.

It is unlikely that Bevin ever put to himself the question, whether or not Britain should assume the leadership of Western Europe. It is more likely that he simply assumed that as a result of the war years, Britain already had it. Probably too he thought of it more as a responsibility that Britain must carry for urgent practical reasons, rather than as a role to be played on the world stage. Probably, again, he saw no conflict between Britain's responsibility towards Western Europe and its responsibility towards the Commonwealth – except over the specific question of merging Britain in a European federal structure. Like Churchill, he may have thought of Britain's Commonwealth connection as a source of strength to Western Europe.

During 1946, the more doctrinaire members of the Labour Party who had been badly disappointed in their hopes that Labour, in power, would somehow follow a specifically socialist foreign policy, and who were worried by rapidly worsening relations with the Soviet Union, started pressing the idea of a 'Third Force' policy. In November 1946 the Labour rebels tabled an amendment to the Reply to the Throne in the House of Commons, on the Labour Government's foreign policy. They said it should 'provide a democratic and constructive Socialist alternative to the otherwise inevitable conflict between American capitalism and Soviet Communism . . .'.[14] This 'Third Force' policy was aimed at securing support from the socialist parties of Western Europe. Bevin, it seems, considered this idea seriously and at one time was inclined to like it. But he decided against it because 'he could see in a Third Force no possibility of building in the time available a stable power strong enough to meet and check the encroaching power of Russia.' He thought American partnership in the security of Europe essential.[15]

Bevin therefore set out to organise the defence of Western Europe with the long-term private aim of bringing in the United States when American opinion was ripe. He had first to stand up to attacks, from Soviet propagandists and from Labour Party critics, against plans for a 'Western bloc' in a purely European sense. In February 1946, after the Moscow conference of Foreign Ministers, Bevin told the House of Commons that he had told the Russians, in connection with the idea of a Western Union, that Britain wanted friendly neighbours in its street as much as Russia did in *its* street; such a union would not in the slightest degree constitute a threat to Russia.

In March 1946, after de Gaulle had withdrawn from power, the new French Prime Minister, M. Gouin, urged the conclusion of an

Anglo-French Treaty of alliance on the lines of the French-Soviet Treaty which de Gaulle had negotiated in Moscow during the war. The new French Prime Minister's statement was publicly welcomed by Bevin. He told Parliament that Britain had always wanted the closest possible friendship with France, and had for a long time thought that relations should 'at an appropriate moment' be cemented by a treaty of the same character as the Anglo-Soviet Treaty, which would provide further security against any renewal of German aggression. In early April talks started in Paris about the treaty. Communist propaganda attacks on Western 'blocs' and 'ganging up' continued. Attlee, speaking in Parliament in June, said that friendship with neighbours was not 'ganging up'. Britain, he said, wanted the closest friendship with Holland, Belgium, Scandinavia and above all France.

On 4 March 1947 the Anglo-French Treaty was signed at Dunkirk, as if to wipe out painful French memories of the British withdrawal through Dunkirk in 1940. It was a fifty-year treaty specifically aimed against German aggression. If either party became involved in hostilities with Germany, the other would at once give all the military and other support and assistance in its power. At the Dunkirk ceremony, Bevin spoke, with obviously sincere emotion, of the misunderstandings between the two wars which allowed the resurgence of an aggressive Germany. 'We will strive to avoid misunderstandings and to understand the new France,' he went on. 'I see so much in common between our two countries. . . . Why should we not march together at all times?' Bevin said his signature was a pledge that his country would never leave the side of France.

Although the treaty spoke of German aggression, Bevin still seemed to think it might arouse Soviet suspicions. So he felt it necessary to say that Russia would realise that it was not a 'Western bloc', but an attempt to make a contribution to European peace. Later, in the House of Commons, he said he hoped that the treaty would cause French confidence to grow, and at the same time make the new Germany take the right course. He presumably meant that the treaty should help the French to overcome the irrational element in their fear of Germany, but that the Germans would also have to play their part.

At Dunkirk a friendship between Britain and France, even closer than the old Entente Cordiale, seemed to have been formed. The serious strains and frictions of the war years, caused partly by de

Gaulle's determination to establish France's equality of status, partly by his extreme sensitivity to real or imagined slights or encroachments, seemed to have been forgotten. But before long new differences between the two countries arose, in the first place over the question whether Western Europe should be organised on a 'supranational' or 'functional' basis. At Dunkirk Bevin said that Britain was sometimes described as a cool practical race, France as a very logical people; the two could now be combined. This was not so easy; the French logical mind liked the building of 'supranational' structures as the means of creating West European unity; the British liked the 'functional', or practical, step-by-step approach to unity. In the 1950s and 1960s, a much more serious clash became open: a rivalry between France and Britain for the leadership of Western Europe which did serious harm to West European unity.

This Anglo-French difference appeared first in the economic field. In defence, the process of building up a West European system went smoothly for some time. By January 1948 Bevin showed that he thought the time had come to refute Soviet attacks on 'Western blocs' once and for all, and to press ahead. In a House of Commons debate, he sharply criticised the Soviet action in 'cutting off Eastern Europe from the rest of the world and turning it into an exclusive self-contained bloc'. Britain, he went on, had not pressed for a Western Union, and some of its neighbours had been reluctant to press it, hoping that agreement could be reached with the Soviet Union which would close the breach between East and West and so avoid the necessity for crystallising Europe into separate blocs. Bevin then recalled the whole history of British thinking about West European defence, from the war years on, and showed how the Soviet Union had been informed at every stage. When he had told Stalin in Moscow in 1945 that any arrangements with France and other neighbouring countries would not be directed against the Soviet Union, Stalin had said: 'I believe you.'

Now, Bevin said, the nations of Western Europe must draw together. Through the Dunkirk Treaty, relations with France were closer and firmer than ever before. Britain was not proposing a formal political union with France, but would maintain the closest possible contact. The time had come to draw closer to the Benelux countries, Holland, Belgium and Luxemburg, and to conclude treaties with them. Other European countries, including the new Italy, might also be drawn in. 'We are thinking now of Western

Europe as a unity. . . . We shall do all we can to advance the spirit and machinery of cooperation.'

From the Conservative side, Churchill and Eden both gave their blessing to Bevin's statement. Churchill added that European unity could be perfectly well reconciled with Britain's obligations to the Commonwealth.

Things moved fast. Three months later, on 20 March 1948, Britain, France and the three Benelux countries signed the Brussels Treaty, creating Western Union. Like the Dunkirk Treaty, it was to last fifty years. Unlike the Dunkirk Treaty, it was not specifically directed against German aggression. Article 4 said that if any party should be 'the subject of armed attack in Europe', the other parties would afford all military and other aid and assistance in their power. Moscow obviously concluded that the treaty was aimed against the Soviet Union. A fortnight later the Soviet authorities took the first step in the Berlin blockade.

On the basis of the Brussels Treaty the member States started rapidly building their own military structure, which was in fact the foundation of the wider and more complex NATO structure in which it was later merged. In September 1948 the Western Union Defence Ministers met in Paris and set up a permanent organisation, under their own authority, with headquarters at Fontainebleau, near Paris, together with a Chiefs of Staff Committee under the British Field-Marshal Montgomery. The French General de Lattre de Tassigny was appointed Commander-in-Chief Land Forces Western Europe, a British Air Marshal was given the Air Command and a French Vice-Admiral became Flag Officer, Western Europe. Montgomery was temperamentally extremely active; work was rapidly started on joint planning and joint exercises. All this became part of the NATO structure under an American Supreme Commander in 1951.

While the Brussels Treaty was being hatched, Bevin was also hatching a rather tricky plan to involve the United States in defence responsibilities in Europe, in the first place in Greece. At the time of the liberation in October 1944, Britain had undertaken commitments towards Greece for military and financial support. In particular, Britain had helped Greece to build up a fairly efficient and sizeable army. When the Greek Communists launched the so-called 'Third Round' of the civil war in the spring of 1946, the British were deeply involved in the supply of advisers and arms to the Greek army in the long and frustrating struggle against the guerrillas. By the beginning of 1947, British economic weakness, in particular the balance-of-payments deficit, made it essential to cut expenditure overseas. On 28 February it was disclosed that Britain had sent a note to the United States warning it that without immediate economic support, Britain would be unable to carry on its commitments to Greece which would expire at the end of March. It was stated that discussions were going on between the British and American Governments.

Dean Acheson, then Under-Secretary of State, later described the repercussions of the British move in Washington. There were in fact two British communications. 'They were shockers,' he wrote. Their main point was that British aid to both Greece and Turkey would end in six weeks. Britain hoped that the United States could take on the burden for both. The Greek economy would be in need of substantial sums in foreign aid for several years. Turkey was stronger but could not finance simultaneously the modernisation of the large army which Soviet pressure demanded, and the country's economic development.[16] After some rapid work in Washington, and a difficult interview with Congressional leaders, President Truman addressed a joint session of Congress. He spoke of the urgent needs of Greece and Turkey and said: 'I believe that it must be the policy of the United States to support free peoples who are resisting attempted subjugation by armed minorities or by outside pressures. . . . I believe that our help should be primarily through economic and financial aid. . . . Should we fail to aid Greece and Turkey in this fateful hour, the effect will be far-reaching to the West.' He asked Congress to approve money for aid, and to agree to sending American civilian and military personnel to Greece and Turkey. Truman received a standing ovation.

Bevin's plan had worked. He had involved the United States directly in the defence of non-Communist Europe, in spite of the instinctive American dislike of European entanglements, especially if Britain was mixed up in them. Francis Williams described him 'holding on with grim patience for the right moment and the right issue'. He had judged Greece to be the right issue and the current of American opinion also to be right. He was correct, even if the first reaction from Washington was a strongly-worded protest from the Secretary of State, General Marshall. He was also probably correct in deliberately using shock tactics which compelled the Americans to take a decision which they would rather have put off.

After the Truman Doctrine had been declared and accepted by

Congress, it became easier to move on towards the wider American involvement in Western Europe for which Bevin had been working. Once again, the Soviet Union played into his hands. Just as Soviet demands on Turkey and the Communist military onslaught in Greece had led, through Bevin's action, to the Truman Doctrine, so Soviet pressures on Norway, coupled with the Communist take-over in Czechoslovakia, followed by the blockade of Berlin, all in 1948, combined to create a climate of American opinion in which Bevin felt the time had come to make the next move. He proposed to the United States an early meeting to discuss a joint plan for Atlantic security and a Mediterranean system of security. Canada strongly supported the Atlantic idea; Truman for the moment felt unable to go beyond public support for Western Union – the Brussels Treaty alliance. However, on 11 June 1948, the Congress rather surprisingly lent a helping hand. It voted overwhelmingly in favour of the Vandenberg Resolution, which urged the US Government to pursue 'association of the United States, by constitutional process, with such regional and other collective defence arrangements as are based on continuous and effective self-help and mutual aid, and as affect its national security'. This resolution was obviously framed to meet the needs of the defence of Western Europe; it was the result of consultations between Senator Vandenberg and the Acting Secretary of State, Robert Lovett.[17]

After that things moved forward in a smooth and orderly way. In July 1948 the United States, Britain and the other Western Union countries, and Canada started exploratory talks on the basis of the Vandenberg Resolution; in December 1948 and January 1949, these talks were continued. On 14 January 1949 the US State Department said that because of the Soviet Union's preponderant strength, support of Western Europe by the United States was essential: 'the geographic position of the Brussels Pact nations brings their strategic and security interests into mesh with those of the United States and Canada.' On 20 January President Truman, in his inaugural address at the start of his second term of office, said: 'we are now working out with a number of countries a joint agreement designed to strengthen the security of the North Atlantic.'

Trouble followed between the US Senate and the Secretary of State, Acheson, over the degree to which the proposed treaty would or could automatically involve the United States in war in Europe – thereby depriving the Congress of its constitutional right to declare war. This was smoothed over; but it was for this reason that the crucial clause of the Atlantic Pact was weaker than the corresponding clause of the Brussels Treaty. Article 5 of the Atlantic Pact was long and tortuous: the parties agreed 'that an armed attack against one or more of them in Europe or North America shall be considered an attack against them all and consequently agree that, if such an armed attack occurs, each of them, in exercise of the right of individual or collective self-defence . . . will assist the party or parties so attacked by taking forthwith, individually and in concert with other parties, such action as it deems necessary, including the use of armed force, to restore and maintain the security of the North Atlantic area'. This cautious complex phraseology rather worried the West Europeans but was necessary to safeguard the rights of the Congress, and to avoid offending its sensibilities. The treaty's duration was to be twenty years, automatically continuing beyond that period unless it was denounced, though two years' notice of denunciation had to be given.

The Atlantic Pact was signed on 4 April 1949 in Washington. By that time the original seven countries had been joined by Iceland, Italy, Norway and Portugal. Greece and Turkey, in spite of the Truman Doctrine, felt left out in the cold, and asked for membership. They were accepted in 1951; the fact that they could not possibly be called North Atlantic states was glossed over. In any case the Atlantic Pact allies, in accepting Italy, had already accepted defence responsibilities in the Mediterranean, thereby meeting Bevin's plea for a Mediterranean system of security. West Germany did not become a member until the mid-1950s, after the long dispute over German rearmament had finally been solved.

When Bevin signed the treaty in Washington, he must have felt great satisfaction – even though the American commitment to Western Europe was, for the moment, no more than a political pledge written on paper. (Acheson, in ironic comment on the treaty's lack of 'teeth', recounted that at the ceremony, the US Marine Band played the song 'I've got plenty of nothin' ' out of Gershwin's *Porgy and Bess*).[18] While the signing of the Brussels Pact in 1948 had been followed by the first Soviet move in the Berlin blockade, the signing of the Atlantic Treaty was closely followed by the Soviet ending of the blockade. Stalin had concluded that campaigns of pressure against the West produced the opposite of the desired result.

Britain in a divided Europe

Stalin also cannot have foreseen the repercussions in Europe of the Korean war. This did not merely bring to the forefront of Western planning the question of West German rearmament which might otherwise have lain dormant for some years, but also brought about a firm American decision to keep troops and air forces stationed in Western Europe and to join with the West Europeans in setting up an integrated military structure. In the mood of panic created by the Korean war, willing West European acceptance was certain. At the end of July the United States asked the other NATO countries what they were willing to do to strengthen their own defences. Britain and France promised increased efforts. But the combined European total strength was regarded by the American defence chiefs as far too small. Around this time the French had proposed a far-reaching system in the Atlantic alliance – integrated organs for foreign policy, military command, armaments and economic supply. This was much too complicated and novel a proposal to be readily acceptable to the United States. But the American defence chiefs agreed to send American troops and set up a unified command, provided the West European allies accepted the idea of West German units in NATO.

There were various difficulties to be overcome. Truman felt it would be politically awkward to send more American troops to Europe, over and above those already occupying Germany; at first he publicly denied any intention of doing so. Bevin did not like West German rearmament in the NATO framework; but the British Chiefs of Staff favoured West German military participation in European defence. The Defence Minister, Emanuel Shinwell, wanted Bevin to urge the European allies to accept the American offer to join in an integrated structure in Europe, and backed him when he agreed to do so.

The biggest obstacle was the deep opposition of the French (represented by Robert Schuman and Jules Moch) to West German rearmament. However, the Americans were privately told that the tireless Monnet was already at work on a plan for a European Army, which might solve the problem. So they thought it safe to leave the German question in suspense, and go ahead with the announcement by the NATO Ministers in September of their joint decision to set up an integrated force under centralised command and a Supreme Commander, to ensure the defence of Western Europe. In January 1951, General Eisenhower became Supreme Allied Commander in Europe. His brief from the American Government was that the North

Atlantic Treaty should add the power of the United States to create a true balance of power in Europe, as a stabilising and preventive force.[19] In spite of the many criticisms of NATO, in the twenty years that followed, it clearly succeeded in this aim.

In a further aim set by the American Government, that the treaty should be a vehicle for closer political and economic cooperation with Western Europe, it had much less success. There were two reasons for this. On their side the Americans, given their preponderance of power, and given the constant tension between President and Congress, never developed the habit of serious political consultation with the West European allies on non-European problems; they asked for the support of their allies, but not for their views in advance of decision or action. On the other side the West Europeans – or an important group of them – wanted more and more to go their own way in the political and economic fields. The idea of a real Atlantic community, which had been one of Bevin's many dreams, never took root.

The more realistic West Europeans, however, saw that their freedom to go their own way rested ultimately on the foundation of the American commitment to defend Western Europe through NATO. If this foundation crumbled away, their freedom of action might crumble too. That was why all the NATO allies, even including de Gaulle's France, wanted the North Atlantic Treaty to continue after its twentieth birthday in April 1969. Bevin, in helping to create NATO, helped to build a solid and lasting structure.

9 Bevin, West European economic recovery, and West European integration

Progress in European economic recovery, with large-scale American aid, was surprisingly quick and successful from 1948 onwards; and it was efficiently coordinated through the Organisation for European Economic Cooperation (OEEC), in which Britain played a big part. But from a very early stage, the question of economic cooperation in Western Europe became inextricably entangled in the dispute over the kind of structure which West Europeans wanted to build for the purpose of banding together in some form of economic or political union. The idea that Western Europe should create a federal or supranational union came up repeatedly, and the man who was either in the forefront of the struggle or active behind the scenes was the remarkable French economic planner, Jean Monnet, whose brilliant brain delighted in devising federal or supranational structures for all purposes. He certainly did not do this to embarrass or annoy the British; he wanted the British to join in and he always believed that sooner or later they would be converted to his views and would accept supranationalism. However the British usually *were* embarrassed or annoyed, because they preferred to feel their way forward step by step in one specific field after another, in a 'pragmatic' way.

This clash between the British pragmatists and the continental federalists or supranationalists was not serious in the immediate post-war years. But gradually, as it became mixed up with the underlying rivalry between France and Britain for the leadership of Western Europe, it caused a great deal of bad feeling and damaging divisions between theoretically allied countries.

In the first two years after the war, the economic difficulties of Western Europe, including Britain, were so vast that there was not much time for argument about structures. Owing to the destruction and disruption caused by the war, normal trade patterns had been shattered; channels of trade were blocked; supplies of food, coal and raw materials were very short; industrial production was low; countries could not export enough to pay for essential imports. In particular there were very few dollars available to pay for imports from the United States, so there was a great deal of talk about the 'dollar gap'. Britain, though less devastated by war than some continental countries, had particular balance-of-payments problems. Not only were its exports down to one-third of the pre-war level but its invisible exports, which had always been a very important item in the balance of payments, derived from investments abroad, insurance, shipping and other services, had also dropped heavily. There were large wartime debts to be paid off. The United States was not at first in a mood to be helpful to Britain. Some influential Americans (for instance, Admiral Leahy, Truman's Chief of Staff in 1945) thought that Britain was already down and out (and therefore presumably not worth helping), while more Americans refused to believe that Britain was in serious difficulties and thought it must be concealing hidden wealth. Many Americans were also in the traditional state of moral indignation over supposed British imperialist schemes.

However, Attlee and Bevin continued to try to work as closely as possible with the United States. They were nervous that alarm or offence might be caused by Churchill's famous Fulton speech, in Missouri, in March 1946, in which he pointed dramatically to the Soviet danger, at a time when most Americans still preferred to ignore it. The speech caused a shock, but pleased Truman. It did not awaken the Americans to the urgent need to help Western Europe back to economic health and stability.

Bevin felt bitterly frustrated by British helplessness in the matter of aid to the continental countries. At the Trades Union Congress in September 1947, he said that ever since he had been Foreign Secretary, he had been wondering how Britain could assist in the rehabilitation of Europe. Do you realise, he asked the trades unionists, that this is the first time in British history for 400 years that Britain has not been able to do anything either with goods, money or coal? Bevin recalled (inaccurately) that Churchill had said 'Give me the tools and I will win the war'; 'I say in peace,' Bevin went on, 'give me the tools of production and their full results, and I will change the foreign policy of Europe.'

However, Bevin was realistic enough to know that British frustration would not help Western Europe. American dollars were needed, and in June 1947, General Marshall, then Secretary of State, gave a signal, in a speech at Harvard which had been carefully drafted on the basis of alarming reports received from American representatives in the West European countries about the dangerous state of their economies. Marshall said:

It is evident that before the United States government can proceed much further to alleviate the situation and help start the European world on the way to recovery, there must be some agreement among the countries of Europe as to the requirements of the situation, and the part those countries themselves will take in order to give proper effect to whatever action might be undertaken by this government. . . . This is the business of the Europeans. The initiative must come from Europe. The role of this country should consist in friendly aid in drafting a European programme and of later support of such a programme, so far as it may be practical to do so. The programme should be a joint one agreed by a number, if not by all, European nations.

At a press conference a few days later Marshall said he counted Russia as a European nation.

The American signal was so discreet – presumably because of the great sensitivity of the US Congress – that its importance was not immediately striking. But Bevin, when he read the first press reports of the speech, was delighted. (He had in fact had an advance tip-off about it from Acheson.) According to Francis Williams, he said it was 'like a lifeline to a sinking man'. He went across to 10 Downing Street to see Attlee straight away, resisted a suggestion from the Foreign Office that he should ask the Washington Embassy for clarification of the Marshall speech, and, instead, told the Ambassador to see Marshall at once, express Britain's deep appreciation of the offer and say that Britain would immediately consult France about how it could best be implemented. He then telephoned Paris to ask the French Foreign Minister for his co-operation, all by noon of the same day. On 13 June, at a Foreign Press Association lunch in London, Bevin publicly welcomed the Marshall offer. He paid a special tribute to France, but spoke also of its 'terrible difficulties' (there was a prolonged French Government crisis because of the expulsion of Communist Ministers who had supported damaging strikes). He then went on to say that he thought that the initiative devolved on the British Government to try to lead Europe back to a healthy state.

Bevin thought not only of Western Europe but also of the possibility of using this opportunity to heal the breach with the Soviet Union and Eastern Europe. Once he knew that Marshall was willing to include the Soviet Union in his plan, he got Molotov invited to meet Georges Bidault (the French Foreign Minister) and himself in Paris. When Molotov accepted, Bevin kept saying: 'perhaps they *will* play after all.' In his speech to the Foreign Press Association, he said that when the United States threw a bridge to link East and West, it would be disastrous to frustrate 'that great endeavour' for ideological or other reasons. However, Stalin did not allow Molotov to play; nor did he allow the East European governments to play, as some of them clearly wanted.

Already on 13 June *Pravda* was attacking the Marshall offer as a plan for political pressure with the help of dollars and for interfering in the internal affairs of other countries. This was the line subsequently followed by Molotov at the Paris meeting. He also argued that there should be no 'all-embracing programme', but that each country should decide for itself how best to rehabilitate its economy; moreover, those who had suffered most from the Germans (presumably, that is, the Russians) should get the lion's share of any aid that was going. Later, the Poles particularly attacked the idea that Germans should participate in Marshall aid.

Soviet opposition to the Marshall plan was so intense that in September 1947, at a meeting in Warsaw, the Communist Information Bureau (Cominform) was set up by the Soviet Union, six East European countries including Yugoslavia and the communist parties of France and Italy – the two most powerful in Western Europe. The Cominform was, at least in part, a counter-measure directed against Marshall aid and the consequent economic organisation of Western Europe. The Warsaw conference attacked Marshall aid as merely part of an overall United States plan of world expansion.

When the Soviet Union rejected the Marshall offer and forced the East Europeans to do the same, this was one of the big turning points of the post-war history of Europe. As a result of Stalin's decision, the East–West division in Europe was hardened and institutionalised. The denial of American aid to the East Europeans widened the gap between their standard of living and the West European standard, a gap which was still wide in 1970 and was particularly serious in the case of Czechoslovakia. The Soviet Union set up Comecon as an East European counterpart to the OEEC, but it did little to help economic advance in Eastern Europe – though it helped Russia to bind the East European countries to itself by economic ties which in some cases were a form of economic bondage.

Britain in a divided Europe

Bevin's hopes of healing the East–West division were dashed. Perhaps they had never been very bright. At least it was easier to get on with business without Molotov's stone-faced stalling.

After Molotov's walk-out from the Paris three-power conference, Bevin and Bidault, early in July, invited all the European states (except Spain) to take part in framing a joint reply to the Marshall proposal. Albania, Bulgaria, Czechoslovakia (after first accepting), Finland (wishing to remain 'outside international conflicts'), Hungary, Poland, Rumania and Yugoslavia (after first saying it would like to cooperate) all refused. Fourteen countries came to the Paris conference on 12 July 1947. Bevin, refuting Soviet charges, said that Britain and France were not seeking to exercise hegemony over other countries; to accuse them of interfering with the sovereignty of small nations, after their record in two world wars, was nonsense. On the following day the meeting adopted the Anglo-French proposal to set up a sixteen-nation Committee of Economic Cooperation. Before the end of September, this Committee had completed a four-year plan for economic reconstruction, in the form of a report to the American Secretary of State.

It was at this point that there came into the open the clash between British and French ideas about the form to be given to the proposed European economic organisation. The report began, innocuously, by saying that the participating countries, with a total population of almost 270 million, would aim at four things: a strong production effort, especially in agriculture, fuel and the modernisation of equipment; internal financial stability; economic cooperation among themselves; and an ending of the payments deficit with the United States, mainly through increased exports. So much was common ground. So also was the undertaking to aim at rapid removal of abnormal restrictions on trade between themselves, and at a sound and balanced multilateral trading system. However the report then went on to say that the formation of a European Customs Union (or unions) had been studied – but obviously without agreement; although the idea contained 'important possibilities', it was merely referred to a special Group for 'careful and detailed study'.

The report also contained some of the British arguments against the idea: the European balance of payments problem was a world problem; it could not be solved without the closest possible economic cooperation with countries outside Europe; the development of trade with the American continent and the rest of the world, including Eastern Europe, was of crucial importance.

The key phrase was perhaps this: 'special problems also arise for countries with a high proportion of their trade outside any proposed Customs Union.' Bevin had put things more plainly to the Trades Union Congress earlier in September. A European Customs Union, he said, would not solve Britain's problem, even if it went far to solving the problems of the continental Europeans. Only 25 per cent of Britain's trade was with Europe, the other 75 per cent was extra-European. And he went on to suggest, not perhaps very seriously, a Commonwealth customs union.

As things turned out, the customs union idea got lost in the long meetings of the Study Group during the following months; Britain participated on the understanding that it would take no firm commitments because it was not only a European power but also an extra-European power. The French–Italian Customs Union which was announced later was abortive.

A further British–French argument went on about the kind of continuing organisation which the sixteen nations should set up. The French wanted some supranationalism in it, in particular a strong executive board working full time, and an international secretariat with a Secretary-General with the power to take initiatives in important matters. The British – not only the politicians but also the civil servants – wanted to keep decisions firmly under the control of the member governments. That is, they wanted a council of ministers, working on the basis of unanimity, with most of the work being done by committees of experts provided by member governments. The British won. On 15 March 1948 the sixteen nations met again in Paris. Bevin said that the four-year recovery programme must succeed; if it did, 'I do not believe that we shall break apart; I believe that our cooperation will go on'. During the four years, 'the habit of voluntary cooperation' would have grown so strong that it would continue after the pressure of economic need had slackened. He also talked about the new organisation as a club, in which there must be tolerance and a contribution from each as the price of taking part.

The resulting Organisation for European Economic Cooperation, set up in Paris on 16 April 1948, conformed roughly with British ideas. Decisions were to be taken 'by mutual agreement of all members'; but to avoid paralysis through lack of unanimity, 'the abstention of any members declaring themselves not to be interested in the subject under discussion shall not invalidate decisions which shall be binding for the other members'. (The unanimity rule was not only the wish of the British; the Benelux countries also pressed strongly for it, so as to safeguard the interests of the smaller countries.) However, there was a (French) Secretary General and a Secretariat, who in practice developed considerable influence.

One of the more important obligations on members was to furnish information requested of them. This enabled the OEEC to exercise very strong influence on member states, in spite of the unanimity rule, through what became known as the 'confrontation technique'. A member state was asked for a detailed report on a specific problem; this was then studied by other members, both by experts and by home governments, and also by the Secretariat. The member state concerned might then have to face strong and well-informed criticism, first from the experts of other member states and finally from ministers. This often proved very effective. 'Repeated examinations of this kind ... have done something to promote agreed standards of financial, economic and trading behaviour. ... The confrontation technique has ... provided a means of bringing organised persuasion to bear against discriminatory national actions or policies.'[20] Any country using the veto might find itself isolated and subject to diplomatic pressure.

In spite of its limitations, the OEEC was remarkably successful in doing the job for which it was first intended. Using American aid, European production was increased, trade barriers (mainly import quotas) were lowered; the West Europeans escaped from the bilateral barter arrangements which they had been forced to use, by means of a system of settling accounts on a collective West European basis, through the European Payments Union created in 1950. At the end of the planned four-year period, dependence on American help was virtually ended and prosperity was returning. By general consent the OEEC carried on, mainly concerned with the job of removing remaining trade quotas and preparing the way for convertibility of West European currencies in the latter 1950s.

Even when the Six created the European Economic Community in 1957 through the Treaty of Rome, the other members of the OEEC wanted it to carry on. By this time however it was disliked by the French as a British-dominated body, and tension between France and Britain was growing. The Americans, who strongly favoured the Six, also came to dislike it. So it was transformed into a different body, the Organisation for Economic Cooperation and Development, including the United States, Canada and Japan. Some of the OEEC's members, including Britain, were sorry to see it disappear.

Bevin's whole attitude over the OEEC was typical not just of the Labour Party, but of general political and official opinion in Britain at that time and for some years after. Personally, Bevin did not have a closed mind; in the summer of 1947 he was willing to discuss privately the idea of a French–British customs union. Adenauer, in his memoirs, quoted Lord Henderson, then Under-Secretary at the Foreign Office, as saying in 1951 that Bevin had always sympathised with the idea of a European federation, though the overwhelming majority in England preferred the functional method.[21] In the House of Commons in May 1948, speaking about Western Union, Bevin said that it did not create a European federated state nor a political union; such a dramatic move might appeal to idealists, but 'in the world of international politics one is forced to proceed step by step'. He had no intention, he said, of being diverted from practical tasks by 'academic discussions about sovereignty'. Francis Williams wrote that Bevin saw federation as the end and not the beginning of a long process of cooperation; he was chary of erecting impressive superstructures until the practical foundations had been laid. He was also afraid to create anything which might stand in the way of wider Atlantic unity. Finally, he did not want to weaken Britain's close links with the Commonwealth. In fact, Bevin wanted to feel his way forward, not to take a leap into the dark – or, as some would have said, into the future.

Britain, the European Movement and the Council of Europe
However much Bevin's caution and reserve may have disappointed or annoyed the federalists or supranationalists in Western Europe, at least they understood his position and knew where they were. What caused confusion, in the early post-war years, was the position of Churchill and other prominent Conservative supporters of the European movement. Churchill, rather at a loose end after six years as war leader, ardently espoused the 'European' cause – the idea of a United States of Europe. As opposition leader, he could talk far more freely and dramatically about it than he could have done in power. But did he or did he not mean Britain to be part of 'Europe'? At some moments this was a puzzle.

Britain in a divided Europe

At Zurich on 19 September 1946, Churchill said: 'we must build a kind of United States of Europe'; it was to be based on reconciliation and partnership between France and Germany. The first step would be to form a Council of Europe. At this stage Churchill did not seem to expect Britain to be a member. Along with 'mighty America' and perhaps Soviet Russia, Britain and the Commonwealth were to be 'friends and sponsors of the new Europe' and champion its right to live.

The next step was a statement issued in London in January 1947 that a United Europe Committee had been formed, with Churchill as chairman. The aim seemed to be to make Britain a full member of a 'unified Europe'. Britain, the statement said, had special obligations and spiritual ties linking it with the Commonwealth; nevertheless, 'Britain is part of Europe' and must be prepared to make its full contribution to European unity. Churchill himself, speaking in the Albert Hall on 14 May 1947, seemed to have no worry about the Commonwealth problem. Why, he asked, should the Dominions not be with Britain in this cause? They felt, with the British, that Britain was geographically and historically a part of Europe and that they themselves had their inheritance in Europe. If United Europe was to be a living force, Churchill said, Britain would have to play its full part as a member of the European family.

In July 1947 a French Committee for United Europe was formed, supported by members of all political parties except the Communists. A joint meeting of the French and British committees was held, and called on the two countries to become 'pioneers for United Europe'. In December an International Committee, bringing in the Belgians and Dutch, was set up with Churchill's son-in-law, Duncan Sandys, as chairman.

The next stage was to hold a 'Congress of Europe' in May 1948. The Labour Government, which wanted to conduct its own gradual approach to European unity, was plainly annoyed about the whole affair. Three months before, Churchill and Attlee exchanged letters. Attlee wrote coldly that it would be undesirable for the Government to back the conference officially. The Labour Party's National Executive formally discouraged members of the party from attending the Hague conference; however, a small group of Labour MPs actually attended the Congress, though the Conservatives played the dominant role, Eden and Macmillan among them. (Other distinguished men present were Bertrand Russell, Lord Beveridge and the poet laureate, John Masefield.) A German delegation came, and also exiles from most East European countries.

Churchill made a moving though vague speech, going back to Henry of Navarre's 'Grand Design'. He foresaw three regional councils – one based on the Soviet Union, or formed by the Soviet Union; 'the Council of Europe, including Great Britain joined with her Empire and Commonwealth'; and one in the Western Hemisphere with which Britain would be linked through Canada and 'other sacred ties'. This did not sound a very practicable scheme. Churchill did not explain himself more clearly.

The Hague Congress declared that the nations of Europe should create an economic and political union, transferring some part of their sovereign rights to secure common political and economic action. They also called for a European Assembly chosen by the parliaments of member countries.

By this time the general impression had been created that the British Conservatives wanted something close to a federal Europe while the Labour Party was dead against it. The issue had also, in Britain, become a matter of party politics, with Conservatives taunting the Labour leaders for their backwardness. (There were in fact many Conservatives far more 'backward' than the Labour Government.) This made Bevin all the more bad-tempered and unhappy about the proposed Council of Europe: it was not his own idea, his opponents were forcing it upon him and anyhow for the time being he preferred his own 'functional' approach.

However, the French had now got the bit between their teeth. At a meeting of the Western Union ministerial council, in October 1948, it was agreed to set up a committee on European unity, under Herriot, then President of the French Assembly. The committee was soon deadlocked by disagreement between the French and Belgians on one side and the British on the other. The French and Belgians wanted an Assembly of members elected by the various national parliaments, voting freely and not on the instructions of their governments, so as to get a 'true consensus' of European public opinion. Britain wanted a Committee of Ministers and a 'conference' of delegations appointed by national governments and voting as national blocs.

In January 1949 the Western Union Ministers reached a compromise: there would be a Committee of Ministers and a 'consultative body', its members chosen as each member country wanted. In May the five Western Union countries were joined by Denmark, Ireland, Italy, Norway and Sweden and, under Bevin's chairmanship, agreed on a Statute setting up the Council of Europe, which was signed on 5 May. By this time the 'consultative body' had become the 'Consultative Assembly'. All member governments were to be represented on the Committee of Ministers; a complex voting procedure was laid down, but 'important matters' were to be settled by unanimous vote. The aim of the Council of Europe was splendidly vague: 'to achieve a greater unity between its members for the purpose of safeguarding and realising the ideals and principles which are their common heritage, and facilitating their economic and social progress.'

Bevin had succeeded in making the Council of Europe quite harmless from the British point of view. How much further other West European governments would really have been prepared to go, if Britain had not acted as a brake and an alibi, is not at all certain. Certainly, if the Council of Europe had demanded a real pooling of sovereignty, it would have had far fewer members. The merit of its harmlessness was that neutrals could join it without fear of compromising their neutrality; it also, in later years, made possible a certain degree of cooperation with East Europeans on special non-political matters of general European interest.

At the first meeting of the Council of Europe's Consultative Assembly, in August 1949, Churchill made a powerful speech in which he said: 'we should make a gesture of practical and constructive guidance by declaring ourselves in favour of the immediate creation of a European army under a unified command, and in which we should bear a worthy and honourable part.' This statement probably made more headlines than anything said in the Council of Europe before or since. It aroused great enthusiasm in some West European countries but turned out to be a snare and a delusion. As Eden wrote later in a splendid under-statement: 'I think this speech may have been misunderstood at the time.'[22] In October 1950 the French Prime Minister, René Pleven, announced the 'Pleven Plan' for a European Defence Community. The Labour Government was reserved and non-commital, as had been expected. When the Conservatives returned to power the following year they had to explain that in spite of what Churchill had said, they were not going to take Britain into the proposed European Army. There was gloom and anger in the West European countries most closely concerned.

M. Spaak of Belgium resigned the presidency of the Council of Europe Consultative Assembly in protest. Churchill himself did not try to explain the causes of a misunderstanding which harmed Britain. They were perhaps to be found in his tendency to be carried away by his own splendid rhetoric, especially when out of power.

Britain and the Schuman Plan
By the time the Council of Europe had been created in the watered-down form which suited Britain, the West European federalists and supranationalists were feeling thwarted. From their point of view, Britain was behaving like a dog in the manger. Britain felt that it could not itself join a federal or supranational structure, partly because of instinctive dislike of what it felt to be a doctrinaire approach to a practical problem, but even more because it felt itself to be an extra-European power as well as a European power. This was true: George Ball, who had little sympathy for Britain, pointed out that in 1950 Britain still controlled 100 million colonial people and manned a string of strategic bases round the world, with 75,000 troops in Egypt alone.[23] Because Britain would not itself become part of a European federal or supranational structure, yet wanted to play a key role in any European organisation, it ingeniously tried to prevent other West Europeans from creating the sort of structure they wanted. Or so it seemed to some West Europeans, both then and later.

The federalists and supranationalists therefore determined that Britain should not have another chance to block their plans. Their next project was the Schuman Plan, which created the European Coal and Steel Community. This resulted from the alliance of two men and the merging of two motives. Monnet wanted to have another try at creating a supranational structure, believing that it would be politically desirable and economically efficient. The French Foreign Minister, Robert Schuman, wanted to find a new way of dealing with the German problem, which had obsessed French politicians since the war. The French had reached the point when it had become clear to them that the United States and Britain were not going to agree to dismember Germany or permanently suppress the Germans. So, as Lord Gladwyn, a former British ambassador in Paris, put it, the emphasis came increasingly to be laid on the idea of 'containing' an always potentially dangerous Germany by the construction of some 'European' body into which it could be absorbed and which it could not therefore dominate.[24] The nub of the Schuman Plan was the placing of coal and steel production in France and Germany under the control of a single High Authority; other European countries could join in. Schuman, at a press conference on the day the plan was announced, 9 May 1950, set it in a wider political context. He said that France had taken upon itself for more than twenty years the role of champion of a united Europe. The new plan would be the first step in the federation of Europe.

It was bound to be disliked by the British Labour Government. For one thing, the nationalisation of the coal industry had been one of the key points of its political programme and was regarded as a major socialist achievement. How, it was asked, could the national-ised British industry be merged with free-enterprise continental industries, and taken from the control of the Labour Government and placed under an alien High Authority? The fact that in both France and West Germany there were at that time Christian Democratic leaders may have been another psychological barrier, though not a very important one.

The way in which Bevin heard of the plan was calculated to make him even more suspicious of it. The American Secretary of State, Acheson, went to Paris on 7 May, before travelling to London for a meeting with Bevin and Schuman. In Paris, Schuman told Acheson about the plan, asking him to keep it entirely secret because he had not yet presented it to the French Cabinet, let alone the Assembly. Since the German question was such a sensitive one, the slightest leak might make things go wrong. Acheson was then in an em-barrassing position: he had to go to London and have talks with Bevin, who was still in poor health after a major operation, without telling him anything about the plan. When it was announced in Paris, Bevin, who had known nothing about it, was very angry at French failure to consult Britain; he also suspected a French–American plot to keep the British in the dark. Acheson had to tell Bevin that he had known about the plan.

The next day, Acheson issued a statement that the objectives of the French plan had long been favoured by the American Government and expressed sympathetic approval. The Foreign Office said that the British Government, having had no notice of the French plan, had had no time to reach any conclusion. How-ever, it also said that Britain had always been anxious that a permanent solution of the age-long feud between France and

Germany should be found. Attlee told the House of Commons on 11 May that the British Government would approach the problem in a sympathetic spirit; but he stressed that it would have far-reaching implications for the economic structure of the countries concerned and would therefore require detailed study.

Later in the month France invited Germany, Britain, Italy and the Benelux countries to negotiations on the plan, on the understanding that those taking part would accept in advance its main principles, including the High Authority's power to make binding decisions. Britain said it wanted first to discuss the scheme fully, before accepting the principles. France did not agree, so the conference was held without Britain. On 16 April 1951 the treaty setting up the European Coal and Steel Community (ECSC) was signed.

One thing that could not be charged against Bevin was that he tried to hinder the Schuman plan negotiations once they had started. In November 1950 the British High Commissioner in Bonn told Adenauer that Bevin was quite sympathetic towards the Schuman plan, that he hoped for an early conclusion of the negotiations and that he planned to make agreements with the new Community as soon as the treaty was signed.[25] In the event Britain announced the setting up of a permanent delegation to the ECSC High Authority on 28 November 1951. Everything settled down peacefully.

Nevertheless, British failure to join the ECSC came to be regarded by many as a turning-point in Britain's post-war relations with Western Europe. Acheson wrote: 'some decisions are critical. This decision of May 1950 was one. It was not the last clear chance for Britain to enter Europe, but it was the first wrong choice – as wrong as General de Gaulle's tragic rejection of the penitent in 1963.'[26]

Certainly it marked the beginning of the split between Britain and the Six which proved so difficult to heal. It also marked the first occasion after the 1939–45 war on which France took a successful European initiative without Britain, and even in a sense against Britain. (The French can hardly have expected Britain to enter the negotiations on the conditions laid down.) It produced a shift in the balance of political forces in Western Europe, increasing the weight of France.

There is no doubt that the Labour Government underestimated the chances of success and long-term importance of the Schuman plan. There were several reasons: an ingrained Foreign Office tendency to be sceptical about ambitious new schemes; possible faulty advice from Whitehall experts on technical problems and prospects; opposition from influential and vocal sections of the Labour Party to any link-up with continental countries which could limit the British Labour Government's freedom to pursue its own socialist programme and to apply economic controls. (This was set out in the National Executive Council's document, 'European Unity', issued in 1950.)

However, when the Conservatives came back to power in 1951, they made no move to reverse the Labour Government's decision, as they had been expected to do. Eden, who became Foreign Secretary, dropped the matter. The change only came ten years later when a Conservative Prime Minister, Macmillan, reversed his own government's policy towards the Common Market. The simple fact was that in the early 1950s Britain still *was* a world power, if a declining one, and was preoccupied with such problems as relations with Communist China, the Communist revolt in Malaya, developments in newly independent India and Pakistan, an oil dispute with Persia, and, in the European context, the strengthening of NATO and of the newly formed West German state in the face of continuing Soviet hostility. If this wide range of major worries is taken into account, it is understandable, if unfortunate, that Britain failed to guess the long-term significance of the Schuman plan.

10 The 'Special Relationship' 1945–50

The surprising thing about the 'special relationship' between Britain and the United States was that it survived the many bitter disputes and grievances that arose. These included the abrupt cutting-off of American Lend-Lease; the size and severe terms of the American loan; the cutting-off of nuclear information to Britain; differences over European integration, over Communist China, and over the Korean war.

On the British side there was inevitably resentment of some American actions and attitudes. The British historian, W. N. Medlicott, probably reflecting official feelings at the time, called American action over Lend-Lease and the loan to Britain 'dollar diplomacy with a vengeance'. He also commented that there was a convenient American theory that economic cooperation within the Commonwealth in the form of preferences was morally indefensible, whereas high American tariffs were a legitimate expression of a healthy national life. Medlicott recalled that in 1946 the American press confidently forecast vast gains for American exporters in the Far East and India, mainly at Britain's expense. Washington thought that Britain should retire from Hong Kong, Singapore and Malaya. 'The moralistic current in American foreign policy,' he wrote, '... now dashed itself for a time against residual imperial barriers, mainly British. The unnecessary violence of this attack was due to something much more concrete than the vague humanitarian sentiments of American liberals. Powerful interests undoubtedly hoped to profit at Britain's expense.'[27]

There was also strong resentment in the Government when Truman cut off nuclear information. This was natural. In the early stages of the 1939–45 war, Britain was ahead of the United States in atomic research. In October 1941 (when the US was still neutral) Britain made an independent decision to make a nuclear weapon. After the United States came into the war, Britain agreed with the American Government and Canada to pool research and resources in order to speed up the process of making the weapon. The main work was to be done in the United States, by joint teams, largely for reasons of safety. This meant that while the British played an important part in the essential research, the actual production of the weapon remained in American hands. The two bombs which were eventually produced were dropped on Japan in August 1945.

Attlee expected the secret wartime agreements on exchange of information to continue. When he met Truman in November 1945 they agreed on 'full and effective cooperation'. When in April 1946 he received a letter from Truman refusing to help Britain in building an atomic energy plant – in effect, ending the wartime nuclear partnership – this seemed a breach of faith. Attlee argued back strongly. But in August 1946, the US Congress passed the MacMahon Act formally forbidding exchange of nuclear information. The Attlee Government decided to make a British nuclear weapon independently. In addition to strategic reasons, at this time it still seemed very possible that the United States might retreat into isolationism; it was therefore important for Britain to have the bomb, in part as a counter-weight to Soviet power. Moreover, a British nuclear weapon might help Britain to retain some influence over American policy, especially in the field of nuclear strategy. It was probably also seen as a means of regaining nuclear partnership with the United States.

The differences between the Labour Government and the United States over Communist China and the Korean war were serious. Britain moved rapidly to recognise Communist China, in January 1950, and wanted to establish some sort of working relationship with the Communist Government. The United States, which had been deeply involved with the Chinese Nationalists, disagreed.

When the Korean war broke out in June 1950, Attlee was prompt to back up the United States decision to intervene, and to send British forces to South Korea. However, he was very worried that the Korean war might distract American energies from more important areas, in particular Europe. He was also afraid that through the Korean war the Americans might become involved in a third world war with the Soviet Union or China. Bevin, for his part, was afraid that the United States might push Communist China into the Soviet Union's arms.

For this reason, he strongly opposed a proposal by the American commander, General MacArthur, for bombing bases in Manchuria. A remark by Truman at a press conference, implying that the United States might use an atomic bomb in the Korean conflict, led Attlee to ask for a personal discussion with the President. He had consultations with the French Prime Minister and Foreign Minister, who were in London on other business, before he flew to Washington. There he urged that it would be suicidal to allow American (and British and Commonwealth) forces to get bogged down in China, 'fighting the wrong people in the wrong place at the wrong time'.[28] He also told Truman privately that the British public would be appalled if the United States was seriously thinking of using an atomic bomb. Truman said this was not in his mind.

On Acheson, who was present at most of the talks, and who had been annoyed by earlier British and Indian peace moves, Attlee created the impression that he was asking the United States to accept defeat in Korea. This could hardly be Attlee's real aim; rather, he was asking the United States to put strict limits on the war and prevent any extension which could fatally weaken American power to resist aggression elsewhere, especially in Europe. In a final private talk with Truman, he secured agreement with him that neither the United States nor Britain would use atomic weapons without first consulting the other. But, as Truman's advisers pointed out strongly, any such undertaking by the President would have caused a storm in the Congress; so a very much watered-down formula appeared in the communiqué.[29]

In spite of all the many difficulties and differences, the 'special relationship' survived during the 1945–50 period, in the form of a very close knowledge and high degree of understanding, on the part of the government of each country, of the problems and ideas of the other. Acheson wrote that each side thought of relations between the two countries, and their management, as part of domestic affairs. He also described his very close relationship with Sir Oliver Franks (later Lord Franks) during his time as Ambassador. The two men had a private compact that they could talk completely freely with each other on the understanding that neither would report back to his government without the agreement of the other.[30] On the other hand, Acheson disliked all talk about the 'special relationship', since it could cause offence to other allies (to say nothing of American opinion, senators, mayors and others). When in May 1950 he discovered that after talks between US State Department and British Foreign Office officials a paper had been written on the 'special relationship', he ordered that all copies should be burnt.

Attlee and Bevin on their side were attacked from within the

D

Labour Party for giving away too much to the capitalist Americans. Attlee was tolerant in his attitude to what he called the 'woolly idealism' about foreign affairs of some Labour supporters. Bevin on the other hand got angry with the critics who, he felt, were always ready to stab him in the back. When Francis Williams asked Attlee if he had not sacrificed too much independence to get America in to Europe, Attlee replied, 'of course not', adding, 'without the stopping power of the Americans, the Russians might easily have tried sweeping right forward'. He used the same argument to justify giving the Americans air bases in Britain from which they could, in theory, use the atomic bomb against Russia. Obviously, Attlee said, it added a certain amount of danger to Britain's own position, but 'we couldn't have asked . . . continental countries to put themselves in a dangerous position while keeping ourselves out'.[31]

Neither sentimentality nor megalomania entered into the British Government's view of the 'special relationship' in the early post-war years. It was thought of as one element in a realistic foreign policy, a policy which was based on recognition of Britain's weakness.

One particularly stubborn difference, which did not become acute until several years later, was over the question of federal or supranational structures in Europe. Britain's dislike of them was often seen in America as somehow morally wrong. Any scheme likely to lead towards a 'United States of Europe' was popular with American politicians who assumed that the USA model could and should be copied elsewhere, however different past history and present circumstances; any such scheme was much more likely to persuade the Congress to vote money for aid than a scheme lacking this glamour. More seriously, successive American governments thought that some form of federal or supranational structure was the best way – perhaps the only way – of securing lasting political stability and strength in Western Europe. As President Kennedy later saw it, only a united Western Europe could be an equal (or nearly equal) partner to the United States within an overall Western alliance.

Given these convictions, Americans were apt to brush aside real and serious British difficulties as trivial or imaginary, and to assume that the Commonwealth could simply be dissolved by a wave of the hand, and that the British pattern of trade and British public opinion could be changed overnight. A few Americans, such as George Ball, came to think that it was America's moral duty to push Britain into Europe by forcing it to 'face realities' and abandon all extra-

European pretensions. America could do this by withholding aid to sterling and nuclear cooperation, and demonstrating forcefully that there was no such thing as a 'special relationship'. Luckily for Britain, American governments did not push their eagerness to get Britain 'into Europe' to quite such drastic lengths; they perhaps realised that a really bad quarrel with Britain would harm the interests of the United States and of the Western alliance. On the other hand, when Britain did at last try to 'enter Europe', American over-enthusiasm for the cause added to British difficulties.

PART III

Britain in Europe in the 1950s:
Time of transition

11   Britain in the 1950s: A weak great power

For Britain, the 1950s were a period of transition and flux in which it was difficult to keep a clear sense of direction. In addition to the new and far-reaching commitments to Western Europe which Britain had taken on in the 1945–50 period, the country started the new decade with a Commonwealth of which it still felt itself to be the undisputed leader and centre, a colonial empire spread so widely that very few people could accurately list the territories that composed it, and a chain of military, air or naval bases or staging-posts almost equally extensive and varied. The two most important bases – which cost Britain most money – were Suez and Singapore. Britain also believed that it held the main responsibility for peace and stability in the Middle East, which was thought to be threatened by a Soviet drive for power in the Eastern Mediterranean, as well as by the unsolved Arab–Israel feud and the internal quarrels of the Arab world. The grant of independence to India was not thought to have weakened the Commonwealth nor the scope of British influence; until the Suez crisis of 1956 Britain regarded India as an important partner in diplomacy in Asia (for instance, both in the Korean war and in the Indo-China crisis of 1954). British success in mastering the communist revolt in Malaya, though slow in coming, gave confidence that the Commonwealth could be held together and British influence maintained around the world. It was not until the Suez crisis that this confidence was seriously shaken. It was also felt that Britain had both a political and a moral duty to provide economic and technical aid to backward Commonwealth countries.

The basic dilemma which Attlee and Bevin had faced, but not solved, between 1945 and 1950 still remained. How was a world-wide role compatible with Britain's economic weakness? Under the Labour Government, Britain had withdrawn from its commitments in Greece, Turkey, Palestine and above all, India; but this had not removed the dilemma. The trouble was that whenever the question pressed for a clear answer, it was put aside because it seemed less urgent than the need to face up to what was seen as a world-wide threat – the threat from the Soviet Union in particular and from 'communism' in general.

It would be unfair to suggest that British politicians were naïve about 'communism'; the Labour leaders were quick to distinguish between the Chinese Communists and the Russians and loath to drive Peking into Moscow's arms. When Tito broke with Stalin, they were ready to help him. Bevin, according to Francis Williams, refused to see every communist uprising as a force of evil. Eden and Macmillan also were capable of discernment and a common-sense approach to 'communism'. On the other hand, Soviet propaganda organs and Soviet spokesmen at the United Nations and elsewhere attacked the Western Powers in vitriolic language on almost every front, and gave praise and encouragement to almost every movement or group, anywhere in the world, which opposed the West. It was therefore easy to see 'communism' as a centrally-controlled monolithic force directed from Moscow and aiming at world-wide disruption leading to world domination. Also, Stalin's ruthless achievement in creating an empire of apparently docile vassal states in Eastern Europe between 1944 and 1948, led to the dubious inference that the Soviet Union could repeat the performance in other parts of the world. All this produced a widespread tendency, even after Stalin's death, to over-estimate the efficiency and coherence of the 'communist bloc' or 'international communism'.

Since the Soviet or 'communist' threat seemed at every turn to make it dangerous for Britain to contract its worldwide commitments too quickly, for fear of opening the door to Soviet or 'communist' expansion, there seemed to be only one way open, during the 1950s. That was to go on spending too much money overseas and to live with a chronically unhealthy balance of payments, relying on American support – especially financial support – when things got too bad. It was all the easier to follow this course, in that during the 1950s Britain experienced a return of prosperity, and what was more, prosperity, in a relative sense, for a much bigger number of people than had ever known it before. This was what lay behind Macmillan's unlucky phrase, 'you never had it so good'.

At the start of the 1950s, however, Britain faced a serious economic crisis. When the Korean war broke out in 1950, Attlee, under strong American pressure, launched an ambitious rearmament programme which had a most harmful effect on the convalescent British economy. It diverted the British industrial effort from exports to armaments, while the prices of raw materials needed for the rearmament programme soared because greatly increased demand created world scarcity. Government spending on rearmament compelled cuts in other fields, including social services, and in April 1951 Aneurin Bevan resigned from the post of Minister of Health in consequence, as did Harold Wilson, then President of the Board of Trade. Luckily, the Americans fairly soon came to see that they had asked too much of Britain and the other West European allies, and had risked undoing the good done by Marshall aid. After a visit to Washington by Hugh Gaitskell, then Chancellor of the Exchequer, in September 1951, during which he warned the Americans of a possible British balance of payments deficit of one billion dollars and rapidly vanishing gold reserves, American pressure slackened and the pace and scale of rearmament were reduced. In this more practicable form, it was continued by the Conservative Government which came to power shortly after.

It seemed strange that Attlee and Bevin, who in 1947 had shown a clear understanding of economic realities by pulling out of Greece and Turkey, should have shown such lack of economic realism three years later. One reason was that they believed that the Korean war meant there was a direct threat of Soviet aggression in Europe so that rearmament must take priority over all other considerations. Another reason was that they felt that they must keep as close as possible to the Americans, so as to be able to influence them more effectively, and to persuade them to limit the Korean war and concentrate their energies on Europe.

On the question of limiting the Korean war, the British had mixed fortunes. In spite of Bevin's pleas that every effort should be made to avoid involving Communist China, Washington allowed General MacArthur to drive north towards the Chinese frontier, thereby bringing large Chinese 'volunteer' armies into Korea and prolonging the war considerably. On the other hand, the British were able to strengthen the hands of those elements in the American Government which were resisting proposals for all-out war against China and possibly also the Soviet Union; the war was at least contained, geographically, within the frontiers of Korea.

As for the defence of Western Europe, the Americans needed little urging, during the panic months following the North Korean attack, to take up new responsibilities. By the end of 1950 General Eisenhower had been appointed Supreme Allied Commander of

NATO forces in Europe and the President had promised to keep American troops in Europe under his command.

The Conservatives, when they took over in 1951, aimed to maintain a world role for Britain, though on a smaller scale than in the past. The Conservative Government resisted all American efforts, during the 1954 crisis of the Indo-China war, to involve Britain militarily in the conflict. It liquidated the vast Suez base and withdrew from Sudan – even if these achievements were off-set by the attempt to turn Cyprus into a large-scale base for Middle East operations and by the Suez operation of 1956.

However, continuation of a world role for Britain, even on a reduced scale, meant a heavy burden on the balance of payments. The well-worn solution was to increase British exports. There were some hopes that Britain, by forging ahead in such fields as peaceful nuclear energy, aircraft and aero-engine construction, electronics and computers, might win new export markets. But there slowly followed a realisation that Britain did not have a broad enough economic and financial base to succeed alone in these scientifically and technologically advanced fields where the cost of research and development was high. Hopes of finding world markets for British nuclear reactors were disappointed – often because of more forceful and more powerfully backed American selling methods. In computers, Britain was overtaken and out-paced by the Americans. The balance of payments problem was not solved.

The only solution seemed to be a world-wide partnership in which the Americans supplied the money and the British the experience, know-how and prestige in those areas which had traditionally been under British influence. In these areas, it was assumed that the British would retain the leadership, while the Americans would supply the necessary support in the form of economic and financial aid to governments friendly to Britain, and would withhold aid from governments with which Britain had a quarrel. Where necessary the Americans would demonstrate their political or military solidarity with Britain.

One example of this line of thought was Churchill's proposal to Truman in 1952 for American aid to Britain in carrying its 'heavy burdens' in the Middle East: the United States should put a brigade into the British base at Suez, so allowing the British to withdraw a division for use in other trouble-spots, and at the same time impressing the Egyptians by a demonstration of Anglo-American solidarity; the United States should also stop giving financial aid to Iran, so that Britain could bring its oil dispute to a rapid end. There can be no doubt that Churchill thought that all this would be in the joint Western interest. Truman did not accept the proposal.

It was in fact difficult to foresee how the United States would react to British requests for aid and support in any particular instance. This was because the Americans were split-minded in their reactions to British attempts to carry on a world role. On the one hand, they did not want to be left alone with their own new, rather overpowering, world-wide responsibilities; they wanted an ally, or allies; they feared that if the British withdrew from overseas commitments Soviet power or 'world communism' might fill the void. (Even in the late 1960s they did not want to see Britain withdraw from south-east Asia or the Persian Gulf.) They also had a certain respect for British efficiency or skill in certain fields.

On the other hand, the old instinctive mistrust of British 'imperialism' died hard. The Americans were reluctant to get involved in disputes which they regarded as private British quarrels, even when the British argued that they had a much wider significance in world-wide strategy. On other occasions, they argued that to back up the British (for instance, in the Persian oil dispute or the Suez crisis) would drive the other party into the arms of the Soviet Union. In a country where the Americans felt themselves to be more popular than the British, they felt it their duty to extract maximum benefit from this popularity, if necessary by publicly dissociating themselves from the British.

Finally, there was a growing feeling in Washington, during the 1950s, that Britain, instead of worrying about a world role, should 'get into Europe', as a stabilising and steadying force which would guide Western Europe – or rather the evolving Community of the Six – in the right direction and make it a reliable partner within the wider Atlantic alliance. There again, there was a certain split-mindedness in the Americans; they might, in general, want Britain to give up a world role, but they were much less eager to see Britain give up any one specific overseas commitment, where American interests could be said to be involved.

Another cause of uncertainty lay in personal relationships between leading British and American politicians. Acheson (as he made clear in his memoirs) felt strong personal liking both for Bevin and for Eden, especially Eden; he did not like Morrison or Attlee. As

Secretary of State he found it easy to work very closely with both Bevin and Eden, in spite of occasional storms. On the other hand relations between Eden and Dulles were frankly bad; there was very little understanding between them and Eden obviously thought Dulles both unaccountable and clumsy. 'My difficulty,' Eden wrote in his memoirs, 'was to determine what he really meant and in consequence the significance to be attached to his words and actions.' He added: 'the consequences were unfortunate for Britain, the weaker partner.' Eden's feelings were no doubt reciprocated. Dulles obviously resented and mistrusted the skills which Eden displayed at the 1954 Geneva conference in bringing about an Indo-China settlement, which Dulles refused to sign.

If there had not been such mutual dislike and misunderstanding between Eden and Dulles, it is just possible that Eden would not have launched himself into the very damaging folly of the Suez adventure. It was in part the outcome of bad Anglo-American relations; it made these relations worse than at any time since the 1939–45 war. It also marked the beginning of the end of Britain's effort to go on playing a world role. Sir Pierson Dixon, the British diplomat who had to defend Eden's action in the United Nations, wrote in his diary a year later: 'at the time I remember feeling very strongly that we had by our action reduced ourselves from first-class to a third-class power. We revealed our weakness, by stopping; and we threw away the moral position on which our world status largely depended. We were greater than our actual strength so long as people knew that we went to war in defence of a principle – which is what we did in 1914 and 1939. . . .'[1]

What the Suez débâcle also showed was the uncertainty of American support – whether financial, economic, political or military – for efforts to maintain Britain's position as a weak great power, or as the weaker partner in an American–British partnership. This uncertainty in the American attitude produced uncertainty and some floundering in Britain's own sense of direction and purpose during the 1950s. The unsolved problem of Britain's extra-European role, linked with the equally unsolved problem of the British economy, distracted British attention from the long-term significance of what was going on inside Western Europe during the 1950s, in the emergence of the Community of the Six as a powerful force.

12   Britain and the struggle over West Germany

The first half of the 1950s was taken up with a prolonged struggle
between the West and the Soviet Union over the rearming of West
Germany, which ended in a certain stabilisation in East–West
relations in Europe. The struggle was immensely complicated and
prolonged by the internal struggle within the Western alliance, and
above all inside the French mind, over the creation of an independent
West German State and its acceptance as an equal partner in the
defence of Western Europe. In this dual struggle, Britain played an
unspectacular but important part.

In the early post-war years, the Soviet Union had strongly opposed,
first, the unification of the three Western occupation zones of Germany, next, the inclusion of West Germany within the scope of
Marshall aid and the OEEC, and then the formation of the West
German State in September 1949. (Moscow declared this, in a note
of 1 October, to be a violation of Potsdam; Britain replied that it was
the Soviet refusal to treat Germany as a unit, as required by Potsdam,
which had compelled the West to unify Germany as far as lay within
its power.) At each of these steps it became more and more clear that
the Soviet Union, by cutting off its own zone from the West, had also
cut itself off from the power to intervene in West Germany. But it had
not yet given up hope of influencing the course of events in West
Germany.

The Soviet Union had good grounds for hope. Although there
were in West Germany several million refugees from East Germany,
the territories handed over to Poland, or the former German-
speaking areas of Czechoslovakia, who were bitterly opposed to
communism in every form, there was also a strong and vigorous
Social Democratic Party which was bitterly opposed to Adenauer
and his Christian Democrats. The Social Democrat leaders did not
like the Communists, but around 1950 they seemed to dislike even
more Adenauer's policy of working very closely with the Western
occupying powers and tying the new West German State very closely
into Western Europe. Ignoring the fact that Adenauer was working

for exactly the same end by less open means, they demanded equality of rights for West Germany. But they were genuinely at odds with Adenauer in pressing for the reunification of Germany and apparently really wanting it; in a reunited Germany the Social Democrats could expect a big reinforcement of their political strength in relation to the Christian Democrats. Adenauer professed to want German reunification but he obviously gave much higher priority to the integration of West Germany in Western Europe. The real hostility between Adenauer and leading Social Democrats, especially Schumacher, gave the Soviet Union an obvious opening.

The internal situation in France also offered an opening. After the withdrawal of de Gaulle in 1946, France had had to face a series of political crises, including the expulsion of the Communist ministers and the long and damaging series of Communist-inspired strikes in 1947, and a series of governments unable to command a stable majority in the National Assembly. The one subject which seemed certain to stir profound emotions in French hearts at all times was the threat of a resurgent Germany. Any politician who chose to play on this fear was sure of an immediate response. The powerful Communist Party naturally followed the Moscow line; the Socialists were also strongly anti-German. So the French in general had given up their hopes of the dismemberment of Germany reluctantly, and they watched nervously and with distaste the emergence of the new West German State which basked in American favour. In many Frenchmen there was still a hankering after a partnership with Russia aimed at suppressing Germany; this had been de Gaulle's aim in signing the French–Soviet Treaty of 1944.

In Britain, there were mixed feelings about the Germans. On the far right, the *Daily Express* made a special feature of warnings against the supposed German danger; on the left of the Labour Party and elsewhere among the party rank and file, there was dislike and fear of any sort of German nationalism. The Labour leaders, after successfully luring the United States into pledging itself to the defence of Western Europe, soon found that the Americans were rushing along too fast for them, dragging the reluctant British in their wake.

The Soviet Union might well think that there was a good chance of splitting the new and untried Western alliance over Germany. When the rearmament issue arose, the Soviet Union had of course every interest in preventing it on both military and political grounds. The Russians knew that the Germans were excellent soldiers, experienced in warfare deep inside Russian territory; they did not want twelve West German divisions facing them in the middle of Europe. Moreover, the rearmament of West Germany, on any of the plans proposed in the West, would mean the welding of West Germany yet more solidly into what Moscow saw as a hostile Western bloc. This would end the chance of successful Soviet intervention in West Germany, or elsewhere in Western Europe. Moscow had good reasons to use every political and propaganda weapon to stop West German rearmament by exploiting differences inside the Western alliance.

The first talk about rearming the new West Germany came towards the end of 1949, sparked off by news from East Germany. In October, the decision to form an East German State, or German Democratic Republic, was announced, as a reply to the 'dictatorial policy' of the Western powers in forming a West German State. Soon after reports began to reach the West about the arming of the East German People's Police. Adenauer uttered warnings about the new danger, but little notice was taken until the outbreak of the Korean war. It was then that the American defence chiefs decided that West German soldiers were essential for the defence of Western Europe (see p. 61 above).

When Acheson, Schuman and Bevin met in New York in September 1950, Schuman was most unhappy about German rearmament. However, the three foreign ministers could agree on a communiqué which said that German views on participation in an integrated defence force were being studied. They also declared that the Federal German Government in Bonn was the only government freely and legitimately constituted and therefore entitled to speak for the German people. The immediate reasons for this declaration were legal rather than political, but it became one of the foundation stones of Bonn's foreign policy until the late 1960s, when it became a millstone round the neck of West German leaders trying to reach an understanding with East Germany.

As a counter-move to the extremely cautious New York statement on West German rearmament, the Foreign Ministers of the Cominform countries (Yugoslavia had of course been evicted in 1948), together with the East German Foreign Minister, met in Prague and attacked the New York 'decisions' as 'a threat to Europe' and a gross violation of Potsdam. They proposed that a peace treaty should be concluded with Germany at once and that all occupation troops should be withdrawn within a year thereafter; an all-German constituent council should be set up to prepare the formation of a provisional democratic peace-loving all-German government; the council was to be formed on the basis of parity between the two Germanies (which would of course have given East Germany, with a population of around one-third of the West German population, a quite unfair weight).

This Cominform plan was followed up on 3 November by a Soviet note to the three Western powers supporting it and proposing a four-power meeting to consider the implementation of the Potsdam agreement on the demilitarisation of Germany.

At this point differences appeared in the reactions of the three Western powers. In Washington, Acheson thought that the Soviet Union was simply out to create trouble, delay West German rearmament and split the Western allies; and he advocated a tough and uncompromising response from the West. Bevin was fairly close to Acheson in his assessment of Soviet aims, but wanted a softer and more subtle response, taking account of public opinion in West Germany, France and Britain itself. Already on 25 October, Acheson had publicly denounced the Cominform plan as 'effrontery', and as an attempt to deflect the Western allies from their resolve to build 'real strength' in a free world. It was not until 13 November that Bevin said mildly in Parliament that the British Government did not think the Prague communiqué of the Cominform an adequate basis for dealing with fundamental world problems. But he added that the Soviet Union had, in spite of protests from the West, refused to disband large and heavily armed quasi-military units that had been created in East Germany.

The French were less interested in the Cominform plan than in their own new approach to the problem of West German rearmament. While the Cominform was meeting in Prague, the French Prime Minister, Pleven, had announced his plan (or rather, Monnet's plan) for a European defence force, containing West German units of not more than battalion strength, with a European Minister of Defence and a European Command which, in turn, would come under the NATO Supreme Commander.

This, according to Acheson, caused 'consternation and dismay' at first sight in Washington. To him, the plan appeared hopeless; General Marshall (then Secretary of Defence) and President Truman himself agreed.[2] There were similar feelings in London, except that the British had a better understanding of French misgivings about West German rearmament.

The British also found it hard to take the plan seriously. British officials made fun of it as an ingenious French device for keeping the Germans disarmed. The military experts were sceptical about the usefulness of a force in which the largest national contingent – or at least the largest German contingent – would be a battalion. (By the time the treaty creating a European Defence Community was signed, the limit had been raised to a division.) The Labour Party was bound to dislike the political implication that the European Army would be an important step on the way to a European federation.

As for Churchill, in theory the spiritual father of the whole idea, he obviously saw the EDC as a kind of abortion – something quite different from the grand alliance of European nations which he apparently had in mind. According to Harold Macmillan, he called it a 'sludgy amalgam'.[3] He was still carping at it when he visited Washington as Prime Minister early in 1952. Acheson described how Churchill 'pictured a bewildered French drill sergeant sweating over a platoon made up of a few Greeks, Italians, Germans, Turks and Dutchmen, all in utter confusion over the simplest orders'. Eden patiently explained that the proposal 'did not contemplate any such heterogeneous mixing of nationalities'. But, Acheson wrote, 'each time the subject came up, we went back to the baffled drill sergeant'.[4]

However, out of deference to French feelings, the first American and British public reactions to the Pleven plan were polite. Washington welcomed it and promised sympathetic examination. When in January 1951 France invited all European members of NATO to a conference to discuss the plan, the British Government said that it had 'considerable interest' in the conference; however it was not Britain's 'present policy' to contribute forces to a European Army; Britain would therefore be represented by an observer only.

By this time the plan had come up at a NATO meeting of ministers in Brussels in December 1950, at which it had been left open whether a German defence contribution should be made in the framework of the proposed European Army, or directly in the framework of NATO. Thereafter Adenauer got the impression that while the British were being very reticent, they seemed, like the Americans, to prefer the NATO solution to the European Army solution.

These differences between the three Western governments did not stop them from putting up a solid public front to the Soviet Union.

On 22 December 1950 they sent identical notes about the Soviet proposal for four-power talks. These, they said, should cover not only the German question, but also the principal problems in relations between the Soviet Union and the West. They suggested preliminary talks on an agenda, in New York. On 30 December, the Soviet Union agreed to preliminary talks, but they should *not* be in New York and they *should* be confined to the German question. On 23 January 1951 the three Western governments agreed that preliminary talks could be held in Paris (not New York) but continued to press for a wider agenda than the German question.

At the same time the Soviet Union, in an effort to influence British opinion, was conducting an acrid exchange of notes with the British Government, which it accused of wrecking the policy of Anglo-Soviet cooperation laid down in the Anglo-Soviet treaty. The British Government, on its side, was trying through its notes to Moscow to convince British opinion that West German rearmament was necessary because of the Soviet Union's 'vast military forces' and the rearming of the East European states, including the former allies of Hitler, and because of Soviet aggressiveness outside Europe. British opinion was left confused rather than convinced.

The four-power 'preliminary talks' eventually took place at the Palais Rose in Paris, starting on 5 March. They went on for three and a half months, and to the ignorant outsider seemed to plumb the lowest depths of ingenious futility, as each side put forward, or rejected, very slightly differing lists of points for a four-power conference. The points ranged from the violation of human rights in Hungary, Rumania and Bulgaria to American military bases in Norway and Iceland.

There was, however, a real stake in the game. The United States did not want a four-power conference which, it thought, would inevitably delay the rearming of West Germany and the creation of an efficient NATO defence system. It therefore did not want the Palais Rose talks to succeed; but it wanted Gromyko to appear guilty of their failure. Gromyko, probably hampered by excessively rigid instructions, helped the Americans to achieve this; he was clumsier than his agile and deft Western opponents. The British and French seemed to become fascinated by the game of skill for its own sake, and the Western team played together well. The result desired by the Western players was achieved: no agreement was reached on an agenda for a four-power conference.

After that, there was a lull in the word war between the West and the Soviet Union which lasted until it became obvious to Moscow that progress was being made over the French plan for a European Army including West German units. At first, the discussions started by France early in 1951 moved extremely slowly. But Eisenhower, who had become the NATO Supreme Commander at the beginning of the year and who was eager on military grounds to obtain German units, worked out an ingenious method of fitting the proposed European Army into the NATO integrated command. He also became a strong convert to the cause of European political integration. In Washington, during the summer of 1951, Acheson became converted to the European Army plan as the only possible means of getting the French to agree to rearming West Germany. Like Eisenhower, he also became a champion of West European integration on the lines favoured by the Six. However, this did not lead to direct American pressure on Britain to join the European Army. When Acheson met Robert Schuman and Herbert Morrison in September 1951, what he asked from the Labour Foreign Secretary was 'understanding support' for the plan. Morrison joined the other two in a declaration backing the proposed European Defence Community and saying that Britain wanted 'the closest possible association with the European continental community at all stages of its development'.

Soon after, Eden became Foreign Secretary. He reviewed the European Army question in the rather embarrassing light of Churchill's clarion call at Strasbourg not much over a year earlier. He secured from Eisenhower the view that a British offer to join the European Army 'now' would delay things and therefore be a mistake. Eden then in effect decided to carry on the Labour Government's policy – to keep Britain outside the European Defence Community but to promise close association. This was to be expected, even though when Eden announced it publicly at a press conference in Rome, it shocked the federalists and supranationalists.

From that point on, Eden was busy making plans for various links between Britain and the EDC, so as to overcome French fears of being left to face Germany alone and unsupported. Privately he still thought the plan might fail, and that some less ambitious scheme might be needed. In December 1951 he and Churchill visited Paris and promised support for the EDC. A joint Anglo-French statement forecast the closest possible association between Britain and the EDC including joint training and operations.

How much the plan needed outside help was shown by the mood of a debate in the French Assembly in February 1952. Schuman, as Foreign Minister, defended the EDC by arguing that it was designed to guarantee the security of France, and that if the French rejected it, then Germany would take the place of France in the new defence system. The former Radical Prime Minister, Daladier, attacked it, remarking that with Britain and Scandinavia outside the community, it would apply only to one-third of Europe. Gaullists attacked it as military nonsense, 'a utopian integration of spirits'. A deputy from a centre group attacked it as American-inspired, rather than of European origin. The Communists attacked it as a violation of the French-Soviet Treaty. The Socialist, Jules Moch, a former Defence Minister, said that the absence of Britain was such an important factor that it might influence the Socialists in their final vote on the ratification of the treaty. For the time being, the Government secured the votes of most Socialists by stating conditions for conclusion of the EDC Treaty: one was that the effort to secure British participation should include 'the study of institutions and arrangements likely to bring this about'.

At almost the same moment, there was a debate in the West German parliament, in which the Social Democrats attacked the EDC on the grounds that there would not be equal rights for the West Germans. The Government won a comfortable majority for a resolution in favour of a European federation and German participation in common defence on a basis of equal rights. In fact, the West Germans would not have had equal rights with France in the EDC as planned, but this was glossed over.

Just after these debates, at the NATO council meeting in Lisbon, Eden and Acheson tried to help things forward by letting the ministers of the Six know that Britain and the United States would make a joint declaration guaranteeing support for the EDC against any threat to any of its members from within or without. This was intended as a guarantee to France against trouble from West Germany. Schuman was pleased but not satisfied.

A little earlier, the Soviet Government had decided to launch a new campaign against West German rearmament, by offering a tasty carrot to the West Germans. On 10 March it sent notes to the three Western powers calling for immediate talks to draw up a German treaty and arrange withdrawal of all occupation troops. New points were that reunited Germany should have its own armed forces and be permitted to produce military equipment, though it would promise not to enter any military alliance directed against any Power which took part in the war against Germany (that is, it would be banned from belonging to NATO or the EDC). Former Nazis, except for those sentenced for war crimes, were to have civil and political rights. These suggestions, if intended to entice the West Germans, were bound to displease the French; but Moscow may have thought that the French were in such a muddle anyhow that it was unnecessary to court them.

In the following weeks the three Western powers were carrying on two operations at once – countering the new Soviet campaign and trying to get the EDC treaty signed. In mid-March the European Army conference in Paris asked Britain to sign a separate treaty with the EDC, in addition to the joint Anglo-American declaration of support. Britain responded by offering to extend to the EDC as a whole the commitments which it had made in the Brussels Treaty of 1948, to give military aid in case of attack.

On 20 March, the three Western powers answered the Soviet Union, calling for free all-German elections, to be held after a UN Commission had verified political conditions throughout Germany, as an essential preliminary before forming an all-German government. The right of a united Germany to enter into 'associations compatible with the UN Charter' (which meant NATO) was defended. On 9 April the Soviet Union replied, rejecting a UN Commission and proposing a four-power commission instead. On 13 May the three Western powers said they would prefer an 'impartial commission' to a four-power commission to investigate conditions in Germany. On 25 May the Soviet Union sent further notes accusing the three Western powers of hatching an open military alliance with West Germany through which the West Germans could prepare for a new war.

On 27 May 1952 the EDC treaty and the accompanying documents were at last signed in Paris. The Soviet diplomatic barrage seemed to have failed. The EDC, as defined in the treaty, was to be a typical Monnet-esque structure. It was to be a 'supranational community' with common institutions, common armed forces and a common budget; troops were to wear a common uniform. There would be a Council of Ministers, Assembly and Court of Justice; the

111

specifically supranational institution would be a Board of Commissioners (the equivalent of the High Authority of the ECSC or the Commission of the future Economic Community). This was to be the federal yeast in the dough of intergovernmental ingredients. The basic military unit, composed of troops of the same nationality, would be around 13,000 men. France would be in a special position because of the need to supply occupation troops for West Germany and troops for overseas commitments; it would therefore keep armed forces outside the EDC.

At the same time Eden and Acheson signed the joint declaration that the United States and Britain would regard any threat to the integrity or unity of the EDC as a threat to their own security (this was a guarantee against a West German walk-out), and Eden signed the treaty between Britain and the EDC, extending to the EDC as a whole the pledge of military aid given in the Brussels Treaty. However, Eden rather spoilt the gesture by refusing to allow the new treaty to run for the fifty years of the Brussels Treaty; it was linked with Britain's membership of the Atlantic Pact, and therefore subject to review after twenty years.

It might have been thought that the Americans, in their strenuous effort to get their West European allies to agree to West German rearmament, were now home and dry. This was not so. The EDC treaties still had to be ratified by the various parliaments.

In the House of Commons, the Labour Party was still very uneasy about the whole affair, but was hamstrung by the fact that it was a Labour Government that had originally accepted American policy on German rearmament. In the debate at the end of July 1952, the Labour Opposition approved the general policy of bringing West Germany into 'a continental community within a wider Atlantic community', and of a German defence contribution within this framework; but it declared formal approval of the treaties to be 'inopportune', especially at a time when attempts were still being made by the Western Powers 'to discuss the German problem with the USSR'. Among Labour speakers, the former Defence Minister, Shinwell, said that the possibility of four-power talks should not be cut off. Hugh Dalton, the former Labour Chancellor of the Exchequer, said that the British people had little enthusiasm for German rearmament and in fact had 'considerable repugnance' for the general idea; he gave a warning that there might be a repetition of the Molotov–Ribbentrop deal of 1939. Eden, on the government side, threw cold water on the idea of talks with the Soviet Union, on the grounds that Moscow would never allow free all-German elections and wanted to leave a united Germany in 'dangerous and irresponsible isolation'. The Government won the day with a majority of forty.

It was a different matter in France and West Germany. Adenauer was in no hurry to face his Social Democratic opponents until the French position had become clearer. The French Government approved a ratification bill in January 1953 but was afraid to put it to the vote in the Assembly. It decided that it wanted still more guarantees from Britain. At the beginning of the year Britain had made proposals for practical military cooperation between Britain and the EDC, including training facilities for the EDC in Britain, joint formation training, interchange of officers and coordination of air defence systems. These were discussed with the French Prime Minister, René Mayer, and the Foreign Minister, Georges Bidault, when they visited London in mid-February; the French Ministers countered with proposals for the closest possible cooperation 'with particular reference to the political aspects'. Britain remained determined not to join the EDC but wanted to give France every satisfaction short of joining.

Meanwhile, there were important changes in the world outside Europe. At the beginning of 1953, Eisenhower became President, with Dulles as his Secretary of State. In March Stalin died; this started speculation in the West about big changes in Soviet policy, for good or bad. By the time the three Western Foreign Ministers met in Washington in July, both France and West Germany had decided that they wanted a further bid for negotiations with the Soviet Union before ratifying the EDC treaties. The three Western powers suggested to the Soviet Union a meeting in September. In August the Soviet Union rejected a four-power conference, proposing instead a German peace conference within six months, preceded by formation of a provisional all-German government. It was possible that the new Soviet Government did not want to face four-power talks in which the West would insist on talking about free all-German elections: the workers' demonstrations in June in East Berlin, suppressed by Soviet tanks, had made it clear to the world what the result of free elections in East Germany would be. However, by the end of November the Soviet Union had agreed to a four-power conference; Berlin was eventually agreed as the place.

Britain in a divided Europe

At the same time, the United States was getting badly worried about the endless delays over West German rearmament. Dulles was not a patient man; the Congress, which had swallowed the EDC plan whole, might refuse to vote money for the defence of Western Europe if this bait were withdrawn. Dulles wanted to get the four-power conference over and done with as quickly as possible. He regarded it as a waste of valuable time. In December he said at a press conference in Paris that there might be an 'agonising re-appraisal' of United States policy if France did not ratify the EDC treaty. (He had already talked privately in this strain to Eden.) His remark had exactly the wrong effect on French opinion, which it was intended to influence.

In January 1954 the four-power conference met in Berlin, with Molotov, who had served Stalin for so many years, still representing the Soviet Union. It never had the slightest chance of success. The Western strategy was to hammer away on the need for free elections throughout Germany in order to produce a truly representative all-German government with which a peace treaty could be concluded. A further aim was to secure freedom for a united Germany to link itself with the West through NATO or the EDC. It was obvious that both ideas were repugnant to the Soviet Union. Molotov's brief was to push the peace treaty plan, including the proposal that Germany should have its own armed forces, and to attack NATO and the EDC as designed for aggression against the Soviet Union. There was obviously no meeting-point between the two sides. However, Eden seems to have tried quite sincerely, in private meetings with Molotov, to discover whether there was any possible common ground. Not surprisingly, he found none, nor did he find out anything about the new Soviet leadership.

(One thing, however, Eden did achieve in Berlin: to bring about agreement among the four, overcoming considerable resistance from Dulles, to hold a further conference, including Communist China, on Indo-China and Korea in the following April. It was at this further conference, in Geneva, that Eden again, played an outstanding role, against resistance from Dulles, in helping to bring about an Indo-China settlement which enabled the French to withdraw from a militarily impossible position in relatively good order and by agreement. However, this did nothing to improve Eden's relations with Dulles and little to increase Britain's popularity in France.)

The Berlin conference – or rather its breakdown – theoretically cleared the way for French ratification of the EDC treaty. In April 1954, to help the process forward, Britain moved still closer to the EDC. It signed an agreement on military cooperation in all fields, linked with a unilateral British declaration. Through these, Britain undertook not to withdraw from the mainland of Europe so long as there was a threat to the security of Western Europe and of the EDC; Britain would consult with the EDC on questions of mutual concern, including the level of British and EDC armed forces serving in NATO on the European mainland. Moreover Britain would agree to the inclusion of British army formations and air force units in EDC formations, and vice-versa. Spelling out this agreement, Eden said that a British armoured division would be placed with an EDC corps, and RAF units would participate in European units in each NATO air group. To get over French objections to the fact that the British treaty with the EDC, signed nearly two years earlier, was linked, as regards its duration, with the Atlantic Pact, Britain said that it regarded the Atlantic Pact as of 'indefinite duration' and was confident that it would develop as an 'enduring association' for common action between member states in every field.

This was rather a vague formula. But Eden made it clear that in practical terms British association with the EDC would be extremely close: a British minister would attend meetings of the EDC Council of Ministers, and a permanent British representative would be in constant contact with the Board of Commissioners. This should perhaps have warmed a few French hearts. In fact, it seemed a little odd that Britain, having gone so far, could not take the final step and become a member of the EDC. If Britain had an extra-European role and extra-European obligations, so also had France; in both cases, safeguards were possible. The basic difficulty was that the EDC was declared to be a step to European federation; British opinion was simply not ready for the country to be merged in a federation. (Nor, very probably, was French opinion.) Given this feeling, and given Eden's doubts whether the French would ever ratify, whatever the inducement, it would have been extraordinarily difficult for Britain to take the final plunge into membership. Short of that, the British did all they possibly could to make the EDC plan work.

Nevertheless, some prominent Americans and some West Europeans later blamed the British for the fact that when the EDC treaty finally came before the French Assembly in August 1954, it was rejected, and the whole scheme collapsed. Perhaps if the British had agreed to join the EDC, the Assembly might have felt differently; but this cannot be taken completely for certain. The strong French national feeling, or sense of French identity, which was expressed by de Gaulle a few years later, must have existed in 1954; fear of Germany was not the only reason for French opposition to the EDC. Moreover, the EDC plan was a French plan; when Pleven put it forward, he must have known that Britain would dislike its federal aspect; unless, therefore, he was using it purely as a delaying tactic, he must have thought that it would work without Britain.

The fundamental difficulty was that the French had worked themselves into such a state of inner tension that they were unable to say either yes or no to West German rearmament; they did not want to take the decision themselves, nor did they want others to take it for them; they hoped that some outside event would somehow remove the necessity of making a decision. In other words, the French went through a kind of long psychological crisis, partly as a result of unwise and excessive American pressure. The British tried to help the French over the crisis, unsuccessfully; even if they had gone farther than they did, they might well have failed. In the end the French got over the crisis for themselves by rejecting the EDC treaty; after that they reacted to the German problem far more calmly, without the fears and tensions of the past.

This made it relatively easy for Eden to step in and conduct a rescue operation in the autumn of 1954. By a lightning diplomatic tour of West European capitals and by skilful handling of a difficult conference in London, he played a leading part in producing a complex agreement which brought West Germany into NATO and made sure that the United States would not make an 'agonising reappraisal' of its policy towards Europe and that the Congress would not cut off money for West European defence. Already in October 1954 it was possible for a conference to be held in Paris at which a whole network of treaties, protocols and declarations was completed.

The five-nation Western Union created in Bevin's day in 1948 was expanded into the seven-nation Western European Union so as to include West Germany and Italy, which thereby submitted themselves, along with its other members, to a relatively mild measure of arms control (though Britain and France retained a privileged position). Within this framework Germany was to supply divisions to the NATO command, becoming a full member of the alliance;

Britain promised to keep four divisions and the Tactical Air Force in West Germany, only withdrawing troops in case of urgent need elsewhere or in consequence of serious balance of payments difficulties; West Germany declared that it would not make nuclear, biological or chemical weapons, or guided missiles. This time the French Assembly gave its approval, though the British Government thought it necessary to issue a public warning that if it did not, France might find itself isolated and West German rearmament would nevertheless go ahead. These warnings presumably had some influence on the debates in the Assembly and the Council of the Republic; they can hardly have made the British popular in France.

The Paris agreements came into force on 5 May 1955. At last the process of rearming an unenthusiastic West Germany could begin. The British could reflect that if, as Bevin had strongly urged, Adenauer's original suggestion for an armed West German federal police force had been accepted, it could have happened several years earlier, without imposing such severe strains on relations among the Western allies, perhaps too without such a long, bitter and futile propaganda war with the Soviet Union, and just possibly without such a hardening of the East–West division in Europe. But any such reflections rested on many 'ifs'.

Two days after the agreements came into force, the Soviet Union fulfilled its threats and denounced its treaties with Britain and France. In the following month, it announced that it wanted to establish diplomatic relations with West Germany and invited Adenauer to visit Moscow. Such was Soviet realism.

There was a further consequence; in May 1955, the month when the Paris agreements came into force, the Warsaw Pact was signed. It was a kind of watery mirror-image of NATO, bringing together the East European states and East Germany under a (Soviet) joint command. It was not clear how far this new pact, and the formal and open subordination of the East European armed forces to a Soviet Commander, really added to Soviet armed strength. The Soviet Union had already constructed a web of bilateral defence treaties with the East European States and had from early post-war days sent military 'advisers' to them to secure the necessary coordination. The creation of an overall Soviet command may have increased the general level of military efficiency – in particular through lengthy joint manoeuvres on the territory of the East European states (though in the 1960s independent-minded Rumania resisted these).

Britain in a divided Europe

But it also made for dissatisfaction and resentment in the higher ranks of the East European military hierarchies, as was revealed by the Czechoslovak Colonel Prchlik during the brief 'Prague Spring' of 1968.

The Warsaw Pact did, however, provide the Soviet Union with yet another way of controlling the East European countries, in addition to the controls exerted through 'inter-Party relations' (that is, through the Soviet claim to the right to sack Party leaders of other countries) and through penetration of the secret police and internal security apparatus of other countries. West German rearmament unhappily provided the Soviet Union with the pretext for instituting this additional method of control and pressure on Eastern Europe.

13 Britain and the emerging superpowers: Summitry in the 1950s

During the 1950s the United States and the Soviet Union – mainly through the manufacture of stocks of hydrogen bombs sufficient to create a balance of terror – were moving to the status of superpowers, immensely more powerful than any other countries. Britain, in spite of its decision in 1952 to make its own hydrogen bomb, could not hope to follow them to this power status. Britain was too small and the cost was too great. Nevertheless, the Conservative leaders, Churchill, Eden and Macmillan, all had a taste for diplomacy at the summit level. They believed that Britain, because of its long experience and skill in international affairs, its wartime role and its nuclear status, however modest, was well fitted to span the gulf between the superpowers and bring them nearer together. The two seemed, in the early 1950s, to have taken up completely rigid positions, set hard in postures of mutual hostility. British politicians felt that they still had some room for movement; they could be more realistic and less dogmatic. This approach was in line with traditional British diplomacy, or what Lord Strang called its 'conciliatory quality'. It was also in line with Bevin's way of thinking, in spite of all his genuine toughness towards the Soviet Union. He had privately written to Attlee from Moscow, about the Soviet Union and the United States, 'for us Britishers, between the two of them, our task is very difficult'; he had spoken of his hope that it would in the end be possible to bargain with Russia.

Neither to Bevin nor to the Conservative leaders of the 1950s did this belief in conciliatory diplomacy mean disloyalty towards the United States or other allies. But in the tense and confused atmosphere of the 1950s, British efforts at 'summit diplomacy' were often mistrusted and disliked by allied leaders, especially Adenauer, in spite of British assurances of loyalty. As for the Soviet Union, it had an obvious interest in encouraging British efforts in so far as these tended to cause division or suspicion among the Western allies. But it is also possible that in the period of uncertainty and change inside the Soviet Union after Stalin's death the Soviet leaders may have had a more serious and genuine interest in British approaches. It can, too, be argued that during the Berlin crisis of the late 1950s, Macmillan played a useful part in helping Khrushchev to climb down from a dangerous position in which he was challenging the West. On the other side, it could be argued that the Soviet Union, with its customary realism, did not rate highly Britain's influence in the world, especially after the Suez débâcle had shown up Britain's relative military weakness and the divisions within the Commonwealth; it was therefore unlikely to set much store by British summitry.

Yet even if Conservative leaders in the 1950s had an exaggerated idea of the country's influence and prestige, and even if there was an element of vanity in their summitry, they were also sincere in their wish to establish some sort of contact and understanding with the Soviet leaders, however limited. Moreover, their efforts at summitry were popular with the British public (though less so in Whitehall).

Summitry had first become an established practice during the 1939–45 war, when the Western leaders believed that agreements could only be reached by dealing directly with Stalin. In so far as the military conduct of the war was concerned, the summit meetings served a useful purpose; in so far as they dealt with post-war problems they produced little more than pieces of paper which each side interpreted in a totally different way.

Churchill's Bid for the Summit

It was Churchill who in May 1953 revived the idea of summit meetings as a possible way out of the deadlock in relations between the West and the Soviet Union (he had mentioned it earlier, as opposition leader, in the election campaigns of 1950 and 1951; the idea had then been denounced by Labour as an election stunt). By May 1953 he was once again Prime Minister and was the only survivor of the big three of the war years; Stalin had died two months earlier.

Stalin's death was the starting-point of the speech which Churchill made in the House of Commons on 11 May. He said he would welcome any sign of better relations with Russia; he had been encouraged by a series of 'amicable gestures' by the new Soviet Government. It would be a pity to impede any 'spontaneous and healthy evolution' in Russia. In this context, he suggested a new summit meeting:

I believe that a conference at the highest level should take place between the leading powers without long delay. This conference should not be overhung by a ponderous or rigid agenda, or led into mazes or jungles of technical details, zealously contested by hordes of experts and officials drawn up in vast cumbrous array. The conference should be confined to the smallest number of Powers and persons possible. It should meet with a measure of informality and a still greater measure of privacy and seclusion. It might well be that no hard-faced agreements would be reached, but there might be a general feeling among those gathered together that they might do better than tear the human race, including themselves, into bits. . . . If there is not at the summit of the nations the will to win the greatest prize and the greatest honour ever offered to mankind, doom-laden responsibility will fall upon those who now possess the power to decide.

This was the fine flower of Churchill's style, as in the old days of the war. He was an old man approaching eighty. It was easy to see his proposal as an expression of nostalgia for lost national greatness, or as an old man's wish to achieve one more great deed – a peaceful deed – before the end. However, Churchill received immediate support from Attlee, who as leader of the Opposition said: 'there seems to be a definite departure from the autocracy of Stalin. . . . We want to try to get closer personal relationships. We want a greater understanding by us of them and by them of us.' Attlee went on to say that it was an over-simplification, to which some Americans were prone, to imagine that all nationalist movements – for instance, in Indo-China, or the Arab world – were just a matter of Soviet intrigue.

In Washington, where there was at that time great impatience about French slowness in facing up to West German rearmament, reactions to Churchill's summit proposal were very reserved. The State Department said two days later that the Soviet Union should first demonstrate its sincerity through progress in the Korean armistice talks and over the Austrian treaty: this would 'help to pave the way towards a high-level conference'. Eisenhower told the press that he had no objection to Churchill's idea, but before committing the United States to participation, there should be some evidence of general good faith.

The French liked the summit idea a little better, though they were unhappy about the British attitude to their war in Indo-China. In Bonn, Adenauer was worried that a summit would delay still further the achievement of sovereignty by West Germany.

In Moscow, the official Soviet reaction was given in *Pravda* ten days later. It mixed approval for the summit proposal with attacks on the rearmament of West Germany. Churchill, it said, had made 'constructive proposals regarding methods of examining international problems . . . he did not bind his offer to any kind of preliminary obligations. . . . His rich and long experience in international relations apparently protects him from the elementary mistake that . . . one side can dictate to the other preliminary conditions . . . '. The Soviet Union, the paper said, was always ready to examine any suggestion directed towards assuring peace.

Pravda also pointed to the difference between the British and United States' positions. It was therefore possible to see the Soviet reaction as a piece of wedge-driving or as delaying tactics intended to block the European Army plan. But perhaps, considering how short a time had passed since Stalin's death, it was an attempt by the new Soviet leaders to keep every option open – even including a serious discussion with the West.

Nothing came of Churchill's move. Eisenhower proposed that before any summit meeting with Russia there should be a Western summit – the United States, France and Britain. Churchill agreed, but fell ill; so also did Eden. Lord Salisbury represented Britain at a meeting of Western Foreign Ministers and argued strongly for a top-level meeting with Malenkov – who then seemed in control of Soviet affairs – with a flexible agenda. The Americans and the French would only agree to a four-power meeting of Foreign Ministers on Germany and Austria. In December 1953, the postponed Western summit took place; all that came out of it was agreement on a note to Moscow about a meeting of the four Foreign Ministers.

For the time being, summitry was smothered. However, the House of Commons would not let it die. In April 1954, it returned to the subject. This was the period when, after a series of American hydrogen bomb tests, the general public was getting seriously worried about the new weapons held by the two superpowers. The Labour Opposition put down a motion which spoke of the 'immense range and power' of the hydrogen bomb, and declared that the House would welcome an immediate British initiative for a summit meeting of the United States, the Soviet Union and Britain on the control of armaments. Churchill agreed, with reservations on the word 'immediate'. In June 1954 Churchill was in Washington, mainly to patch up with Eisenhower the differences which had arisen between Eden and Dulles over Indo-China. He failed to make any headway over a summit.

Churchill then made a curious move. On his way home from the United States he sent a personal and private telegram to Molotov (then Soviet Foreign Minister), at the same time informing Eisenhower of his action. He suggested to Molotov that if a three-power summit were impossible, he himself might make contact with the Soviet Government. How would Molotov feel about the idea of 'a friendly meeting, no agenda, no objectives but of living side by side in growing confidence, easement and prosperity'? He spoke of his 'war comradeship' with Molotov. A few days later he received what he later described as 'a very encouraging reply' from Molotov. He then proposed Berne, Stockholm, or Vienna as meeting-place, assuming that Malenkov and Molotov would take part on the Soviet side.

Eden, in his memoirs, did not mention this plan of Churchill's; perhaps, as Foreign Secretary, he found it highly embarrassing, because of its likely effect on some of Britain's allies. A new Soviet move in a different context provided a means of diverting Churchill from his aim. On 24 July 1954 the Soviet Union had sent notes proposing a formal conference of European states and the United States to discuss a proposal for a European security pact. This could be seen as cutting across the Churchill proposal for an Anglo-Soviet meeting – though Molotov insisted in letters to Churchill that it did not. Churchill was induced to put aside his plan. The Soviet leaders seemed to grow cool about the summit idea; early in 1955 Malenkov was deposed, and replaced by the Bulganin–Khrushchev combination.

The next move came, rather oddly, from the French Prime Minister, Pierre Mendès-France. On 3 January 1955, just after the French Assembly had narrowly approved the Paris agreements on West German rearmament and WEU, he wrote privately to Churchill that he still needed help in getting the approval of the Council of the Republic; he therefore proposed that the three Western powers should invite the Soviet Union to a summit, on the understanding that it would only actually be held when ratification of the Paris agreements had been completed. A week later Churchill answered that he was 'whole-heartedly resolved' that there should be no invitation to the Soviet Union 'in any circumstances that we can foresee' until the agreements had been ratified by all the signatories.

In March 1955, the Labour Party again pressed Churchill. It put forward a motion in the House of Commons urging that, since a world war waged with weapons such as the hydrogen bomb would mean the destruction of civilisation, the Government should immediately approach the United States and the Soviet Union to arrange a summit meeting 'with a view to a lessening of world tension and preparation for world disarmament'. Churchill took the same line as with Mendès-France, that a summit must await ratification of the Paris agreements.

In April Churchill resigned and made way for Eden, who thereupon became an ardent 'summiteer', though of a much more orthodox and unadventurous kind than Churchill. Since the Paris agreements came into force in May, it was not difficult for him to carry the American and French leaders with him. The three Western powers sent their invitation to the Soviet leaders on 10 May. The British general election, called by Eden, was held on 26 May. The Conservative Party won a comfortable majority to which the promise of a summit must have contributed something. The summit meeting was held at last in Geneva in mid-July.

The Geneva Summit 1955

One of the Soviet proposals at Geneva was a European Security Treaty. This had blocked Churchill's proposal for an Anglo-Soviet summit the year before. At that time the West regarded it as no more than an attempt to prevent ratification of the Paris agreements. This was certainly one aspect of it. But it also had a more serious aspect, since it survived the coming into force of the agreements and was repeatedly revived in various forms in later years.

It was first put forward by Molotov at the four-power Foreign Ministers conference in Berlin, on 10 February 1954. It was to be a fifty-year treaty (like the Brussels Treaty of 1948, creating Western Union). Article 4 of the Soviet draft treaty was also reminiscent of Article 4 of the Brussels treaty, but rather more of Article 5 of the Atlantic Pact. An armed attack against any party would be considered an attack against all; in the event of such attack, each party, in the exercise of the right of individual or collective self-defence, would assist by all means at its disposal including the use of armed force.

A significant point was that pending the formation of an all-German government, both West Germany and East Germany were to join the pact as parties with equal rights. This was perhaps the first clear sign that the Soviet Union had come to see that it could not block the incorporation of West Germany in the Western alliance, and that it should therefore prepare to fall back on its alternative position – that is, the demand that the West (including West Germany) should accept the division of Germany, and of Europe, as permanent. This would also mean Western recognition of the East German State, as the equal of the West German State.

The Soviet Union also accepted the need for the United States to take part in any European Security Treaty, or conference. A Soviet note of 31 March 1954 said that the Soviet Government 'sees no obstacles in the way of a positive solution of the question of United States participation in an all-European collective security treaty'; in November 1954 the Soviet Union specifically invited the United States to a European security conference.

The Soviet note of March 1954 had thrown in the ludicrous red herring that the Soviet Union should join NATO. This cannot have been intended as anything but a debating point. At the summit in July 1955, however, a more serious Soviet suggestion was made: that there should be a non-aggression pact between NATO and the Warsaw Treaty organisation. This implied that in spite of the repeated Soviet demands for the withdrawal of all foreign troops from Germany and other European countries, the Soviet leaders had begun to think that the existence of the two rival defence organisations could in a sense be a stabilising factor and a safeguard against unintended upheavals; at the very least it would help to perpetuate and harden the division of Europe.

It was often argued in the West that the overriding Soviet objective was to secure the withdrawal of American troops from Europe, by whatever means. But at no time during the 1945–70 period – apart from possible Soviet second thoughts in 1956 – did it seem likely that in order to purchase American withdrawal, the Soviet Union would be willing to withdraw its troops from East Germany and Eastern Europe: the risk of losing control of Eastern Europe would have been too great. In terms of practical politics, therefore, it looked as though from the mid-1950s onwards, the Soviet Union were willing to tolerate, if not to welcome, the continued existence of NATO – provided always that it respected the line of division in Europe.

What Bulganin and Khrushchev wanted out of the 1955 summit, therefore, was a firm understanding with the West on respecting and maintaining the division of Europe. This, in the Western view, had been created by the Soviet Union, by cutting off Eastern Europe and East Germany from all contact with the West; in the Soviet view, it had been created by the West, which had created NATO and included West Germany in it. The sequence of events in time was against the Soviet view. The Soviet leaders were probably hardly aware of this.

They failed to get a pledge from the West to respect the division of Europe, but they probably left Geneva fairly confident that the Western powers, having successfully consolidated their own 'bloc' in Western Europe, had no serious intention of interfering with Soviet interests in Eastern Europe. Sir Ivone Kirkpatrick, who, like most professional diplomats, was sceptical about the usefulness of summits, wrote that the Russians went away with the comforting assurance that the Americans entertained no aggressive designs against them.[5]

Kirkpatrick also said that in so short a time and without any proper preparations it would have been impossible to have reached any satisfactory conclusion. In fact, fairly detailed preparations had been made on the Western side. The Austrian treaty was no longer on the agenda: on 15 May 1955, partly perhaps to sweeten the atmosphere for the summit, the Soviet Union at last joined the Western powers in signing the treaty. (The conclusion of the Warsaw Pact at almost the same moment provided the Soviet Union with an alternative reason for keeping troops in Hungary and Rumania; until then, the need for lines of communication with the Soviet occupation forces in Austria had been the legal pretext.) On Germany, Eden thought that the West should take an initiative of its own. The Foreign Office had worked out a further development of the plan put forward at the Berlin conference of 1954 – which had come to be known as the Eden Plan – for reunification of Germany through free elections under impartial supervision, with freedom for a united Germany to join a regional association (such as NATO). The new element in the expanded Eden Plan was to link German reunification with a plan for European security of a very much less ambitious kind than the Soviet draft for a European security treaty which – so Eden argued – would take years to work out and would postpone reunification indefinitely.

Eden suggested three ways of providing the security element: a security pact between the four powers and a united Germany, by which each would pledge aid to any other party which was the victim of aggression; an area of arms limitation, and limitation of forces, in Germany and neighbouring countries; and a demilitarised zone 'between East and West', in other words, along the existing dividing line. The last of these three ideas, however, caused alarm and despondency in Bonn, where it was feared that it would perpetuate the division of Germany and might lead to withdrawal of American troops. It became known unofficially as the 'bad Eden plan' in contrast to the other proposals, which were labelled the 'good Eden plan'; it was quietly forgotten, and over-laid by a further idea of Eden's for the joint inspection of forces confronting one another in Europe.

As for the 'good Eden plan', it made no headway. Bulganin said flatly, as could have been expected, that the Soviet Union could not agree to a reunited Germany entering a Western military grouping. Bulganin also told Eden at a private dinner that it was not possible for his government to go back to Moscow having agreed to the immediate unification of Germany: neither the army nor the people would understand, and 'this was no time to weaken the government'. Eden thought there was a 'genuine streak' in this. More seriously, perhaps, Khrushchev told Eden over dinner that the NATO countries should maintain their organisation and the Warsaw Pact countries theirs, and all should join the European security treaty. The Soviet leaders were in fact ready to discuss any solution *except* the reunification of Germany.

It seems most unlikely that the Western leaders ever considered among themselves how far they could go in reciprocating Soviet 'realism' about the division of Germany and of Europe. With Adenauer watching the summit like a hawk, on the look-out for any sign of Western weakening, they dared not make any move towards the Soviet position. Towards the East European countries, Eisenhower made a brief gesture at the opening of the summit, saying that the American people believed that the people of Eastern Europe had not been given the right to choose their own form of government in accordance with wartime agreements. When the Soviet leaders refused to discuss the subject, it was quietly dropped. In any case, Eisenhower's move may have been intended to impress the American public rather than the Soviet leaders. As a gesture it was a little perfunctory. It might seem odd that the Western powers should devote so little energy to the problems of all the East Europeans, and so much to rescuing eighteen million East Germans from Soviet control. The reason was that they felt they could do virtually nothing for the East Europeans, while it was a matter of immediate practical importance to them to back up Adenauer in his political struggles at home. Adenauer on his side felt that he could not allow the demand for reunification to be monopolised by his political opponents at home, and that he must constantly demonstrate that he was keeping the Western allies up to the mark, or reproving them if they began to stray – as Britain was often suspected of doing.

So great was Adenauer's strength of character and persistence, and so anxious were the Americans to retain the loyalty of the West Germans, that the Western powers felt that they must repeatedly make public demonstrations of their devotion to the cause of German reunification. For Britain this also meant devising more and more ingenious schemes aimed at combining reunification with security guarantees for the Soviet Union. None of these – either at the 1955 summit or at the Geneva meeting of the four Foreign Ministers in the following autumn, or at conferences in later years – carried any weight with the Soviet Union. But they presumably gave some satisfaction in Bonn, even though they failed to remove persistent West German doubts about Britain's reliability.

Bulganin and Khrushchev in London; from the Summit to Suez
Although the Geneva summit had little to show in the way of concrete results, it temporarily produced a better atmosphere in relations between the West and the Soviet Union. Bulganin told the Supreme Soviet on 4 August that all four powers had shown their desire to end the cold war; the policy of 'positions of strength' had been abandoned. Bulganin also said that he and Eden had discussed a possible exchange of visits of warships and military delegations between Britain and the Soviet Union. Eden also seemed pleased; before leaving Geneva he invited Bulganin and Khrushchev to visit Britain, and they accepted. In spite of violently anti-British speeches made by Khrushchev in India and Burma, towards the end of 1955, the visit took place in April 1956.

In the long conversations between Eden and the Soviet leaders, the familiar arguments about Germany and European security were exchanged, but probably neither side expected any movement. The Soviet leaders may have decided that as a result of the 1955 summit, the European situation had been satisfactorily stabilised. Their interest had therefore switched to other continents, particularly Asia and the Middle East. Eden on his side was preoccupied with Middle

East problems, above all, worsening relations with Egypt. He made a particular point of telling the Soviet leaders that Middle East oil was literally vital to the British economy and that Britain would fight for it. This was intended as a warning to the Soviet Union to respect British interests in the Middle East, and Eden wrote that later events showed that the Russians had heeded it.[6] However, it did not stop the Soviet Union from encouraging and helping President Nasser. Nevertheless, the Conservative leaders, unlike the Labour leaders, seemed to make a big impression on Khrushchev; he told the British Ambassador in Moscow that he had 'great confidence in Eden and Selwyn Lloyd [the Foreign Secretary]', adding: 'I think we are beginning to understand each other.'[7]

In spite of the apparent success of the Anglo-Soviet talks, in the growing crisis between Britain and Egypt during the summer of 1956, culminating in Nasser's expropriation of the Suez Canal, Eden tended more and more to see the evil hand of the Soviet Union. During August, he noted with satisfaction that the Soviet Foreign Minister had recognised, in the course of diplomatic conversations in Moscow, Britain's special interests in the Middle East.[8] However, by the end of August Eden wrote to Eisenhower: 'I have no doubt that the Bear is using Nasser, with or without his knowledge, to further his immediate aims. These are, I think, first to dislodge the West from the Middle East, and second to get a foothold in Africa so as to dominate that continent in turn . . .'.[9] Eden's aim must partly have been to win Eisenhower's support for his tough line towards Nasser, and if possible to get him to over-rule Dulles, who was blowing first hot then cold, thereby frustrating and infuriating Eden. But no doubt Eden also believed in the Bear's sinister activities, and with some reason. However, he failed to sway Eisenhower or Dulles; so the Anglo-French operation started without Eisenhower's knowledge, and the United States took an open stand against it – naturally supported by the Soviet Union – at the United Nations.

It seemed strange that Eden's policy could have led to the unprecedented situation in which the two rival superpowers were aligned against Britain and France. Among the many reasons were the unusually bad relationship between Eden and Dulles and Eden's illness. It was one of the weaknesses, as well as the strengths of the 'special relationship' that because of its intimacy, it depended so much on personal relations between individuals. As things were, American condemnation of Britain had considerable popular appeal inside the United States. Richard Nixon, then Vice-President, said that for the first time in history America had shown independence of Anglo-French policies which reflected the colonial tradition: this 'declaration of independence', he went on, had had an electrifying effect throughout the world.[10]

The Soviet leaders were so tempted by the possibilities of this novel situation that on 5 November Bulganin proposed to Eisenhower that Soviet and American naval and air forces should cooperate in taking 'decisive measures' to stop Anglo-French aggression in Egypt. But by this time Soviet troops were suppressing the Hungarian uprising; the White House said that Bulganin's proposal was unthinkable and an attempt to divert attention from the Hungarian tragedy.

Britain, Suez and Hungary

For some sections of British opinion, the coincidence of the Suez operation with the Soviet repression of Hungary raised agonising doubts or fears. The question was whether, at a crucial stage of events in Hungary, the Soviet Union seriously considered adopting a relatively 'liberal' policy towards Hungary and perhaps also the other East European states – a policy in line with the revulsion against Stalinism which had followed Khrushchev's disclosures in the Central Committee in February 1956; and whether the balance was tipped against such a change of policy by the Anglo-French operation against Egypt. This could have strengthened the hands of the hard-liners and Stalinists in Moscow against the innovators and anti-Stalinists.

The dates looked significant. On 29 October, the Israeli Army launched its attack on the Egyptians in the Sinai peninsula. At this moment the reforming government of Imre Nagy seemed in firm control in Budapest, after the first phase of fighting. On 30 October a remarkable declaration by the Soviet Government was published in Moscow, stating Soviet willingness to consider withdrawal from Hungary, together with wider and deeper reforms in relations with the East European states.

On military relations with Hungary and other Warsaw Pact countries, the declaration said that it was common knowledge that Soviet units were stationed in Hungary and Rumania under the Warsaw Treaty, and in Poland under the Potsdam agreement as well as the Warsaw Treaty. There were no Soviet units in the other East

European countries. With the aim of safeguarding the mutual security of the socialist countries, the Soviet Government was ready to examine with the other members of the Warsaw Treaty the question of the Soviet forces stationed in those countries. In doing so, the Soviet Government based itself on the 'universal principle' that the stationing of forces on the territory of other states was done 'only with the consent of the state on whose territory and at whose request those forces have been so stationed'.

Dealing specifically with the Hungarian crisis, the declaration said that the Soviet Government, like the whole Soviet people, deeply deplored the fact that developments there had led to bloodshed. It then claimed that Soviet troops had entered Budapest at the Hungarian Government's request, but went on: 'bearing in mind that the further stationing of Soviet military units in Hungary may provide a pretext for making the situation more tense, the Soviet Government has instructed its military command to withdraw the Soviet military units from the city of Budapest as soon as the Hungarian Government finds it necessary.' 'The Soviet Government,' the declaration went on, 'is ready to enter into appropriate talks with the Government of the Hungarian people's republic and the other parties to the Warsaw Treaty on the question of the stationing of Soviet forces in Hungary.'

On the same day, 30 October, that Britain and France sent an ultimatum to Egypt and Israel, Soviet troops started moving out of Budapest. On 31 October Britain and France started their air offensive on Egyptian airfields and other military targets in preparation for landings. Also on 31 October, the Hungarian Prime Minister protested to the Soviet Ambassador against the movement of Soviet troops and armour *into* Hungary and asked the Soviet President to name a day for negotiations on Soviet withdrawal from Hungary, which wished to withdraw from the Warsaw Pact and become neutral. (The mention of neutrality was of course a fatal error.) On 4 November the Soviet troops attacked Budapest in strength.

It could be argued that the aim of the Soviet declaration of 30 October was merely to mobilise the other Warsaw Pact governments to bring pressure to bear on Hungary to remain a docile ally, in the interest of 'the mutual security of the socialist countries'; perhaps also to gain time for the arrival of Soviet reinforcements in Hungary for the decisive assault on Budapest and the occupation of the whole country. Soviet tactics twelve years later in Czechoslovakia – when invasion followed a period of apparent dithering and flirtation with a relatively liberal policy – seemed to strengthen this interpretation. There were phrases in the 1956 declaration which could be taken to foreshadow the 'Brezhnev doctrine' of 1968.

Nevertheless, there were big differences between 1956 and 1968. In 1956, power was held by Khrushchev, an unaccountable man ready to take risks and experiment with new ventures, very different from the ultra-conservative, orthodox and cautious rulers of 1968. Eight months earlier at the Twentieth Party Congress he had denounced Stalin and the wrongs of the Stalin era, and had given the appearance of turning over a new leaf, in relations with the East European countries as well as inside the Soviet Union. In April he had dissolved the Cominform, which existed as an agency for keeping other communist parties in line with Moscow. The Soviet Government's declaration of 30 October based itself on the Twentieth Congress, denouncing 'violations and mistakes which had belittled the principle of equal rights in the relations between socialist states'. It said that the Soviet Government intended to put into effect the 'historic decisions' of the Twentieth Congress, one of which was that friendship between socialist countries should rest on 'the immutable basis of respecting the full sovereignty of each socialist state'.

In the economic field, the Soviet Union said it was ready to discuss with other socialist states measures which would 'remove any possibility of violation of the principle of national sovereignty, mutual benefit and equality in economic relations'. In particular, it was ready to discuss the 'desirability of the further stay' (that is, the withdrawal) of Soviet advisers – 'engineers, agronomists, scientific workers and military advisers'. (The Soviet declaration said nothing about the 'advisers' on internal security and secret police matters, who had been one important cause of the quarrel between Tito and Stalin in 1948, and who may well also have been a factor in the Soviet–Czechoslovak quarrel in 1968.)

The whole tone and scope of the Soviet declaration therefore suggested something more far-reaching than just a tactical move in the struggle to subdue Hungary, perhaps a genuine move towards a less arbitrary and unequal relationship with the East European allies – though Moscow would almost certainly not have accepted the Hungarian declaration of neutrality.

It is also likely that there were differences inside the Soviet leadership over Hungary. Sir William Hayter, who was British Ambassador in Moscow at the time, believed that there was 'a certain hesitation and perhaps a division' in the Soviet Government about what to do next.[11] When on 30 October, the order was given for Soviet troops to leave Budapest, the Soviet Defence Minister looked very bad-tempered, made the 'famous Russian dismissive gesture of the hand' and said to the American Ambassador, 'let them [the Hungarians] get on with it as best they can'. It looked, Sir William Hayter commented, as though the strong-arm party had been over-ruled. Then came the Anglo-French intervention and Nagy's declaration of neutrality for Hungary. It was the second of these two events, he thought, which determined the switch in Soviet policy in Hungary – but the first 'contributed something'.[12]

Certainly at the time of Suez there were feelings of guilt over Hungary among a good many people in Britain. When Eden broadcast his defence of the Suez operation on 3 November, he did not talk about Hungary. When the Labour Party leader, Hugh Gaitskell, broadcast on the following day, he immediately linked Hungary and Suez: 'I cannot but feel, hearing today's heart-breaking news from Hungary, how tragic it is that at the very moment when the whole world should be united in denouncing this flagrant, ruthless, savage aggression by Russia against a liberty-loving people, we, by our criminal folly, should have lost the moral leadership of which we were once so proud.' A few days later, Eden had taken up the theme of Hungary, for a rather different purpose. In his Guildhall speech of 9 November, he spoke of the world's shock and horror over Hungary, adding, accurately enough: 'the world stood powerlessly by, unable to help except by such medical supplies as it may be possible to distribute. . . .' A week later he was denouncing the 'nauseating hypocrisy' of the Soviet Government in condemning Anglo-French action in Egypt while it was itself engaged in 'enslaving the Hungarian people', and was contrasting Britain's good behaviour in accepting U N observers and a U N force for Suez with the Soviet rejection of any U N intervention in Hungary.

This argument hardly answered British self-questioning about the possible link between Suez and the Soviet repression of Hungary. However, for the failure of the outside world to intervene in Hungary, whether through the United Nations or in any other way, Britain can hardly be blamed. Even if there had been no Suez operation, it is most unlikely that the United States would have been willing to go beyond verbal denunciation of the Soviet Union. It had drawn the logical conclusion of Soviet possession of the hydrogen bomb – that any military move across the dividing line in Europe would be too dangerous to risk. World opinion had little weight with the Soviet Union when the latter felt that important Soviet interests were at stake.

Another question was whether the Soviet Government at any time seriously thought of military intervention in the Suez affair. On 5 November Bulganin sent a letter to Eden – and simultaneously published it – saying that the British Government 'must put an end to the war in Egypt'; otherwise 'war might spread to other countries and become a third world war'. Bulganin appealed to Parliament, to the Labour Party, to the trade unions and to the 'people of Britain' to stop aggression, and said the Soviet Union was fully determined to restore peace 'through the use of force'. This, according to Eden, weighed very little in his decision on 6 November to order a cease fire. Certainly its tone and its immediate publication suggested a propaganda purpose rather than a serious threat. On 10 November, Moscow publicly threatened to allow 'great numbers' of Soviet volunteers to go to Egypt if the British and French did not withdraw their troops. This again had a strong propaganda flavour; the aim was probably to gain credit for the Soviet Union for the inevitable British and French withdrawals.

However, even if there was never any serious question of Soviet military intervention, it was obvious that Eden's activities at the summit did nothing to restrain the Soviet Union from exploiting the whole Suez crisis to the full, politically and in propaganda. The Soviet Union established for itself a strong position of influence in Egypt, and did whatever it could to undermine Britain's position throughout the Arab world.

The Suez adventure had another consequence. The joint action had the effect of worsening Anglo-French relations, rather than consolidating them. What France wanted above all was the removal of Nasser, whom it held responsible for most of its troubles in Algeria. The operation failed to remove Nasser and if anything strengthened his position. This, the French could argue, was because the British moved too slowly and stopped too soon. Moreover, what had started as an Anglo-French gesture of independence of the United States ended with British submission to American wishes, or so it seemed to the French. The resulting coldness between the two countries had its effect on the long negotiations over the economic structure of Western Europe in the late 1950s.

Macmillan and Summitry

Summitry as practised by Eden had been of strictly limited value. His highly-polished diplomatic virtuosity had not carried enough weight. He resigned on health grounds in January 1957 and was succeeded by Macmillan who, for some months, was extremely cautious in his approach to the matter. His first aim was to restore relations with the United States. It was no moment for Britain to risk further misunderstandings with allies by independent diplomatic moves.

However, the Soviet leaders had acquired a taste for summitry. In April Bulganin – in spite of the unpleasant things the British and Russians had said to each other over Hungary and Suez – made an approach to Macmillan. He sent him a long, polite and conciliatory letter, recalling pleasureably his visit to Britain with Khrushchev a year earlier; the Soviet Union, he said, recognised the importance of British economic interests in the Middle East, but thought that they should not be pursued by the use of force; he wrote approvingly of the Eden plan for demilitarised zones and areas of restricted armaments in Europe. Bulganin ended flatteringly: 'for the maintenance of peace in Europe and throughout the world, it is exceptionally important that the present tension in relations between the Soviet Union and Britain should be replaced by good friendly relations.' He suggested Anglo-Soviet talks.

Macmillan obviously regarded this letter with some suspicion. It was widely thought at that time that the Soviet Union was anxious to persuade the world to forget Hungary and to climb back to respectability. Britain itself had achieved this feat after Suez with unexpected speed. After a Macmillan–Eisenhower meeting in March, Anglo-American relations had returned to normal. Macmillan was not in a mood to give the Soviet leaders a helping hand. He waited two months before replying to Bulganin's letter, and then said that while he welcomed its conciliatory tone, he would not be frank if he did not express a certain disappointment at the lack of any new and constructive proposals. He was ready to consider means of improving relations but he suggested a long list of actions which the Soviet Union should undertake in order to show good faith, and said that in the Middle East it was still pursuing a policy harmful to Britain's well-being. Rebuffed, Bulganin replied a month later expressing his 'profound disappointment' at Macmillan's views and his failure to make any constructive proposals whatsoever. He made a sharp attack on NATO and particularly on plans for the 'concentration of atomic weapons in Europe'. Two months passed before Macmillan replied, once again coldly: 'it is sometimes better that disagreement should be openly expressed, not camouflaged in obscure wording: in this way we may find a basis for agreement.'

Then came an event which had wide political repercussions: the launching of the Soviet Sputnik on 4 October 1957. It greatly increased Soviet prestige throughout the world, caused some alarm in the West, and gave great self-confidence to the Soviet leaders. At the same time, the Soviet Union – as Bulganin had said in his second letter to Macmillan – reacted strongly against plans which were being discussed among the NATO allies for arming the NATO forces with atomic weapons, both tactical and intermediate range, with the nuclear warheads kept under American control.

The combination of these things produced a positive explosion of Soviet diplomacy in favour of every kind of summit meeting. Bulganin sent notes in all directions, both before and after the meeting of NATO Heads of Government (yet another summit) in December 1957, which announced the decision to establish stocks of nuclear warheads in Europe to be 'readily available' in case of need, together with an American offer of intermediate range missiles to NATO countries which wanted them.

First, Bulganin sent notes to eighty-two members of the United Nations, pressing for an atom-free zone in central Europe, as originally proposed by the Polish Foreign Minister, Rapacki, in the previous October. He also sent notes to the fifteen NATO Heads of Government warning them of the danger of Soviet 'retaliatory action' against atomic bases in European countries. To Eisenhower, Macmillan and the French Prime Minister, Gaillard, he sent notes saying he was ready for a summit meeting to discuss an atom-free zone and other Soviet proposals.

All this was in December 1957. In January 1958 Bulganin sent notes to nineteen governments, including all NATO countries, proposing a summit meeting within the next two or three months. In addition to the NATO and Warsaw Pact countries, countries such as India, Afghanistan, Egypt, Sweden, Yugoslavia and Austria were to be invited. Bulganin was against a preliminary meeting of foreign ministers.

The Soviet diplomatic offensive in favour of a summit continued until the late summer of 1958. Although until March it was conducted in the name of Bulganin, the offensive bore the mark of Khrushchev's personality. At the end of March 1958 Bulganin handed over the post of Prime Minister to Khrushchev who denounced him a few months later as a member of an 'anti-party group', along with Malenkov, Molotov and others. From April onwards, Macmillan was in correspondence with Khrushchev; the Western leaders were holding out for a preparatory meeting of foreign ministers before a summit. In July came the American–British intervention in Lebanon and Jordan. Khrushchev proposed a five-power summit including Nehru. Macmillan suggested a summit-level meeting of the Security Council. Khrushchev then suddenly dropped the summit idea, proposing instead a special meeting of the United Nations Assembly. Macmillan disagreed. The correspondence then lapsed. It had become a little absurd. In November 1958 a speech by Khrushchev opened a new Berlin crisis.

Macmillan and the Berlin Crisis
The Berlin crisis brought Macmillan back to summitry, at a moment when the Soviet Union and the West seemed to be heading for a direct clash. It was perhaps surprising that for over nine years after Stalin lifted his blockade of the city, there had been relatively little trouble over Berlin. It seemed an inevitable trouble-spot since both sides were highly vulnerable. The access routes to Berlin from the West could at any moment be harassed or cut by the Soviet Union or the East Germans by all sorts of devices. On the other side, since there was still freedom of movement between the Western and Eastern parts of the city, the stream of refugees from East Germany to West Berlin, or through West Berlin to West Germany, showed up dramatically the unpopularity of the East German Communist regime; it also sapped East Germany's economic strength, since many of those who went West were young and highly skilled. Both the Soviet Union and the Western powers were therefore very sensitive on the subject of Berlin. Possibly that was why the lull lasted so long.

It would have been political logic for the Soviet Union, when in 1955 it recognised West Germany and granted sovereignty to East Germany, to argue that the position of the three Western powers in

Berlin had become an anomaly and an anachronism, and that they should withdraw. But the Western powers, in granting sovereignty to West Germany, had specifically reserved their rights in respect of Berlin as well as German reunification. The West Berlin Mayor and Senate remained legally subject to the three Western Commandants in Berlin, not to the Bonn Government. For economic and political reasons, the Western powers allowed West Germany to develop very close links with West Berlin, including the right for West Berlin to send non-voting representatives to the parliament in Bonn; but they did not allow these links to undermine their own rights as laid down in wartime agreements with the Soviet Union.

In 1955, the Soviet leaders decided not to challenge these rights. This was the time just after the Geneva summit; there was a lot of talk about the 'Geneva spirit'. When the Soviet Union signed a treaty with the East German Government on 20 September 1955, the Western position in Berlin was safeguarded. The treaty said that the control of traffic of troops and material of the Western garrisons in West Berlin would 'temporarily be exercised by the command of the Soviet troops in Germany, pending the conclusion of an appropriate agreement'. This was confirmed in Soviet notes to the three Western powers in October. Although the word 'temporarily' sounded threatening, no pressure was exerted on the West to change the position until Khrushchev's speech of 10 November 1958.

Whether at this moment Khrushchev deliberately planned to start a major crisis is not altogether certain. He was making an emotional, hard-hitting speech in East Berlin, attacking the 'militaristic circles' in West Germany and the supposed delivery of American nuclear weapons to the West Germans. He then said that the time had obviously come for the Potsdam signatories to renounce the remnants of the occupation regime in Berlin, so as to create 'a normal situation in the capital of the German Democratic Republic'. There were signs that Khrushchev's remarks were impromptu rather than carefully prepared. However, seventeen days later the Soviet Union sent notes to the three Western powers stating Soviet demands in more formal terms (and correcting Khrushchev's errors in his presentation of the case). The Soviet Union said that the 'occupation regime' in West Berlin must be ended; West Berlin should become a demilitarised free city guaranteed by the four powers; in other words, the Western garrisons should withdraw. West Berlin's communications with the outside world would cease to be a Soviet responsibility and would depend on the good will of the East German Government. Finally, the Soviet notes set a time-limit of 'half a year' for the necessary arrangements to be made between the two parts of Berlin and the two German governments. The Western powers were apparently to have no say in the matter.

This was a direct challenge to the West by Khrushchev. On 14 December the three Western governments said they were determined to maintain their position and their rights in Berlin. On 31 December, they sent notes to the Soviet Union, saying, of the 'half a year' time-limit, that they could not discuss matters with the Soviet Government under menace. On 10 January 1959 the Soviet Union published a draft peace treaty for Germany, providing a special status for West Berlin as a demilitarised free city; it also said it was willing to have 'a preliminary exchange of opinion' with the Western powers. The 'half a year' time-limit was neither reaffirmed nor withdrawn. But there was still an implied threat: 'no one can hinder the Soviet Union from relinquishing the function which it performs in respect of Berlin . . . by means of an agreement with the German Democratic Republic.' That meant that the Soviet Union might at any time abdicate its responsibility for maintaining Western access to Berlin, and leave the East Germans free to cut it off.

Macmillan decided that this potentially dangerous situation gave an opening for a British diplomatic initiative at the summit. On 5 February he told the House of Commons that he had had it in mind for a long time to visit the Soviet Union. When Bulganin and Khrushchev had visited Britain in 1956 they had invited Eden to pay a return visit; later Macmillan himself had been invited. 'Recent international developments,' Macmillan said, had made him feel that a visit would be of value. He was not going to conduct a negotiation on behalf of the West; but he hoped his conversations with the Soviet leaders would give them a better knowledge of the Western point of view, and make it easier to understand what was in their minds. On leaving London, he said: 'we are going to search out the hearts and minds of the Russian leaders.'

Macmillan was in the Soviet Union from 21 February to 3 March. There were some unpleasant moments during the visit; Khrushchev made a speech calling the Western attitude on Berlin absurd. Two days later he had a sudden tooth-ache which prevented him from accompanying Macmillan to the Ukraine. However, the visit ended up in an amiable and cheerful atmosphere and Macmillan appeared on Moscow television. The joint communiqué said that the two sides were unable to agree about the juridical and political aspects of the Berlin question, but recognised that it was of great importance for peace and security in Europe that the matter should be urgently settled; they therefore acknowledged the need for early negotiations. Above all, they 'endorsed the principle that differences between nations should be resolved by negotiation and not by force.' Macmillan left Moscow feeling that the Soviet time-limit had been lifted. Three days later Khrushchev said, half-jokingly, at a press conference that he agreed that the Western powers had lawful rights for their presence in Berlin and that one of the reasons why he had proposed a German peace treaty was to extinguish these rights. The four powers, after some argument, agreed that their Foreign Ministers should meet in Geneva in May.

It was hard to judge how much Macmillan had achieved by his summit meeting with Khrushchev, unless it could first be assessed just how dangerous the crisis really was before he went to Moscow. After the event, it could be argued that Khrushchev's near-ultimatum over Berlin was a 'try-on' rather than a serious threat. He had strong reasons for wanting to change the position of West Berlin as a Western outpost and shop-window deep inside Soviet-controlled Eastern Europe and was also probably under heavy pressure from Ulbricht, the East German leader, to take action. He may have hoped to create panic among the Western powers, so that they would quarrel among themselves and end by giving him what he wanted. He may never have had any intention of risking war in Europe.

At the time, Khrushchev's unaccountability and impetuousness created an unpleasant feeling of uncertainty about what he might or might not do next. Four years later, the Cuba missiles crisis showed that he sometimes pushed things dangerously far. At the very least, it was a useful safety measure for Macmillan to go and 'search out' his heart and mind.

There was also no doubt that Macmillan, whose style of leadership and speech had some Churchillian echoes, had been waiting for the right opportunity for a gesture which would show that Britain was still a great power, if not a superpower, and was still capable of acting independently of the United States though as a loyal ally. Unfortunately, this particular independent gesture was not at all welcome to the leading European allies; it was regarded with suspicion or disapproval in Bonn and Paris, in spite of all Macmillan's assurances After returning from Moscow, Macmillan had to go to both capitals to try to make his peace with Adenauer and de Gaulle. The whole affair did nothing to improve Britain's already difficult relations with the two leading Common Market countries, strained by the long and frustrating negotiations over a wider European free trade area, which had collapsed a few months earlier. Macmillan's Moscow visit served no British national interest in the narrow sense. But it may to some degree have served a wider European interest by de-fusing an explosive situation.

Summitry was by now in fashion, especially with the Soviet Union. It had a strong appeal to Khrushchev's extrovert, even exhibitionist temperament, and his liking for human contacts, big audiences and plenty of publicity. He did not suffer from inhibitions nor from the fear of making a fool of himself. Probably this was why he so deeply shocked orthodox Soviet Communists and officials.

The four Foreign Ministers met in Geneva throughout the summer, discussing the German question in general and Berlin in particular. Selwyn Lloyd, for Britain, tended to take up a more conciliatory and optimistic attitude than his Western colleagues, who felt that any change in the existing Western position in Berlin was bound to be for the worse. Adenauer, who was watching closely from the side-lines, advised extreme caution. In any case, the Foreign Ministers' efforts were cut short by President Eisenhower's rather unexpected conversion to summitry and his invitation to Khrushchev to visit him in the United States. The Foreign Ministers left Geneva in early August saying that the positions of the two sides on certain points had come closer, and that their discussions would be useful for the further negotiations needed to reach agreement. Gromyko said that he looked forward to a summit to settle matters.

Khrushchev's visit to the United States in September 1959 obviously made a big impression on him, as he showed in a speech to a mass audience on his return to Moscow. His intimate talks with Eisenhower at Camp David seemed friendly and successful. The result was an understanding that negotiations on Berlin would be resumed. Khrushchev seemed to be looking forward to an early four-power summit with pleasure. There was apparently a new mood in Soviet-American relations.

Macmillan too wanted an early summit. The fact that there was an election campaign in Britain in September 1959 provided the

141

context for his promise that the date of the summit would be fixed within a few days. In October he was less optimistic. He told the new House of Commons, resulting from the election, that he wanted a summit as soon as possible, 'in order to keep up the momentum'. Tension had been lowered and he did not want it to increase again. Macmillan went on to say: 'I hope we shall succeed. It will not be for want of trying.' Eisenhower seemed to feel the same way.

However, de Gaulle and Adenauer remained cold and deplored the willingness of Eisenhower and Macmillan to negotiate over Berlin, rather than risk war. De Gaulle also wanted his own turn in the game of summitry, and insisted that Khrushchev must visit Paris before any four-power summit could take place.[13] This caused a delay of some months. During the spring of 1960, the atmosphere of relations between the West and Moscow began to go sour again.

Then came the shooting down over the Soviet Union of the American U2 spy plane on 1 May. There was a loud outcry in the Soviet Union. The incident may have strengthened the hand of Khrushchev's critics and opponents who disliked his activities at the summit and mistrusted his hob-nobbing with Western capitalist leaders, but nevertheless Khrushchev went to Paris for the four-power summit fixed for May. Perhaps in order to protect himself against his critics at home (and in Peking), he felt it necessary to obtain some form of public apology from Eisenhower, which the President of the United States felt unable to give. The summit collapsed in some disorder. Macmillan left Paris in a mood of philosophic gloom over the unkindness of fate. However, Khrushchev, before he left Paris, had made it clear at a mammoth and interminable press conference that he was not going to set any new time-limit for a Berlin settlement.

The later phase of the Berlin crisis, which opened when Khrushchev met the young and untried President Kennedy in Vienna in June 1961 and gradually petered out when Kennedy had shown he was not going to be intimidated, offered no opening to Macmillan to play an independent role at the summit. His part was to give Kennedy, with whom he was on good personal terms, such friendly support as he could. He also thought it important that Britain should keep in step with the European allies. This had become particularly important since in the summer of 1961 Macmillan had decided that Britain should try to enter the Common Market.

Britain and the emerging superpowers: Summitry in the 1950s

British efforts at summitry in the 1950s sprang from the belief that even if Britain was not in the same class as the two emerging superpowers, it nevertheless had a special status which was more than that of a second-class power, and also more than that of other European powers. British political leaders believed that it was in the British interest, in the interest of the Western alliance and in the interest of world peace that they should make use of this status to make independent moves from time to time. In particular, they thought that Britain was the only European power to which the Soviet Union would listen seriously.

Although these ideas contained an element of wishful thinking, they were not symptoms of megalomania. By the end of the 1950s Britain's standing in the world was much diminished, though it was still the only European nuclear power. But in the years following Stalin's death in 1953 – which were probably the crucial years, from the point of view of relations with the Soviet Union – Britain did still have a certain special status, by virtue of the Commonwealth, the decision to make the hydrogen bomb (delivered to the RAF in 1958) and past history.

The difficulty was that for British summitry to be successful Britain would have had to feel free to advance some small way beyond formally agreed allied positions, so as to be able to explore the outer limits of Soviet willingness to change policies or make concessions. There had to be some room for flexibility and manoeuvre. The United States, obsessed with the novel and difficult task of keeping troublesome European allies in line, was afraid of flexibility. Moreover Adenauer, who came to hold a powerful position within the Western alliance, was extremely suspicious of independent moves on the part of his allies.

This outward rigidity of the West was imposed by the need to weld together fifteen widely different nations, and to line up fifteen governments, each with its own political problems at home. The Western allies naturally and rightly gave first priority to building up a solid defence system in Western Europe, but because of the political rigidity of the alliance as a whole, they were unable to make any real effort to reach an understanding with the Soviet Union in the important years after Stalin's death. Instead, they concentrated all their efforts on completing and strengthening the Western defence structure. Each move that the West made in doing this gave the Soviet Union a pretext to make a corresponding move in Eastern Europe,

143

so that at every step it could tighten its control on the East European countries. At the same time the Soviet Union, because it could control its East European allies much more effectively than the Americans could control their West European allies, was able to show much greater apparent flexibility than the West in the field of what could be called diplomacy by propaganda.

This put the Western allies, including Britain, at a disadvantage. Moreover, because the problem of Western defence had become hopelessly entangled with the German problem, the Western allies tended to concentrate all their attention on Germany to the exclusion of the much wider East European problem. They campaigned endlessly for the reunification of Germany, which few of them, in their heart of hearts, really wanted; they did very little to claim for the East European peoples their normal political and human rights. Efforts to discuss this problem with the Soviet Union seemed half-hearted and purely formal.

Yet there were signs, in the years after Stalin's death, that some of the Soviet leaders sometimes thought that they would have to re-shape relations with the East European countries – possibly by allowing them limited political and economic independence while safeguarding the Soviet Union's security requirements. If at this time British and Soviet leaders could have got away from the usual East–West dialogue of the deaf and had a real discussion, this might just conceivably have helped those Soviet leaders who were willing to risk change. The British, however, tended to fall between two stools. They risked unpopularity with their allies because of their enthusiasm for summit meetings and their liking for conciliatory diplomacy. But they could never achieve a breakthrough in relations with the Soviet Union, nor even discover if such a thing were possible, because they had too little freedom of movement. They were constrained by the rigid positions of the alliance – to which they were entirely loyal, whatever the suspicions of some of their European allies.

When de Gaulle tried his hand at summitry in the 1960s, he produced no more concrete achievements than the British in the 1950s. Yet he escaped the unpopularity among his allies which the British had incurred, even though his attitude to the alliance was quite different from Britain's. For Britain, the label of *'perfide Albion'* seemed to be written in indelible ink.

14 Britain and West European economic integration in the 1950s

A few weeks after the general election, our economy began to feel twinges at its most sensitive point, the balance of payments. . . . Increases in wages agreed earlier in the year were influencing prices. More directly harmful were the strikes . . . and especially the dock strike. They held up our exports and held down the rate of industrial output. . . . The economy of Britain . . . was getting out of balance again. . . . World trade was rapidly expanding, yet Britain . . . was scarcely balancing its payments. . . . We were consuming too much of our increased production and exporting too little.

This was written about the mid-point of the 1950s, just after the 1955 general election, by Eden. It was typical of the economic pattern of the 1950s – and not only the 1950s. From the moment the 1939–45 war ended, the biggest economic worry of successive British Prime Ministers had been the balance of payments. In the economic field, the need to tackle this problem had overridden every other requirement, including the need to re-equip and modernise industry or to develop new and more profitable industries, in particular the advanced science-based industries. The need to increase exports to the maximum, at once, had to come first. In the immediate post-war years, the alternative was seen as national bankruptcy.

Britain, along with other West European countries, saw the problem first and foremost in terms of the 'dollar gap' – their dependence on food, raw materials and machines from the United States and their incapacity to earn the dollars needed to pay for them. The American £1000 million loan of 1945, given to stave off disaster after the sudden cut-off of Lend-Lease aid, was exhausted within two and a half years. Marshall aid to Europe came just in time. Thanks, in part, to British energy in helping to organise the European response to the American offer, it achieved a very large measure of success. By the time that Marshall aid to Britain ceased in December 1950, the British export trade had revived rapidly, at the price of strict controls and austerity at home.

The Korean war and the subsequent unrealistically massive

rearmament programme (the target was to spend £3600 million in three years, soon increased to £4000 million) was a bad setback to recovery, diverting Britain's energies, resources and manpower away from the export trade. But before long the programme was seen to be unrealistic and was scaled down. In 1953 and 1954, the economy seemed again to be progressing very satisfactorily (though food rationing could not be ended, even by a Conservative Government, until the summer of 1954). *De facto* convertibility of the pound sterling came early in 1955, full convertibility at the end of 1958.

However, British governments continued to be obsessed with the balance-of-payments problem and the need to increase exports faster. In the mid-1950s, they thought of it mainly as something which could be handled by 'stop–go' methods such as manipulating the bank rate, hire purchase terms, home loans, and similar techniques. At the same time, there was a lot of discussion about the new problems created by the new economic condition of full employment, which both Labour and Conservatives alike were pledged to maintain. This created different attitudes on the part of both employers and workers, who did not respond suitably to the monetary levers of control. By 1957 the idea of a prices and incomes policy had emerged; this remained an important aim, never satisfactorily achieved, of successive governments in the 1960s.

Because British economists, inside and outside the Government, were preoccupied with these internal problems, and with arguments about the degree of economic planning and government intervention which was desirable or tolerable, they were rather slow to examine Britain's problems in the context of the outside world, and in the West European context in particular. But in the second half of the 1950s both governments and economists became very conscious, first, of the impact of Britain's overseas commitments on the balance of payments, and next, of the failure of the British economy to keep pace with the rapid growth and striking success of the Common Market countries.

The Economic Burden of Defence
Within the context of overseas commitments, defence spending loomed large; defence commitments overseas swallowed up foreign exchange and swelled the balance-of-payments deficit; it diverted manpower and resources from industrial production for export. In the 1950s Britain's defence spending was the highest of the European

NATO countries (though in 1957, France's was slightly higher in terms of Gross National Product).[14] In terms of GNP Britain's defence spending rose sharply from 7·1 per cent in 1948 to 10·4 per cent in 1952, and then declined gradually to 7·7 per cent in 1958. The economist Andrew Shonfield, in his widely-read book, *British Economic Policy since the War* (1958), said that British military expenditure abroad in the mid-1950s was about £160 million a year, and the total cost in foreign currency of overseas military and political commitments, including grants and subsidies to Middle East countries, was about £200 million. The general argument was that without this expenditure, Britain's balance-of-payments problem would vanish.

The Defence White Paper of 1957 (the Government's annual policy statement) showed sharp awareness of the situation. Britain's influence in the world, it said, depended first and foremost on the health of the internal economy and the success of the export trade. Without these, military power could not in the long run be supported. It was therefore in the true interest of defence that the claims of military expenditure should be considered in conjunction with the need to maintain the country's financial and economic strength. The White Paper then said that over the past five years defence had on an average absorbed 10 per cent of Britain's GNP. About 7 per cent of the population were either in the armed services or supporting them. One-eighth of the metal-using industries, upon which the export trade largely depended, was devoted to defence. An 'undue proportion' of scientists and engineers was engaged on military work. 'In addition the retention of such large forces abroad gives rise to heavy charges which place a severe strain upon the balance of payments.'

The answer to the problem offered by the White Paper was the withdrawal of British troops from Korea and Jordan, partial withdrawal from Libya, reductions in garrisons in the colonies, and, after due consultation with WEU and NATO, a cut in British troops in West Germany from 77,000 to 64,000 within twelve months. A Central Reserve was to be created in Britain, capable of great mobility. Perhaps most important of all, the call-up for military service was to end in 1960; from then on Britain was to rely on a professional army.

As a counterpart to this pruning of the British conventional (non-nuclear) defence effort, the 1957 White Paper said that the RAF already held a substantial number of atomic bombs, and a British hydrogen bomb had been developed and would shortly be tested; thereafter a stock would be manufactured. The implication was that this was not going to cost much. In the following year, the Defence White Paper reported that after successful tests at Christmas Island, the hydrogen bomb was being produced and delivered to the RAF.

The 1958 White Paper also paid tribute to the pass-word of the day, 'interdependence', which had been formally proclaimed by Macmillan and Eisenhower at their Washington meeting in October 1957, and later approved by the NATO Heads of Government. In other words, the streamlining of the defence effort, aimed at easing the burden on the British economy and improving the British export performance, required closer cooperation with the United States – or, it could be said, greater dependence on the United States. As the 1958 Defence White Paper said, it was 'now necessary' to coordinate operational plans with the US Air Force; Britain would also accept the American offer of intermediate range missiles (needed to carry Britain's nuclear weapons as bombers became obsolete).

It was therefore, ultimately, the need to strengthen Britain's economic position which led the Government, first, to put more stress on nuclear weapons while cutting down conventional forces, and next, to rely more heavily on the United States. Eisenhower had agreed at the October 1957 meeting to try to restore the nuclear partnership with Britain which Truman had cut off in 1946. This resurgence of the 'special relationship' in the nuclear field had long-term consequences; for instance, it was the part-cause, or pretext, of de Gaulle's veto on British membership of the Common Market in 1963.

The Pattern of Britain's External Trade in the 1950s

The effort to improve Britain's balance of payments by holding down defence spending had only limited success. In the latter 1950s, the Government and the economists also began to study seriously the problems of Britain's relatively slow rate of economic growth and the overall pattern of Britain's foreign trade. It was noted that the growth rate of West Germany, in particular, was much faster. Many reasons were suggested for Britain's failure to match the rate of growth of other West European countries or Japan – among them, failure to invest in long-term projects designed to increase production and productivity, which in turn was thought to be due, in part, to concentration on the short-term aim of maximising exports and the uncertainties of 'stop–go' policies. The rival attraction of investment overseas was thought to be another factor; there were some people who argued that this should be curtailed and strictly controlled. There was also a political argument; those on the Right claimed that Britain's weakness stemmed from too much government interference in industry, or excessive government restraints, those on the Left claimed that there was not enough long-term planning by the Government, and that there should be more centralised direction and control. There seemed no simple clear-cut answer to the problem.

Towards the end of the 1950s, some economists, inside and outside the government apparatus, thought that a good deal of the trouble lay in the fact that Britain was sticking fairly closely to its old-established pattern of foreign trade, as a supplier of manufactured goods, including textiles, to countries which were producers of foodstuffs and raw materials, mainly in the Commonwealth and the rest of the sterling area. Since the Ottawa conference of 1932, there had been preferences for certain British exports in Commonwealth markets, in return for free entry for Commonwealth exports into Britain. This pattern of trade was comfortable and dependable, providing Britain with cheap foodstuffs and safe markets for traditional exports. It was recognised that the market for British textiles was fading away, and by the mid-1950s textiles were being replaced by increased exports of machinery, transport equipment and chemicals; but this did not change the overall pattern.

The harsh fact was that Britain's share in world trade in the 1950s was slowly but steadily falling; this fall was worrying, even within the context of the rapid expansion of world trade as a whole. Before the 1939–45 war, Britain's share in exports of manufactures by the main exporting countries had been 22 per cent; by the mid-1950s it was down to 18 per cent, at which point it was level with the rapidly rising West German share.

What was more, the trade of Britain's traditional partners – its Commonwealth sterling area partners – was growing a good deal more slowly than the trade of the West European countries, which was growing very fast. And Britain's traditional trade partners took nearly half its exports, while the West European countries, taken together, took just under a quarter. Of the West European countries, the Six (Common Market) countries took around 14 per cent, the Scandinavian countries and Switzerland (the future European Free Trade Association group) took around 10 per cent. These figures showed little change from the pre-war pattern. So the position, at the moment at which the Common Market was coming into existence, was that the pattern of Britain's foreign trade was 'very dependent on Britain's own import demand, on traditional sources of supply, outlets for British capital, and economic and political links with the Commonwealth'.[15]

Towards the end of the 1950s, a sufficiently large number of important people looked far enough ahead for a decision to be reached that fairly big changes in the pattern of Britain's external trade would be desirable, healthy and stimulating to economic growth. Up till that point, the Government aimed at a compromise which would combine the advantages of Britain's existing trade with the Commonwealth/sterling area with a bigger and growing share of West European trade, and which would avoid both the disadvantages of being shut out of the Common Market, and the discomfort to Britain (and damage to the Commonwealth) of actually joining it.

Britain's Absence from the Creation of the Common Market

The British were caught out by the remarkable speed with which the Six agreed on the shape and form of the Common Market and actually brought it into existence. The total fiasco of the European Defence Community had made the British rather sceptical and superior about continental efforts at supranationalism or federalism; the success of Eden's rescue operation in creating WEU made them smug about their own realism and common sense. They overlooked the fact that it was just the fiasco of the EDC which made the Six determined to show the world that they could mount an efficient operation and carry it through; the French in particular wanted to make good the harm done to their international prestige by their rejection of their own brain-child.

In April 1955 (just before the Paris agreements creating WEU came into force) the Dutch said that the Benelux governments would soon propose a conference on West European integration. On 20 May the Benelux governments presented a memorandum proposing both a Common Market and a similar system for transport and atomic energy. On 2 June the Foreign Ministers of the Six met at Messina. West Germany was represented by State Secretary Hallstein; this was because the Bonn Government was split between Adenauer, who was all for European integration on political grounds, and Erhard, the father of the West German 'economic miracle', who liked the OEEC (and never really reconciled himself to the Common Market, even when he became Chancellor).

The Messina conference, basing itself on the Benelux memorandum, set up an intergovernmental committee under Spaak to prepare a detailed plan. Early in July the committee met, in Brussels; in the following spring (1956) it submitted a report to the Ministers of the Six, which they considered when they met in Venice in May. Drafting of the treaties setting up the European Economic Community and Euratom followed; they were signed in Rome in March 1957 and ratified by the Six (there was no great difficulty in France) in the following months. On 1 January 1958 they came into force.

This progress of the Six was far quicker and smoother than the British had expected; nor did many people in Britain realise, even when the treaties came into force, that the Common Market was likely to become the magnetic centre of Western Europe, not only in the economic field. After the conclusion of the Paris agreements of 1954, Eden had hoped that the Western European Union 'would take its place as a leading authority in the new Europe'. He intended it to have a scope and responsibilities wider than the defence field.[16] As Eden himself wistfully recorded, it did not work out that way. This was because, just at the moment when WEU came into existence, Britain's six WEU partners started putting their energies into the creation of the EEC and Euratom, and so had little interest in developing WEU into something more than a defence organisation, which in any case tended to be swallowed up in NATO. The British, with some support from some of its members, tried to turn WEU into a forum for regular political and economic consultation and coordination of policies between the seven members, through frequent meetings of permanent representatives in London, as well as periodic meetings of ministers; but even in the early days, before the open clash between France and Britain which developed in the 1960s, WEU was mildly useful rather than important.

At the start of their work on the EEC, in 1955, the Six certainly did not want to shut out Britain; on the other hand, they did not mean to let Britain take control and water down their plans to suit British tastes. At the Messina conference, they said that Britain 'as a State belonging to the Western European Union and associated with the European Coal and Steel Community', would be invited to participate in their work from the start. At this time the French, anxious for help in the development of nuclear energy, wanted Britain in.[17]

On this occasion, the Six did not ask Britain to make any advance commitment to the supranational idea, as they had done over the Schuman Plan. However the Foreign Secretary, Macmillan, who in opposition had been a noted 'European', replied with great caution. There were special difficulties, he said, for Britain in any proposal for a European Common Market. The British Government would be happy to examine the many problems 'without prior commitment and on their merits'. He sent an under-secretary from the Board of Trade to represent Britain on Spaak's intergovernmental committee. He may have thought that if anything came out of the discussions, Britain could have a treaty of association with the new Community, as it had with the ECSC, on Churchill's 'with' but not 'of' principle.

The basic differences between the British and the Six soon became clear. The Six wanted a common external tariff against the outside world, so that they would be a single unit in their trade dealings with other countries. This, among other things, would give them far greater weight in bargaining. (They proved this in the Kennedy Round negotiations for tariff cuts in the 1960s.) Britain would not accept a common external tariff, mainly because it would mean putting up barriers against Commonwealth imports. Britain also wanted to keep the OEEC in being as a wider West European economic organisation with the main responsibility for tariff-cutting. This annoyed the Six, especially the good 'Europeans', such as Spaak, who wanted to create a supranational organisation which was to some degree independent of governments, unlike the British-moulded OEEC which was intergovernmental.

When in November 1955 the work of the Spaak committee was being reviewed, Britain took up a very chilly, neutral attitude. It said that the difficulties which Britain would have in entering a Common Market still seemed real and did not seem to be growing any less; the Government had reached no final decision and wanted to study further the questions involved. This depressed and disappointed the Six, and the British withdrew from the intergovernmental committee.[18]

This came to be regarded as a second important turning-point in Britain's relations with 'Europe', the first being its refusal to take part in the Schuman Plan. If so, very few people in Britain realised it at the time. Eden was preoccupied with summitry and relations with the Soviet Union, with the Middle East and Cyprus and with internal economic problems at home. He had little time left over for the Spaak committee. The general public took little notice of it. Nor did most of the professional economists. It was not until the beginning of 1957 that Sir Roy Harrod wrote: 'it may be said that Britain for the first time believes that the continental countries mean business, and that she feels that it would be gravely to her disadvantage to have a common market formed on the Continent while she was left out in the cold.'[19]

However, at the end of 1955, some experts in Whitehall seem to have come to the conclusion that the Common Market could harm Britain. At a special unofficial meeting of the OEEC, a British delegate was said to have argued, in warning tones, that if the Six went ahead with the Common Market, they might come into conflict with the OEEC.[20] This angered the Six and strengthened their will to push ahead. In the early weeks of 1956 Selwyn Lloyd, now Foreign Secretary, visited Washington, and was told that the United States thought Britain wrong to oppose the Common Market. Dulles was a strong supporter of the Monnet approach to European integration. British opposition was dropped and Macmillan, now Chancellor of the Exchequer, began to study the alternative courses open to Britain.

Britain and the Plan for a European Free Trade Area
During the spring of 1956, there was discussion in London and elsewhere of the idea of a free trade area bringing the Common Market together with Britain and the other OEEC countries. (A free trade area would be like the Common Market in aiming to remove tariffs between member countries, but would be unlike the Common Market, in that it would allow each member to maintain its own tariffs towards the outside world.) In March, Spaak said this would be a possibility, provided it did not mean any weakening of the Common Market.

The British themselves had not originally liked the idea. They still thought Commonwealth trade much more important than trade with Western Europe. But it had been pressed upon them by those OEEC countries which wanted a lowering of tariffs. In the end, a free trade area seemed the only course open to Britain. The OEEC, at a meeting in July 1956, decided to make a special study of the idea. In October, the Eden Government presented a British plan for free trade in all goods except foodstuffs.

Britain's backing for a free trade area aroused suspicion in 'good

153

Europeans' such as Spaak, who feared it might distract attention and energies from the Common Market and make agreement among the Six more difficult. The fact was that the idea of a European free trade area, as an alternative to the Common Market, not just as a sort of outer covering for it, appealed strongly to some influential West Europeans, including West German industrialists and above all Erhard, who called the Common Market both economic nonsense and European incest. It also appealed to some Frenchmen, notably the former Prime Minister, Mendès France, who did not like supranationalism. In a debate in the French Assembly in January 1957, he argued that the Common Market would give excessive power to an external authority and criticised the Government for failing to try to work out a plan with Britain. Other speakers in the debate seemed willing to accept the Common Market only if there were a firm prospect of later agreement with Britain and other OEEC countries. In the final ratification debate in the French Assembly, many speakers said they hoped a free trade area would soon supplement the Common Market.

The Six took little notice of the fact that Britain's conversion to the free trade area plan marked a considerable advance by Britain, and an abandonment of the protectionist, high-tariff elements in its policy in trade with non-Commonwealth countries. This was not surprising, since British Government spokesmen, to ward off criticism at home, stressed all the advantages Britain would obtain, not the concessions it would make. It would, they said, gain a free market in Western Europe, while keeping the traditional special arrangements for Commonwealth trade. They also stressed their determination to exclude agriculture from the proposed free trade area.

In the House of Commons in November 1956 Macmillan, as Chancellor of the Exchequer, said that Parliament would never agree to Britain's entering arrangements which would prevent it from treating imports from the Commonwealth at least as favourably as those from European countries. The aim of the free trade area would be to stop 'discrimination' against British exports by the Common Market. (Macmillan, though one of the most ardent Conservative champions of the European Movement in the late 1940s and early 1950s, had always feared and disliked the idea of a closed supranational community of the Six as harmful to British interests, just as Napoleon's 'Continental System' had been a century and a half earlier.)[21] Harold Wilson, from the Opposition front bench, supported Macmillan, on the ground that 'we can't stay out'. On the other hand Roy Jenkins, later Chancellor of the Exchequer in the Wilson Government, who was an early and convinced 'European', questioned the Government's intention to make it an industrial free trade area only, excluding agriculture: 'this will be a pretty difficult thing for some of our partners to swallow.' He was right.

At the beginning of 1957 Macmillan became Prime Minister. He was determined to get a free trade area; if the Six would not agree, he was prepared to oppose the Common Market.[22] The negotiations, held within the OEEC, threw up many of the differences between Britain and the Six which were serious stumbling-blocks in the later negotiations about British entry into the Common Market. Over agriculture, Britain found itself isolated, with the other OEEC countries siding with the Six. In the end, early in 1958, Britain proposed an agreement for cooperation to bring about freer and increased trade in agriculture, though there were to be special safeguards for 'traditional channels of trade including trade with third countries' (which meant the Commonwealth); there were to be annual reviews of production, consumption, trade and prices. By that time the negotiations had got so bogged down that the British proposal was never seriously considered.

Even more difficult was the question of tariffs against the outside world. The Six, particularly the French, wanted the free trade area to have something as close as possible to a common external tariff such as the Common Market was to establish. At the very least, they wanted the free trade area countries to agree only to change their tariffs with the outside world by agreement; otherwise, they argued, one country might gain an unfair lead over other members through unilateral tariff reductions, which would upset the overall built-in balance of advantage among members. The British on the other hand wanted to retain freedom of action on tariffs and on trade policy towards the outside world, though towards the end they were willing to agree to a 'code of good conduct' and consultation on tariffs, rather on the OEEC model.

It was later argued that Britain should have accepted a common external tariff in principle and then negotiated exceptions for Commonwealth exports to Britain, and that agreement could have been reached on that basis. Similarly some people argued that during the 1961–63 negotiations on joining the EEC, Britain should simply have 'signed the Treaty of Rome' and then dealt with the special problems of the Commonwealth from inside the Community, instead of trying to do things the other way round. At the end of the 1960s it was being argued by some people, both in Britain and France, that Britain should simply accept all the decisions of the Six on agriculture without arguing about the excessive financial burden which this would lay on Britain, and should rely on the fact that the countries of the Six knew that their agricultural system was in a mess and would have to be changed soon anyway.

This kind of argument was unrealistic. Given the relationship between Government and Parliament in Britain, such tactics simply would not work. Any government which used them would have to defend itself in Parliament against charges either of failing to protect the national interest, or else of bad faith and insincerity in dealings with friendly allied countries; and it would find it hard to defend itself successfully.

It could however be argued much more convincingly that Britain committed psychological and tactical blunders. It paid too little respect to the Six and to their united determination to press ahead with the Common Market without outside interference. It assumed that everyone wanted Britain 'in Europe' so badly that it could push through its own terms. The British tried to bring the free trade area and the Common Market as close together as possible, in particular by demanding that both should start tariff-cutting simultaneously, ignoring the fact that the Six, especially the French, wanted to mark a very clear distinction between the two and to stress the privileges and advantages of belonging to the Common Market. The British also – by sins of omission – belittled the 'European' political aims of the Six. All in all, they offended both the 'good Europeans' among the Six, who suspected them of attempted sabotage, and also the French, whether 'good Europeans' or not.

The Struggle between Britain and France over the Free Trade Area
In the long run, it was the French who were decisive. With the 'good Europeans' the British might, by belated concessions, have come to terms. In the final phase, the negotiations took on the form of a duel between Macmillan and de Gaulle, Britain and France, or a struggle for the leadership of Western Europe between a British-dominated free trade area, based on the British-dominated OEEC, and a French-dominated Common Market. Most West Europeans very

probably wanted neither the one thing nor the other, but stood rather helplessly on the sidelines. When the climax came, the other Common Market countries stood by France, determined to preserve and develop their Community at all costs.

There were some solid reasons for French dislike of the free trade area plan. French industrialists thought it would expose them to the risks of competition with British manufacturers – who would have the 'unfair' advantage of low costs because of cheap food imports – without any of the safeguards or balancing advantages built into the Rome Treaty. Since French industrialists were already nervous about free competition within the Common Market, especially with West Germany, they felt that, with the free trade area, they would be asked to swallow two doses of nasty medicine at once. The French in general saw the essential element in the Rome Treaty as a carefully worked out balance of interest: French 'sacrifices' in opening French markets to foreign industrialists were to be compensated by corresponding gains in secure and profitable markets – and financial support – for French farmers in the other Common Market countries. The free trade area idea upset this concept of balance.

In the last half-year of the negotiations, however, it was political motives which determined French policy. In June 1958 de Gaulle was called back to power to deal with the grave crisis over Algeria. Macmillan feared that this event would cause the free trade area negotiations to 'fall to the ground'. He knew – he wrote later in his memoirs – that during the war de Gaulle had been obsessed by 'his almost insane hatred for Roosevelt and even for Churchill' and by his 'jealousy of Britain'.[23] Nevertheless Macmillan set out to win over de Gaulle by a series of long personal letters and a personal visit. He also tried direct appeals to Adenauer, at first with some success.

The dice seemed to be loaded against him. In the same month that de Gaulle returned to power, the US Congress finally passed amendments to the MacMahon Act which restored nuclear cooperation between America and Britain; France was excluded. This put an end to French hopes of American help in carrying out the decision of the government of Félix Gaillard, announced two months earlier, that France should make nuclear weapons. De Gaulle's reaction was characteristic. During his first few months of power, he was deeply engaged in the Algerian drama. Nevertheless he found time to send to Eisenhower and Macmillan, on 14 September 1958, his proposal for a three-power directorate of the United States, France and Britain at the head of the Atlantic alliance, which would plan strategy – including nuclear strategy – on a world-wide basis, not just within the North Atlantic area.

This idea, according to Acheson, was first put forward in 1951 by René Pleven, as Prime Minister, on a visit to Washington. At that time Acheson pointed out that already the pre-eminent position of the three powers was causing painful jealousy to other NATO allies. The idea was not pressed.[24] In the autumn of 1958, de Gaulle's proposal produced very similar reactions in Eisenhower and Macmillan who did not want to cause offence to other NATO allies, in particular the West Germans and Italians. Their response was therefore embarrassed and evasive, boiling down to an offer of tripartite consultations on specific problems or areas.

This can hardly have pleased de Gaulle, even though he later wrote in his memoirs that it was just what he had expected and that the purpose of his move had been to 'hoist the flag' of French independence and give warning of his long-term intention of taking France out of the NATO defence structure.[25] Whatever de Gaulle's exact motive, the incident cannot have made him feel any more kindly towards Britain.

In any case he had already determined his policy for Europe: to get the Common Market into operation, to bring about political coordination among the Six states and to prevent Britain – regarded as a 'centrifugal force' – from 'dragging them towards an Atlantic system which would be incompatible with a European Europe'. He had in no way been softened by Macmillan who, at a meeting in late June, had recalled Napoleon's trade war against Britain and had declared with much emotion that the Common Market was a continental blockade and that Britain would not accept it. Macmillan had begged him to 'renounce' it; de Gaulle had replied soothingly, deploring exaggeration.

This at least was de Gaulle's later account.[26] According to Macmillan's account, what he did was to plead that de Gaulle should allow the free trade area negotiations to go ahead. Obviously feeling that he had made little impression, Macmillan re-stated his appeal in a letter which he wrote at the end of the meeting. Europe, he wrote, was already tragically divided from Stettin to Trieste; 'I am very anxious to avoid any further division.'[27]

The more Macmillan pressed his case, the more firmly de Gaulle resisted him. As his special partner in Europe, de Gaulle selected Adenauer. Receiving him at his country home at Colombey-les-deux-Eglises on 14 September – the same day that he sent his memorandum on a three-power directorate to Eisenhower and Macmillan – he enlisted Adenauer's support for his plans for the Europe of the Six. In particular, Britain must be kept out and French agricultural requirements must be met. Adenauer answered that West Germans in general did not like the common agricultural policy and wanted to give satisfaction to Britain. However, he promised not to allow these things to impede the union of the Six.[28] As for supranationalism, Adenauer was quite happy to join de Gaulle in throwing it out of the window, though he admitted to him that he was grateful to Monnet and Robert Schuman for the gifts they had presented to Germany.

Soon after this meeting, Adenauer must have learnt of de Gaulle's memorandum to Eisenhower and Macmillan. De Gaulle had arranged for it to be shown to the West German and Italian ambassadors, apparently not realising what resentment it would cause. When Macmillan visited Bonn early in October, he found Adenauer very concerned about it.[29] Macmillan thought that Adenauer might back the free trade area plan more strongly in consequence. As late as 3 November, Adenauer seemed sympathetic to it.[30]

By this time, however, Macmillan had privately reached the conclusion that the outlook for the free trade area was bad, that France was determined to exclude Britain and that de Gaulle was 'bidding high for the hegemony of Europe'.[31] He was correct. De Gaulle was simply waiting for the right moment to end the negotiations over which a British Minister, Reginald Maudling, was presiding with the aim – as de Gaulle saw it – of 'drowning' the infant community of the Six in a 'vast area of free trade'. On 10 November Khrushchev opened the new Berlin crisis by his speech in East Berlin. This gave de Gaulle a stranglehold on Adenauer. On 14 November the French Minister of Information, Soustelle, without warning to the other OEEC countries or even apparently to the Six, told the press that it was 'not possible' to form a free trade area as had been wished by the British without a common external tariff.

This was a body blow to the negotiations and to Maudling in particular. However, meetings continued. Then on 26 November de Gaulle again met Adenauer together with the unhappy and helpless Erhard. The two sides agreed to end the Maudling negotiations. Divisions inside the Bonn Government had presumably been eliminated by the overriding need to resist Khrushchev. In exchange for Adenauer's support in ending the free trade area negotiations, de Gaulle promised French support over Berlin.[32] After a final bad-tempered clash between British and French ministers, the negotiations stopped. Britain was in effect defeated.

The Common Market came into operation on 1 January 1959. The British were left complaining about the dangers of the new 'division of Europe' and calling for a long-term solution. In April 1959 the Council of Europe Consultative Assembly in Strasbourg called for a reopening of negotiations between the Six and the other West Europeans. But by this time the Six, secure in strong political backing from the United States, also knew that the Americans did not look kindly on the idea of a wider European economic grouping which would be a fresh barrier to American exports to Europe without displaying any of the political virtues which they saw in Monnet-type integration. The Six therefore saw no need to re-open negotiations and concentrated on their own very successful business.

Britain and EFTA

Britain turned to the only obvious alternative plan – to form a group with other interested OEEC countries. Britain and the Scandinavian countries often had the same way of looking at problems. Switzerland and Austria, though closely linked by trade to the Common Market countries, especially West Germany, felt debarred by their neutrality from joining a body with a strong political colour. Britain, the three Scandinavians, Austria and Switzerland had often worked together during the free trade area negotiations and were sometimes known as the 'outer Six'. After the breakdown of the negotiations in December 1958, British and Swedish industrialists, through their respective organisations, called for the immediate establishment of an 'Outer Six' trading group.

By the early summer of 1959, the British Government had decided to go ahead with this plan and some sort of action was therefore required. In July 1959 ministers of the seven countries (by this time Portugal had been asked to join in) reached agreement, and on 4 January 1960 they signed the Stockholm Convention creating the European Free Trade Association, through which industrial tariffs and quotas were to be totally eliminated by the end of a transition period. (Agriculture was excluded but Britain made special arrangements with Norway over fish products.) The Stockholm Convention was a very short simple document, compared with the immensely long and complex Rome Treaty; it contained no supranational element; unlike the Rome Treaty, which was of indefinite duration, it provided that a member could give twelve months' notice of withdrawal.

The aim was to match EFTA tariff cuts to those of the Six, so as to keep as closely as possible in step, and to make eventual agreement on a wider West European basis as easy as possible. When they signed the Convention, the Ministers passed a resolution on their relations with the Six. They recalled the successful part which the OEEC had played for over ten years in Europe's post-war expansion, and said they were determined to avoid a new division in Europe and regarded EFTA as a step towards agreement among all the OEEC countries.

EFTA aroused little enthusiasm in Britain. Perhaps the Government's dramatic warnings of the dangers of an economic division of Western Europe had been all too successful. In the House of Commons, in December 1959, some Labour members criticised it because they thought it would not help, but rather hinder, negotiations with the Six. Experts outside Parliament thought the same. Few people took much notice of EFTA's own real, though modest, virtues and advantages, or the usefulness of expanding trade with countries which took around one-tenth of Britain's exports. From late 1959 on, the Macmillan Government started an effort to 'build bridges' between EFTA and the EEC. But the United States was beginning to be worried about the prospect of any fresh barriers to American exports to Europe. Its own balance of payments problem was building up and politically, EFTA had no appeal. The French had no interest in a wider West European trade group, and wanted to get rid of the British-influenced OEEC, as did others in the Six. By the end of 1960, the OEEC had been replaced by a new, and different, Organisation for Economic Cooperation and Development, with the United States and Japan as members. This was of course no longer a European group, but a group of the rich industrial nations, consulting together and criticising one another's economic and financial policies at home and abroad. It did nothing to heal the West European economic split. Britain had no special status and, in the 1960s, had to suffer some searching criticism of its poor economic performance.

At the end of the 1950s, Britain found itself rather remote from the new centre of West European affairs, watching important developments from the side-lines, with little influence on them. The 'good Europeans' among the Six tended to look on Britain as a sort of moral delinquent or an unconverted heathen who had failed to see the light, though given every opportunity. (Monnet himself took a kindlier and more optimistic view, believing that when Britain saw that the EEC worked, it would join – and should be admitted.) The French, under de Gaulle, were beginning their quest for full national 'independence' and equality of status (with whom, it was not exactly clear), and the diplomatic defeat of Britain in the free trade area negotiations was seen as a step along this road.

As for the British themselves, apart from Macmillan and those of his advisers who were 'European'-minded, no one seemed to take much notice of the setback to British policy in Western Europe. In 1959, summitry was of greater interest; in 1960, in addition to the failed summit, the 'wind of change' in Africa. Curiously, as 'decolonization' went ahead, and the Commonwealth changed its character from a small, tightly-knit club of the 'white Commonwealth' countries into a much looser and larger grouping of independent countries of all races, it became more and more interesting to the general public. Labour supporters in particular developed a strong affection for the Commonwealth and a sense of moral responsibility towards it. Some young people found in it an outlet for thwarted idealism. For a few years, the creation of a new multiracial Commonwealth seemed a challenge, an adventure, something supremely worth doing. It was an aim, or a dream, which diverted attention from Western Europe.

In the general election of October 1959, British voters gave the Conservative Government an increased majority. It did not look as though they had noticed any failure in the Government's policy towards Britain's closest neighbours in Western Europe. It was to Macmillan's credit that he did take note of this failure, and drew from it the conclusion that Britain must make a fresh start.

PART IV

Britain in Europe in the 1960s:
Movement and change

15   The outlook for the 1960s

Britain entered the 1960s in an atmosphere of growing prosperity in spite of the unsolved balance-of-payments problem. The 1959 election had been the 'never had it so good' election. Britain was still the centre of the sterling area; the pound and the dollar were still the two leading currencies for world trade, in spite of the pound's periodic bouts of instability. The British Government was on good terms with the United States, and still claimed to speak to the Soviet Union as a near-equal partner. In April 1961, Britain and the Soviet Union, as co-chairmen of the 1954 Indo-China conference, jointly summoned a fourteen-nation conference on Laos and appealed, successfully, for a cease-fire between the warring Laotian factions. On the other hand, Britain was on distinctly cool terms with France and West Germany, or, more strictly, with de Gaulle and Adenauer, partly because of Macmillan's efforts at summitry, and partly because of the unpleasantness created by the abortive free trade area negotiations.

Britain was one of the three countries possessing the hydrogen bomb – even though it was already in serious difficulty over the means of delivering it, as bomber aircraft became obsolescent and long-range missiles or nuclear-powered submarines were needed to replace them. This did not prevent Britain from joining the United States and the Soviet Union, as a junior partner, first, in a voluntary ban on nuclear tests in the atmosphere (broken by Khrushchev in August 1961) and then in the negotiations leading to the nuclear test ban treaty of 1963. The British played a smaller part in the later negotiations for a treaty to stop the spread of nuclear weapons, but worked hard to remove political obstacles.

Finally, Britain entered the 1960s in a mood of hope and even enthusiasm about the development of a new-style multiracial Commonwealth. The split in the Commonwealth over Suez seemed more or less healed; the exit of South Africa over apartheid in 1961 seemed if anything to strengthen the Commonwealth by reinforcing its interracial character and beliefs. The new split over Rhodesia lay ahead in the mid-1960s.

Nevertheless, as the 1960s opened, a few politicians, officials, experts and journalists saw that the key question before Britain was the choice between Western Europe and the Commonwealth as the basis for the country's future development. Until then, the answer of British political leaders had either been that the Commonwealth bond was unquestionably of overriding importance, or else that bonds with the Commonwealth and Western Europe were equally important and perfectly compatible. For some time after the beginning of the 1960s, the proposition that the two were entirely compatible continued to be stated. However, the free trade area negotiations of the late 1950s had shown that the Six – or some of the Six – did not agree.

Some people also saw that the key problem for Britain, in its dealings with Western Europe, was its relationship with France. The underlying rivalry between France and Britain for the leadership of Western Europe had been dormant until the return to power of de Gaulle in 1958. Till then, France had been distracted by political instability, lack of economic self-confidence, and preoccupation with overseas problems – first Indo-China, then North Africa, in particular Algeria. De Gaulle gave France strong government with every appearance of permanence; his return to power coincided with an economic surge forward; he solved France's overseas problems, even if it took him four years to do it.

In spite of the enormous difficulties, internal and external, which he had to master in order to bring about an Algerian settlement, from the moment of his return to power he staked out France's claim to equal status with the United States and Britain, in particular, through his proposal for a three-power directorate to plan world-wide strategy. He devoted his energies to asserting the full national independence of France, on his own terms. This required the exclusion of 'les Anglo-Saxons' from the affairs of Western Europe and the firm establishment of French leadership there. He saw Britain partly as an agent of the United States in its interference in European affairs (through NATO and by economic penetration) and partly as the only serious rival to France within Western Europe. West Germany, burdened by the guilt of the Hitler period and maimed by the country's division, was seen as no more than a biddable junior partner to a forgiving but unforgetting France.

These were the considerations likely to influence de Gaulle in his response to any effort by Britain to recover the ground lost by opting out of the Common Market negotiations and failing in the free trade area negotiations, and to 'enter', or perhaps rather re-enter, 'Europe'.

Yet as the 1960s opened, few people in Britain looked at the future in this perspective. It had been an axiom of British policy, from the war years on, that it was a very important British interest that France should be strong. This was re-stated, with unquestioning sincerity, by Prime Ministers and Foreign Secretaries from Churchill and Eden onwards. The British also believed that there were, or must be, particularly close bonds between the two countries. Two world wars had proved this, and it was why the British Cabinet had unhesitatingly accepted the idea of a union of Britain and France in 1940. The British were slow to realise that their 'elder brotherly', somewhat superior attitude was wounding and unacceptable to some people in France, especially de Gaulle, who set out to prove that it lacked all foundation. He made France strong but saw no reason why its strength should be in Britain's interest.

16 Britain's first attempt to join the Common Market

The British Approach to a Decision

The British Government reached the decision to open negotiations about joining the Common Market by a series of diagonal moves. In January 1960, the Foreign Secretary, Selwyn Lloyd, made a speech at the Council of Europe Consultative Assembly which blew hot and cold about Britain's relations with the Common Market. The British, he said in the well-worn phrase, regarded themselves as part of Europe, for reasons of sentiment, history and geography. They also had another bond: their Queen was the Head of the Commonwealth. But that did not disqualify them from European status. It had perhaps been a mistake for Britain not to join the ECSC; as for the EEC, Britain welcomed the Rome Treaty, since a strong political unity of the Six was 'good for Western Europe and for Britain'.

However, Selwyn Lloyd went on, if the Six were to become protectionist, there could be a trade war in Western Europe; and if they failed to consult their allies over major issues such as disarmament or East–West relations, the Western European Union might not survive and NATO might be profoundly affected. (This was the tone of implied threat which was normally most distasteful to members of the Six.) Selwyn Lloyd went on to say that he had been assured by the Six that things were not going to go that way. The question was: if he believed these assurances, why did he think it necessary to air his doubts and warnings publicly?

Also at the beginning of 1960, a committee of senior British civil servants of the ministries concerned started a searching review of the various ways in which Britain's relations with the Six could develop. Their general conclusion was that on political grounds – that is, to ensure a politically stable and cohesive Western Europe – there was a strong argument for joining the Common Market. The economic argument was seen as less important, though it was thought that the wider market of the Six would provide a spur to British industry to become more competitive. However, although officials were moving in this direction, the Cabinet itself was divided. A Macmillan–Eisenhower meeting in Washington in March produced little new; the United States was known to favour the Six. But havoc was created by a public remark of Macmillan's (an echo of his remark to de Gaulle in June 1958) which was taken as a threat that Britain might have to lead a new coalition (presumably against the Common Market) as in the days of Napoleon. Strenuous denials were issued in London. 'What I have pleaded for,' Macmillan told the House of Commons at the beginning of April, 'is that we should not allow an economic gap, a sort of division, to grow up which, gradually . . . will make another division of Europe. . . . We have seen over and over again how fatal that is. . . .'

Although Macmillan was not ready to show his hand, the idea of joining the EEC soon began to be discussed in the press. By June, 1960, *The Economist* was writing that Britain would be wise to become a full member. A junior Foreign Office minister talked about the possibility of Britain's joining Euratom and the ECSC. But in the House of Lords, Lord Strang, former permanent head of the Foreign Office, expressing what had been the traditional Foreign Office view, said that British policy should be the widest, closest and most intimate cooperation with continental Western Europe on an intergovernmental basis; but the British should hesitate, except in specified cases and within defined limits, to agree to subject themselves to majority decisions (as called for by the Rome Treaty). It would be dishonest, Lord Strang said, to join the EEC unless Britain was prepared to face eventual political integration.

On 25 July the House of Commons discussed the matter. Selwyn Lloyd again proclaimed his devotion to the idea of a politically and economically united Europe, but added there were different ways of achieving this. After talking about the problems of Commonwealth trade and British agriculture in relation to the Common Market, the Foreign Secretary said he had not pronounced against going into some form of European institution, but 'we have to be careful . . .'. This was hardly likely to arouse enthusiasm either in the British public or among the Six. For Labour, both Harold Wilson and Denis Healey seemed in general agreement with the Government's cautious approach to the Common Market problem. Healey, however, went so far as to say that there was no longer anyone in the House of Commons who thought it inconceivable that Britain should join the Common Market; the sort of 'Pharisaism' which both the main

Britain in a divided Europe

British parties had shown towards European unity for so many years after the war was completely dead.

While Macmillan continued to hold his hand, he showed the way his mind was moving by putting noted Conservative 'Europeans' in Ministerial office. Duncan Sandys was put in charge of the Commonwealth Relations Office, Christopher Soames became Minister of Agriculture and Edward Heath became Lord Privy Seal with special responsibility for European affairs. At the Council of Europe Consultative Assembly in late September 1960 Heath said that the British Government had been examining the problem of joining the Common Market, and looking at the practical effects on the British economy and on Britain's international links. Britain was maintaining an open and flexible attitude to all possible solutions. But, because of the Commonwealth, it would be impossible for Britain to sign the Rome Treaty in its existing form.

During 1960, the British Government was dipping a cautious toe in the Common Market pool, but no more. The next important development was that Kennedy became President in succession to Eisenhower in January 1961. Kennedy took a close and lively interest in European affairs – which eventually emerged in July 1962 in the 'two pillars' concept: the idea of a Western community formed by two equal partners, the United States and a united Europe. Kennedy chose as Under-Secretary of State for European affairs a devoted friend and disciple of Monnet, George Ball, who believed fervently in the federal or at least supranational solution to the problem of European unity, and had opposed the plan for a free trade area on the grounds that it discriminated against America without any of the political benefits of 'true European integration'.

For the moment, these events had little impact on the British Government. In February, at the WEU Council, Heath was faced with a resolution from the WEU Assembly declaring that Britain should join the EEC; he could only say that the Government did not wish to express a view but had an open mind. In March, in the Council of Europe Consultative Assembly, the French Foreign Minister, Couve de Murville, said something which seemed intended to encourage the British. The Common Market, he said, remained open to any other European country that wished to join: 'we persist in hoping that certain refusals, though repeated, will not be maintained.'

On 30 March, George Ball was in London and had a meeting with

Heath, together with senior officials. Heath told him that the British Government had had 'preliminary conversations with certain members of the Six'. It now wanted to know how the Kennedy Administration would react if Britain were to apply to join the Rome Treaty. George Ball, speaking for himself, was enthusiastic. The United States, he said, had always regretted that Britain had not been willing to accept fully the Rome Treaty. So long as Britain remained outside the European Community, it was a force for division rather than cohesion, since it was 'like a great lodestone drawing with unequal degrees of force on each member State'.[1]

This Heath–Ball talk was intended to prepare for Macmillan's meeting with Kennedy in Washington at the beginning of April. George Ball later gave a graphic description of this meeting, at which he was present. The Prime Minister lost little time in repeating Heath's question: how would the United States react to British entry into the Common Market? Kennedy turned to Ball; at the President's request Ball gave the same answer as he had given to Heath in London. Macmillan then made it clear that Britain would try 'very soon' to 'go into Europe'. At a dinner the following night, Macmillan twice drew Ball aside to repeat that he was determined to sign the Rome Treaty. According to Ball, Macmillan then said: 'we are going to need some help from you in getting in, but we are going in. Yesterday was one of the greatest days of my life.'

Even after this, a further period of consultation and preparation was needed; but heavy hints were dropped. Heath told the House of Commons on 17 May that the course which he found most attractive, of those available, was full membership of the Common Market, if proper arrangements could be made for Commonwealth trade, British agriculture and Britain's EFTA partners. At the end of June, EFTA Ministers met in London, to discuss an approach by Britain to the Common Market. Some were naturally afraid of being left out in the cold. However, they agreed to coordinate their actions and remain united throughout any negotiations. EFTA was to remain in being until arrangements had been worked out to satisfy the legitimate interests of all its members. The aim was that all should enter an 'integrated European market' at the same date.

In July, Macmillan sent out three of his ministers to tour Commonwealth capitals and sound out the ground. There were objections from many quarters for many reasons to the idea of British entry into the Common Market. The strongest at that time came from the 'white Commonwealth', especially Canada and Australia. But Macmillan did not feel that they were big enough to stop him from going ahead.

On 31 July 1961, he at last announced his decision in the House of Commons, with the minimum of drama. He seemed to want to damp down emotions – certainly not to arouse enthusiasm. He said it was necessary for Britain to make a formal application for membership of the Common Market, under Article 237 of the Rome Treaty; but the final decision on joining would only be taken after negotiations had been completed, and would have to be approved by the House of Commons; there would also have to be full consultation with the Commonwealth countries. There was no guarantee of success. If a new relationship between Britain and the Six were to disrupt the 'long-standing and historic ties' with the Commonwealth, 'the loss would be greater than the gain'.

As to the positive aim of his move, Macmillan said that it was to contribute towards securing the closest possible unity within Europe. During the debate, two days later, he said that the dominant considerations were political. There was no security in isolation, and it was better that Britain should play its role fully and use its influence for the 'free development of the life and thought of Europe'.

The reactions in Parliament to Macmillan's announcement were as cautious and reserved as Macmillan himself. However, one Conservative MP, Gilbert Longden, went so far as to say, on 31 July, that 'everyone who has not got to be dragged kicking and screaming into the twentieth century will welcome this belated decision'.

Macmillan had of course reasons for stating his aims in a discreet and rather obscure way. There were so many people he could offend – the Six, the Commonwealth, British farmers, highly patriotic Conservative backbenchers, and others. It is likely that in his heart he still believed that Britain could enter the Common Market and yet remain a great power, the adviser and confidant of the United States, the centre of the Commonwealth, all at the same time. The old 'three circles' concept of British policy would then still be valid; the new element would be that Britain, within the Common Market, would guide it in the direction of becoming the equal partner of the United States within the Western alliance, in accordance with Kennedy's ideas.

Macmillan's mood was certainly not defeatist. In 1961, it was not obvious that Britain's prestige was shrinking rapidly. Macmillan was not the sort of man who would want to go down to history as a leader who had accepted a lowering of Britain's status or a retreat to the rank of a medium European power. Nor was there any need for immediate economic alarm; the impact of the much-feared 'discrimination' by the Common Market against British exports had been less than expected.

If however Macmillan had publicly stressed a belief that Britain could remain a great power and keep a special relationship with the United States, he would have given de Gaulle weapons to use against him. He would also have offended 'good Europeans' among the Six, who wanted Britain to become truly 'European-minded'. He was bound in any case to discourage them because, to avoid alarming Parliament, he had to play down the supranational aspects of the Common Market. He spoke of his approach as 'a purely economic and trading negotiation', and not a political or foreign policy negotiation. On 2 August, he said that the amount of sovereignty to be delegated in adhering to the Rome Treaty would be small. The Labour leader, Hugh Gaitskell, underlined the point. There was no question whatever, he said, of Britain's entering a federal Europe 'now'; British opinion was simply not ripe for this.

The British Labour Party and the Common Market

The Labour Party was perhaps the least of Macmillan's headaches. In 1961 it had still not fully recovered from the great quarrel over unilateralism – whether or not Britain should unilaterally give up nuclear weapons – which had led to Gaitskell's defeat at the 1960 party conference and which had been patched up in a fuzzy compromise statement on defence in February 1961. At the 1961 party conference which reversed Gaitskell's defeat, unilateralism was still the big emotional issue. Thereafter the party became almost equally split over the Common Market. Most, though not all, of its left-wingers opposed it on ideological grounds, since they saw it as an exclusive rich man's club; a group headed by Douglas Jay opposed it mainly on economic grounds; a group of convinced 'Europeans', mainly young intellectuals such as Roy Jenkins, were strongly pro-Market, on both economic and political grounds.

Gaitskell at first seemed closer to the 'marketeers', who included some of his close friends and personal supporters. In the debate following Macmillan's announcement of 31 July 1961, he criticised the Government on tactical grounds for not acting earlier, when entry

173

would have been easier; he did not attack Macmillan's decision. Thereafter he supported the Government's aims, though without much enthusiasm, and on the basis of the Government's three conditions (satisfactory terms for the Commonwealth, British agriculture and EFTA) together with two Labour conditions – independence for Britain in foreign policy and in economic planning.

These conditions left the anti-marketeers free to develop an active campaign. A Fabian pamphlet appeared in April 1962 by William Pickles, a distinguished political scientist of the London School of Economics, attacking the Rome Treaty, the 'undemocratic' institutions of the EEC and the relations of mistrust and antagonism between its members. He argued that the Treaty, if applied to Britain, would take away the sovereignty of Parliament, 'hard won in centuries of struggle against arbitrary rule, from Magna Carta to the Act of Settlement'. A 'rigid, inturned, single-race or single-continent grouping' could be a threat to peace; the Commonwealth, not the EEC, was therefore the right grouping for Britain; 'from Britain's point of view, the EEC is the wrong body, doing the wrong job, in the wrong way.'[2]

This kind of view was fairly wide-spread, not only in the Labour Party. However in May 1962 Gaitskell was still saying that 'to go in on good terms would . . . be the best solution to a difficult problem'. Even at the end of July, Sir Pierson Dixon, Ambassador in Paris and head of the British negotiating team, under Edward Heath, visited London briefly and got the impression that Gaitskell believed that British entry was essentially right and that he would probably not make it a party issue.[3]

Yet Gaitskell was moving to a point where he found himself at odds with his pro-Market friends, while they found themselves in a minority in the Parliamentary Labour Party. Within the shadow cabinet, the balance was even more strongly against them. Among the 'anti-marketeers' were Denis Healey, Michael Stewart, Patrick Gordon Walker, James Callaghan and Harold Wilson. (Wilson, like Gaitskell, never came down firmly against Common Market membership, but he blew more cold than hot, In a speech in the House of Commons on 3 August 1961, insisting on the need for full loyalty to the Commonwealth, he said, 'if there has to be a choice, we are not entitled to sell our friends and kinsmen down the river for a problematical and marginal advantage in selling washing machines in Dusseldorf.' A little over a year later, in the *Sunday Express* of 16

September 1962, he declared that 'a dying government does not possess the right, constitutionally or morally, to take a divided nation into the Common Market'.)[4] The chief of the 'marketeers' in the shadow cabinet was George Brown, who was supported by Ray Gunter and Douglas Houghton.

It was the Commonwealth question which most influenced Gaitskell. On the eve of the conference of Commonwealth Prime Ministers, he and his colleagues met leaders of Commonwealth Labour parties, on 8 September. (Canada, Australia, New Zealand, Singapore, Tanganyika and some West Indies territories were represented.) The meeting issued a joint statement that if Britain were to enter the Common Market on the basis of what had so far been agreed in the negotiations, 'great damage would inevitably be done to many countries in the Commonwealth and thereby to the unity of the Commonwealth itself'. Britain, the statement said, should not enter until better terms had been firmly agreed. After the meeting Gaitskell said that Labour had always recognised that, while the economic arguments were evenly balanced, there were important political considerations which could be said to favour entry; but he warned the Government strongly against going in on terms which Labour regarded as unacceptable.

Thereafter it was not difficult for Gaitskell to unite the party behind him at the 1962 party conference, on the basis of a document intended as a compromise between the 'marketeers' and 'anti-marketeers' in the party leadership. This said that if Labour's demands were met, 'as we still hope', Britain should enter the EEC. However, Gaitskell himself made a passionate speech to the conference, appealing to past British history, which created an anti-market mood at odds with the carefully-balanced compromise document. George Brown tried without much success to restore the balance.

Gaitskell may in part have been influenced in his shift against the Common Market by the wish to avoid a second split in the party which, coming so soon after the 'unilateralism' quarrel, could have done great harm to Labour's electoral chances. But there was no doubt that his 'Britishness' and his feeling of loyalty to the Commonwealth were entirely sincere. Public opinion in the autumn of 1962 was swinging in the same direction – partly because of the unpleasant impression created by the apparently unfriendly attitude of the Six, especially the French, in the negotiations.

By December, Gaitskell seemed actively opposed to the Common

Market. At the beginning of the month, when the negotiations were going very badly, he visited Paris. He failed to see de Gaulle, but, according to Sir Pierson Dixon, he left the Prime Minister, Pompidou, in no doubt about his feelings. Later in December he sent a carefully written statement to President Kennedy explaining the Labour Party's negative attitude. Gaitskell died, in January, before Kennedy had sent an answer.[5]

Sir Pierson Dixon's view was that Gaitskell's change of front played conveniently into the hands of the French Government, adding to the myth that Britain was not ready for admission. If the Macmillan–Kennedy nuclear agreement had not turned up as a pretext for de Gaulle's veto on Britain, he might have used the Labour Party's reluctance instead.[6] If he had, there would have been bitter recriminations between the parties in Britain, perhaps also inside the Labour Party. But this was avoided.

There were of course anti-marketeers inside the Conservative Party as well as the Labour Party. There were strong champions of the Commonwealth link and of the interests of British farmers. Some, as in the Labour Party, feared the loss of Britain's sovereignty and independence – though the most impassioned warnings came from Gaitskell himself. But on the whole Macmillan kept the Conservative Party well in line, and at the party conference in the autumn of 1962 he was helped by the fact that the Labour Party conference had taken up such a negative stand; he won an overwhelming majority. But by then public opinion polls were showing a trend in the other direction.

The Negotiations between Britain and the Common Market, 1961–3
The negotiations between the British Government and the EEC were too complicated for the general public to follow in any detail. It was necessary to learn a new vocabulary to understand them. They also moved slowly, so that it was difficult to keep track of developments. On 10 October 1961 Heath made a formal statement to the Six in Paris, in much warmer terms than Macmillan had used in the House of Commons two and a half months earlier. It included such phrases as 'our destiny is intimately linked with yours', and 'we desire to become full, whole-hearted and active members of the European Community in its widest sense and to go forward with you in the building of a new Europe.' Thereafter little happened for the rest of the year. The West Germans were busy with an election. More important, the Six were busy trying, with great difficulty, to agree on

a common agricultural policy, which involved fixing target prices for Common Market agricultural products, a system of levies on agricultural imports from outside Common Market and the creation of a European Agricultural Fund, which would support farm prices inside the Common Market, subsidise agricultural exports, and – in the long term – finance the modernisation of agriculture. All this was of great importance to the French, determined as they were to obtain all possible advantages for their farmers as part of the built-in 'balance' of the Common Market. They were also clearly determined to get a firm agreement with their partners before serious negotiation with Britain started; there was an obvious conflict of interest between France and Britain over agriculture; and Britain, if admitted to the Common Market, could be expected to strengthen resistance to French demands. (A very similar strategy was followed by France over Common Market agriculture before the opening of negotiations with Britain in 1970.) The Six finally reached agreement on agricultural policy in mid-January 1962.

This agreement had a considerable influence on the negotiations with Britain which started in earnest in the spring of 1962 and soon ran into difficulty over agricultural imports from the 'temperate zone' Commonwealth countries, Canada, Australia and New Zealand, all potential competitors of France, especially Canada and Australia as grain exporters. Sir Pierson Dixon took the view that behind the apparent struggle between Britain and the EEC was a struggle between West Germany (a grain importer) and France (a grain exporter). France had won this battle in January, thereby gaining a dominating position as the 'granary of Europe'.[7] The French did not want to re-open the question by negotiating with Heath about the admission of Commonwealth agricultural products, especially grain. Heath found himself forced to fall back on a plea for assurances of good will towards the various Commonwealth countries, and acceptance by the Six that New Zealand, because it was so heavily dependent on the British market, must be treated as a special case. Unfortunately, assurances of this sort were unlikely to impress either the Commonwealth countries concerned or the Labour Party.

However, progress was made over manufactured imports from developing Commonwealth countries and the special problems of India, Pakistan and Ceylon; some progress was also made over the question of associated status for those Commonwealth countries (mainly African) who decided that they wanted it. (This was the solution which France had found for its former colonies in Africa.) By the time the negotiations were adjourned on 5 August, the outline of a possible future deal for the Commonwealth could be seen; there was as yet no firm agreement.

However, Macmillan felt able to face the Commonwealth Prime Ministers when they met in London on 10 September 1962, and to wear a fairly cheerful face. He told them that he rejected the idea that Britain was confronted with the choice between Europe and the Commonwealth; the Commonwealth remained an association of 'cardinal importance and great value' both to its own members and to the world as a whole. On the economic side, the pattern in the Commonwealth was already changing: some Commonwealth countries had made a big industrial advance, while Britain was producing more of its own foodstuffs. Britain's main value to the Commonwealth was in the markets and the capital which it provided. If Britain grew richer through joining the EEC, the Commonwealth would benefit. There would also, Macmillan said, be a manifest political advantage: if Britain had been 'more closely involved in the European political scene' in 1914 and 1939, two world wars might have been avoided. Once inside Europe, Britain could help to shape its evolution.

The Commonwealth Prime Ministers, with varying degrees of forcefulness, re-stated their fears and objections. Ghana, Nigeria and the three East African Commonwealth countries rejected the idea of association with the Common Market. However, a final communiqué was produced in which, though they recorded their anxieties, they said that they recognised that the responsibility for the final decision rested with the British Government. Macmillan felt free to press on.

The negotiations reopened early in October. The discussion of Commonwealth problems was continued, with some further progress. Then British agriculture came up; tension rose. Britain wanted a fairly long transition period, so as to allow for a gradual change-over from the British system of cheap Commonwealth food imports, low food prices and deficiency payments to British farmers, to the Common Market system of relatively high food prices and levies on all agricultural imports. The Six however asked that Britain should change over on the day of entry into the Common Market and that the wheat price in Britain should at once be raised to the French price level. They argued that a transition period would give British farmers unfair advantages. Both France and West Germany had domestic political reasons for this stand; their own farmers were creating trouble. But the demand was obviously one which Britain could not accept; quite apart from parliamentary and public outcry, the insecure British economy could not be expected to stand the shock.

The French urged the Six to stand firm. Towards the end of the year, people were beginning to think that they were trying to force the British to break off the negotiations; others thought that by a prolonged bout of feverish haggling – which seemed to have become the Common Market's normal method of progress – an overall package deal would eventually be negotiated.

De Gaulle settled the question by delivering his veto at his press conference on 14 January 1963, at a moment when Heath was just going to propose a package deal on unsolved tariff questions and to suggest a transitional period for agriculture ending by 1970.

Macmillan and de Gaulle: Negotiation or Duel?

Some people have argued that from the start de Gaulle meant to prevent British entry into the Common Market. When Macmillan announced his approach to the Six on 31 July 1961, Healey, from the Labour benches, pointed out that de Gaulle had recently said that Britain would only be welcome in the Common Market if there were no conditions attached. Healey asked if it was not dangerous for Britain to enter formal negotiations with the Six without first having an assurance that this was not the final decision of the French Government. Macmillan answered that there were of course dangers on all sides; 'I think that, great as the risks are, it is far better to bring this matter to an issue.'

Macmillan therefore seemed to expect opposition from de Gaulle, but presumably did not think that it would be decisive. It is possible that he also thought that he could win over de Gaulle by establishing an alliance with him against the federalists or supranationalists who wanted to press ahead towards a political union after their own pattern. In the debate on 2 August 1961, he spoke approvingly of de Gaulle's 'Europe des patries' (de Gaulle's actual phrase was 'Europe des Etats'); 'this seems to me a concept more in line with the national tradition of the European countries, and, in particular, with our own'.

The idea of a supranational European political union dated back some years. Plans for a European Political Community of the Six had been carried a considerable way in the early 1950s; but since they were closely linked with the EDC scheme, they collapsed with it. Britain had of course remained aloof. After the EEC was firmly established, some members of the Six wanted to make a new effort in the political field. However, de Gaulle took the initiative, determined to shape things in his own way. In a broadcast of 31 May 1960, he said that he aimed to help build Western Europe into a 'political, economic, cultural and human group, organised for action'. The path to be followed was to be 'organised cooperation between States'. Western Europe, organised in this way, could be an indispensable condition of world equilibrium. One day, de Gaulle said, there could be a European Entente from the Atlantic to the Urals.

The key phrase was 'cooperation between States'. This was not what the 'good Europeans' wanted. In September 1960 de Gaulle went further, at a press conference. He said there should be a Council of Heads of Governments, a permanent secretariat in Paris, an Assembly of delegates from national parliaments, and specialised commissions dealing with specific fields, including defence. Britain was not mentioned. Nor was WEU.

This scheme worried other members of the Six in two ways. There was no supranational element in it and it looked as though de Gaulle was even trying to get rid of the supranational element in the Rome Treaty. He also seemed to be undermining NATO by bringing defence under the umbrella of the proposed new organisation. Moreover, de Gaulle seemed to be moving towards the exclusion of the Americans from Europe. Even if the Americans were unpopular in some Common Market countries, very few people apart from communists liked the idea of facing the Soviet bloc without them.

However, a summit conference of the Six was held in February 1961 in Paris, and a committee on political cooperation was set up under a French chairman, Christian Fouchet. A further summit, in Bad Godesberg in mid-July, resulted in a compromise statement: the Six wanted to organise political cooperation leading to a common foreign policy; but they also declared their attachment to the Atlantic alliance.

This was the situation when Macmillan announced Britain's approach to the EEC. The Fouchet committee (later the Cattani committee) carried on its work. In November the French Government produced its own draft treaty for a 'Union of States'. The Dutch and Belgians did not like it any more than they had liked de Gaulle's original ideas. They thought a second French draft, in January 1962, even worse. It seemed to imply even more strongly a divorce from

NATO. All five Common Market partners pressed France to accept a provision by which the proposed treaty could be revised in the direction of federalism.

On 10 April Britain intervened. Heath told the WEU Council that Britain was prepared to assume all the political obligations of the Rome Treaty, and would also like to be associated with the consultations among the Six on political union. A week later, Foreign Ministers of the Six met in Paris, made some progress over the NATO problem, but came up against the refusal of the Dutch and Belgians to sign a treaty until the British had joined the EEC and were able to take part in political consultations. They were ready to sign a treaty for a supranational union without Britain, but if the treaty was not to be supranational, they wanted Britain in. The discussions among the Six then lapsed. The French suspected the British of sabotage. De Gaulle turned to wooing Adenauer and preparing for the French–German Treaty of January 1963 as a sort of 'Union of States' in miniature.

If, therefore, Macmillan had hoped to establish a common front with de Gaulle over a non-supranational political union, the hope was vain. He himself could never have gone along with de Gaulle in taking defence responsibility away from NATO and placing it in the new union. In any case, the signs were that de Gaulle would rather have no European Union at all than one which included Britain.

There were also rumours that Macmillan hoped to win over de Gaulle by dangling the bait of Anglo-French nuclear cooperation. It was said that when he met de Gaulle at the Château de Champs in June 1962, he had hinted at this possibility. Lord Gladwyn, who was British Ambassador in Paris until 1960, commented on this story that if Macmillan did make such a suggestion, it could only have been within a scheme which made it compatible with the Atlantic alliance; and this was something which the General could never accept.[8] Certainly Macmillan, on his side, set far too much store by his good relations with Kennedy and by the Anglo-American nuclear co-operation re-established in 1958 to expose them to risk. On the other side, whereas France in the 1950s would very much have welcomed cooperation with the Americans or British in the nuclear field, de Gaulle in the 1960s seemed determined to reject both, so as to develop a totally independent French nuclear force. He would presumably have liked to detach the British from the Americans, but it was doubtful whether he would ever have been willing to pay the price of pooling the French nuclear force, when it came into operation, with the British nuclear deterrent.

In the event, things turned out most unluckily for Macmillan. Developments in the United States, quite unconnected with the Common Market, forced him to go to Kennedy in December 1962 and ask for American help in keeping a viable British nuclear deterrent (see p. 194 below). Although Macmillan told de Gaulle in advance what he was going to do, at a meeting at Rambouillet, this provided de Gaulle with a pretext for breaking off the negotiations between Britain and the Six at a moment when the outcome still hung in the balance – and when some of the negotiators, including Heath, thought there was a fair chance of success. The fact that Kennedy offered the same help to France as to Britain made no difference; de Gaulle rejected the offer, in spite of repeated pleas from Macmillan transmitted through the Ambassador, Sir Pierson Dixon.

It could, in the final count, only be a matter of guesswork whether de Gaulle was irrevocably determined, from the moment of the British application, to keep Britain out. Lord Gladwyn wrote that the last time he saw de Gaulle as Ambassador, in September 1960, the General made it clear, in answer to a direct question, that 'he did not think, in view of our Commonwealth commitments, that we could possibly join the EEC, anyhow for a considerable time.'[9] Both Lord Gladwyn and Sir Pierson Dixon thought that de Gaulle had firmly made up his mind by the spring of 1962 to exclude Britain. In March the Algerian conflict had been settled; he had gained fresh freedom of movement. It was at this time that Dixon began to suspect that de Gaulle's tactics were to play for time until the constitutional referendum planned for the autumn and end things off with a 'political veto' after that.[10]

It was during this 'playing for time' period that he met Macmillan at the Château de Champs in June, and apparently on Pompidou's prompting, set out to soothe away British fears. Pompidou perhaps had his eye on the internal political situation: open hostility to Britain would not be popular in France. De Gaulle won the October referendum and the November general election. He then felt free to act. At his meeting with Macmillan at Rambouillet in mid-December he seems to have revealed something of what was in his mind; when Macmillan told him of his coming request to Kennedy for help, the General's reaction was 'grim' – or so Macmillan told Dixon immediately afterwards. At this point, Dixon thought, Macmillan must at last have become convinced that de Gaulle was going to keep Britain out – though he had ignored earlier warnings from the Ambassador.

De Gaulle himself had probably enjoyed keeping Macmillan guessing about his real intentions. On his own account, the two men had a series of intimate friendly discussions on Britain and the Common Market. Macmillan told him that Britain was no longer the England of Queen Victoria, Kipling, the British Empire and splendid isolation, and pleaded that the West Europeans, faced with the threat from the enormous Soviet bloc, should try to restore the balance without permanent dependence on the United States. De Gaulle's answer was to ask whether the British were really willing to shut themselves up with 'the Continentals' inside a common external tariff: 'you who eat the cheap wheat of Canada, the lamb of New Zealand, the beef and potatoes of Ireland, the butter, fruit and vegetables of Australia, the sugar of Jamaica – would you consent to feed on continental – especially French – agricultural produce, which would inevitably cost more?' De Gaulle also queried Macmillan's sincerity in wanting to join a truly 'European Europe'; given Britain's 'privileged ties' with the United States, would it not want to drown 'Europe' in some sort of Atlanticism? Macmillan declared his will for European independence, but de Gaulle – on his own account – remained sceptical, and the Macmillan–Kennedy nuclear agreement finally 'justified his circumspection'.[11]

Macmillan, on his side, may have thought that his own powers of persuasion together with memories of wartime comradeship would win de Gaulle over in the end. If so, his own memories of de Gaulle in war-time must have become a little dim. Alternatively he may have believed that French opposition could be overcome or by-passed, perhaps relying on the other Common Market countries to achieve this. But he underestimated the power of cohesion of the Six and overestimated their internal differences. He must also have overestimated the enthusiasm of the five partners of France for British membership. The Benelux countries certainly wanted Britain in, and the Dutch and Belgians were prepared to be obstinate about it; the Italians also wanted Britain in, as a counter-weight to possible French–German overlordship. In West Germany, the Christian Democratic Government was split between its pro-British and pro-French members; the pro-French, headed by Adenauer, were stronger. In the final count, not one of the five was prepared to put the Common Market itself in danger; the amount of influence they could exert on de Gaulle was therefore small.

After the veto, the five all showed genuine regret; they refused to accept the French assertion that the negotiations had been proved to have no chance of success. So also did the EEC Commission. But their resentment against the General's high-handed action was probably greater than their sorrow about Britain's exclusion.

The British Government sensibly refrained from any effort to mobilise a revolt of the five against France, which would almost certainly have boomeranged. Instead, it took the line that a break-up of the Common Market would be against the European interest and therefore against Britain's interest. At the final meeting with the Six on 29 January 1963, Heath said: 'we in Britain are not going to turn our backs on the mainland of Europe or on the countries of the Community. . . . We shall continue to work with all our friends in Europe for the true strength and unity of the continent . . .'. Britain's application for membership was not withdrawn. The Government wished to demonstrate that it regarded the question as still open.

Heath had won the trust and respect of his fellow-negotiators, who regarded him as both sincere and competent. On 2 April 1963, following in Churchill's footsteps, he received the Charlemagne Prize in the West German town of Aachen, in recognition of services to Europe.

Macmillan had gambled and lost. But the British public as a whole did not blame him; they blamed de Gaulle, who had conveniently acted as a lightning conductor for any feelings of anger or resentment. Few people were seriously disappointed, because the Common Market had come to appear less and less attractive during the long months of complicated, almost incomprehensible, negotiation. The friendliness towards Britain shown by the five was an immediate balm. There was very little sense of national defeat or humiliation. De Gaulle's veto was a nine days' wonder. The Conservatives lost the 1964 general election, but not because of defeat over the Common Market.

Macmillan showed courage in making the gamble and risking his popularity and reputation. He achieved certain things. He made the more sophisticated sections of the British public begin to take an interest in the Common Market. He made them realise what he himself had probably not realised before – that at some point a choice *would* have to be made between the Commonwealth and Western Europe, as the basis for Britain's future development, and that it was useless to go on hoping blithely that the West Europeans would welcome the Commonwealth connection as a general European asset (as it certainly was in two world wars). The British also made the discovery that one West European political leader could say no, and they could find themselves helpless; this made them take a more realistic view of their power and position in the world. The Commonwealth countries, for their part, began to diversify their trade more energetically and to seek alternative markets to Britain; the image of Britain as the mother-country faded rapidly.

For the Six – or rather, for the five – the experience of the General's first veto was rather like a serious illness in adolescence. By the time they had recovered from it, they found themselves wiser, older and sadder, but also stronger. In the economic field, the EEC went ahead successfully by means of hard bargaining and occasional crises. But in the political field, the Six marked time. There was the inevitable antagonism between the supranationalists and de Gaulle; there was also a fairly widespread feeling among the five that if there was to be some form of political organisation, it would be natural and right for Britain to be inside it, not outside it. Moreover, in spite of failure, Macmillan's venture created in Western Europe a certain sense of the historical inevitability of Britain's eventual membership of the European Community. De Gaulle himself, three days after his veto, was reported to have said at a reception in Paris that Britain would enter the Common Market 'one day' – 'but no doubt I shall no longer be there'.

17 The British nuclear deterrent and the defence of Western Europe

The Argument over the British Nuclear Deterrent

The argument about Britain's status in the world was focused, in the early 1960s, on the British 'independent nuclear deterrent' rather than on membership of the Common Market. It was an argument which had several sides – strategic, political and economic. In the field of strategy it raised the question whether the British nuclear arm – whatever form it might take – had value only as a small component in the overall nuclear deterrent of the Western alliance; or whether, either alone or together with a French nuclear arm, it could ever protect Western Europe. In other words, could it only serve a useful purpose if closely linked with the enormously larger American nuclear armoury, or could it serve any purpose independently of the American deterrent?

In the political field, it raised the question of whether the effort to keep up a British nuclear arm forced Britain into permanent dependence on the United States, so turning the 'special relationship' into something which was not only unequal but degrading; or whether, on the other hand, it could ever serve as an important asset for a West European community which would be allied with the United States, but far more independent than the European NATO countries were in the 1950s and 1960s.

In the economic field, there was the simple question: could Britain, a country which, through its failure to solve the balance-of-payments problem, was forced unwillingly to devalue the pound in 1967, afford the luxury of a nuclear deterrent; or, on the other hand, could it be regarded as a form of defence on the cheap?

For some, especially young people, in the early 1960s there was also a moral question: whether it could in any circumstances be right for Britain to possess a weapon of such appalling destructive power. There was, on the whole, curiously little argument about the question whether possession of the nuclear arm made Britain itself more or less safe from nuclear attack.

No clear answers to these questions came out of the 1960s. The statements of politicians tended to add to general muddle. By 1970, few people could have said whether Britain did or did not possess an independent nuclear deterrent, in any real sense. By that time too the main argument had shifted to another problem: should Britain concentrate all its manpower and resources on the defence of Western Europe, or should it still try to keep a small military 'presence' East of Suez? This was a matter of rather artificial dispute between the political parties.

When the Attlee Government made its decision in 1946 to manufacture a British atomic bomb, no one questioned it. It seemed the natural and inevitable consequence of Britain's wartime work on the bomb, in partnership with the United States. American repudiation in 1946 of the two secret wartime agreements between Churchill and Roosevelt on nuclear cooperation seemed if anything to strengthen the argument for Britain's pressing ahead. In October 1946 Attlee told the House of Commons that a research and development establishment for all aspects of nuclear energy was to be set up at Harwell. In May 1948 the Minister of Defence told the House that all types of modern weapons, including atomic weapons, were being developed. The announcement aroused no excitement; there was no criticism.

In the autumn of 1949 the Soviet Union carried out its first atomic test, earlier than expected. This made it seem likely that the United States might resume nuclear cooperation with Britain. But the arrest of Klaus Fuchs, a British subject, on a charge of passing nuclear information to the Soviet Union, put an end to this hope. The British went on alone, saying very little about it. Churchill, as Opposition leader, rather unfairly criticised the Attlee Government for slowness in producing a bomb.

Britain did not carry out its first atomic test until 3 October 1952 – nearly a year after the Conservatives had come back to power. It had become an atomic power alone, without American help. Both political parties had supported the undertaking without question; so also had the distinguished scientists who had done the pioneering work. In Attlee's mind, at least, there was also the thought, in the early post-war years, that the United States might withdraw again from Europe and retreat into isolationism, as it did after the first world war; Britain must therefore have its own nuclear weapon. He also seemed to think that it would give Britain more power to influence the United States – as perhaps it did, when Attlee visited

Truman in Washington to urge that there should be no extension of the Korean war.

Just a month after Britain conducted its first atomic test, the United States tested its first hydrogen bomb. The nuclear race moved into a new, far more deadly phase. The second American test was a year and a half later. By this time the world was beginning to realise how 'the entire foundation of human affairs was revolutionised', as Churchill put it. In the spring of 1955 the Defence White Paper recorded that the decision had been taken to develop and produce a British hydrogen bomb. This, Churchill said in the House of Commons, would 'greatly reinforce the deterrent power of the free world, and ... strengthen our influence within the free world'. He clearly meant influence with the United States. He also had in mind British influence in joint planning of nuclear strategy. Macmillan, then Minister of Defence, argued against the idea that Britain should drop out of the nuclear race: 'politically, it surrenders our power to influence American policy ...'. He also spoke of possible use of the British deterrent in the Middle East and Far East.

The Defence White Paper in the spring of 1957, announcing that a British 'megaton weapon' had been developed, placed this in the context of the need for Britain to economise in its overseas expenditure on defence. The implication was that the hydrogen bomb would maintain Britain's defensive strength relatively cheaply. This was the theory which came to be associated with the man who was then Minister of Defence, Duncan Sandys. It soon proved to be over-optimistic.

On 15 May 1957 Britain carried out its first test of a hydrogen bomb – as with the atom bomb, without American help. In October, Macmillan met Eisenhower in Washington; the President agreed to ask the Congress to amend the MacMahon Act so as to allow the nuclear partnership with Britain to be renewed. Since the first Soviet Sputnik had just been launched, the Congress could be expected to agree. The 1958 British Defence White Paper said it was now necessary to coordinate operational plans with the US Air Force (obviously this meant joint targeting for hydrogen bombs). The Congress acted on the MacMahon Act in June 1958. The amendment was carefully phrased to allow information to be passed to Britain only.

The Aims of the French Deterrent
Just over a fortnight earlier, de Gaulle had returned to power in

France, at a moment of acute crisis and under the threat of civil war over Algeria. He must nevertheless have taken immediate account of the MacMahon Act amendment. Two months earlier, his predecessor, Félix Gaillard – the last Prime Minister of the Fourth Republic – had ordered the final preparations for the first French atomic explosion in 1960. The original decision to undertake preparatory work on nuclear weapons had been made by Mendès-France, as Prime Minister, in December 1954. At that time Mendès-France apparently saw a French nuclear weapon as a safeguard against domination of France by a rearmed Germany.[12] The first public statement that work was being done on nuclear weapons – as distinct from the peaceful use of nuclear energy – had been made in 1957. De Gaulle was in full agreement with the decisions of his predecessors.

France, like Britain, had to make its atom bomb and hydrogen bomb without American help; like Britain, the French felt that through the wartime work of their scientists on the joint allied project, they had earned the right to help. They would also have liked help from the British. Before the war, Frédéric and Irène Joliot-Curie had done advanced work in the nuclear field; Joliot-Curie had sent some of his closest collaborators to work with British scientists at the Cavendish Laboratory in Cambridge, and later in North America. France, however, lacked wartime agreements with the United States – not surprisingly, considering the extreme acidity of relations between Roosevelt and de Gaulle for most of the war period. The question of making nuclear weapons was a delicate one in the early post-war years in France, when Communists were either in the Government or playing a powerful role outside it. However, an atomic energy programme was started in 1945, to cover the whole field of research, and was at first dominated by Joliot-Curie; he was removed in 1950 because of his Communist Party affiliations. The question of the bomb remained politically controversial; all the public emphasis was therefore laid on the peaceful aspects of nuclear research. The Mendès-France decision of 1954 on the bomb was not announced. At the Geneva summit of 1955, the French Prime Minister, Edgar Faure, said that France would in no circumstances manufacture nuclear weapons. The British diplomat, Sir Ivone Kirkpatrick, who was there, remarked that he was 'struck by the attitude of open contempt' with which Khrushchev greeted Faure's declaration.[13]

Certainly, de Gaulle would never have made it. Four months after the MacMahon Act was amended to permit the United States to resume nuclear partnership with Britain, he sent his letter to Eisenhower and Macmillan, proposing a three-power directorate to plan world-wide strategy. This was later described by General Beaufre, who was at one time French representative on the three-power NATO Standing Group in Washington, as a proposal that 'the three nuclear powers in the alliance should devise a joint nuclear strategy'.[14] De Gaulle presumably thought it irrelevant that France would not test its first atom bomb until 1960.

The chilly answer he got from Washington and London, because of fears of strong resentment in Bonn and Rome, strengthened de Gaulle's resolve to press ahead with the creation of a French *force de frappe*, later to be re-named *force de dissuasion*. He also developed the doctrine that France must be able to conduct its own defence by its own means, and could not leave 'its destiny and its very survival' to be decided by others; this doctrine was publicly stated in a speech of November 1959 and shown in practical terms in his refusal to have foreign (American) atomic weapons stocked on French soil.

The British Deterrent in Difficulties: from Blue Streak to Nassau
By the time the first French atomic test took place, in 1960, the British were already getting into serious difficulties over the means of delivery for their new stock of hydrogen bombs. This problem did not appear to have preoccupied Duncan Sandys at the time of the 1957 Defence White Paper, which linked manufacture of the hydrogen bomb with economies in defence expenditure. It turned out to be the biggest obstacle in the way of Britain's hope of being a nuclear power in the great power class, if not in the superpower class. To make first the atom bomb and then the hydrogen bomb had taken time, but had been a job within the range of Britain's economic resources. To make the vehicles which would carry the bombs to their targets – or would be known by the potential enemy to be capable of doing so – was a very different matter. It involved immensely complex calculations of the potential enemy's development of its own delivery vehicles, and its defences against incoming vehicles, for some years ahead; each new delivery vehicle, however costly, risked becoming obsolete as soon as the potential enemy had invented a means of knocking it out on the ground, in the air or at sea. The cost, in money and economic, scientific and technological resources, would be so great that a country of Britain's size could not hope to

bear it alone. By 1963 the problem had brought Britain close to being knocked out of the nuclear race altogether.

In the late 1950s, the vehicle for the British hydrogen bomb was the V-bomber. But V-bombers were expected to become obsolete by the mid-1960s. In 1958 Britain began to develop a British version of the American Atlas missile – a 2500-mile range missile, to be fired from a fixed site, named Blue Streak. Macmillan could therefore conduct his summitry in 1959 and 1960 as representative of a power which was still in the nuclear running. But the Defence White Paper of 1960 was already showing some caution about Blue Streak; in April 1960 it was scrapped, on the ground that a missile fired from a fixed site in Britain was too vulnerable. Britain then agreed with the United States on the development of the American Skybolt, which was to be an air-launched missile with a range of 1000 miles, and was to prolong the nuclear usefulness of the American and British air forces. The United States was to bear the development cost; Britain was to buy a relatively small number of the missiles.

This arrangement was criticised in the House of Commons and outside it on the ground that it showed Britain had to depend on the United States for maintaining a so-called independent deterrent; or that it was in fact the end of the independent deterrent. Harold Wilson, speaking in the House of Commons on 27 April 1960, quoted the *Financial Times* as saying: 'we should leave to General de Gaulle the fatuous search for national prestige through the belated and technologically inferior production of weapons that belong in the arsenals of powers richer than ourselves.' Wilson then asked: 'after the disaster we have debated today, does the British deterrent ... impress our nuclear neighbours any more than France's Sahara bomb impresses us?' (This was a not very tactful reference to the first French test.)

The Labour leaders were probably pleased to have grounds for attacking the Government, for they themselves were by this time in serious trouble with their own supporters over the hydrogen bomb. In the late 1950s feelings of horror and repulsion had been aroused, not only inside the Labour Party, by facts and speculation about the bomb's destructive power. To calm this turmoil of feeling, the Party had fought the 1959 election on the rather unconvincing plan that Britain should offer to give up the bomb as part of a world agreement, under which all countries except the United States and the Soviet Union should promise not to make or possess nuclear weapons. This did not satisfy the many Labour supporters who wanted Britain to scrap the bomb unconditionally. It was estimated that in 1960 there were 45 'unilateralists' in the Parliamentary Labour Party and 70 more who had leanings in that direction.

Gaitskell himself was obviously uneasy. At times he followed the line taken earlier by Attlee, and recalled the argument that Britain needed an independent deterrent so as to have more influence on the United States. In the House of Commons on 1 March 1960, he spoke about 'fear that an excessive dependence on the United States might force upon us policies with which we did not agree', and also about 'doubts about the readiness of the United States ... to risk the destruction of its cities on behalf of Europe'. But he did not accept these as clinching the case for an independent deterrent. In the following autumn he refused to accept the 'unilateralist' vote against him at the party conference as final, and fought successfully to get it reversed, on the basis of an uneasy compromise formula, at the 1961 party conference.

By the time that Skybolt got into trouble, in late 1962, Macmillan perhaps had less to fear from Labour than from his own Conservative supporters, many of whom were firm believers in the independent British deterrent. Kennedy's Defence Secretary, Robert McNamara, arrived in London on 11 December and told the Government that five attempted test flights of Skybolt had failed. The American press had already begun to talk about the probable scrapping of Skybolt. British ministers hinted to McNamara that the Skybolt agreement had been part of a package deal which included British acceptance of an American Polaris submarine base at Holy Loch near Glasgow; but McNamara probably did not take the implied threat seriously. On 12 December, Kennedy said publicly that he expected that Britain would play 'a significant role' as a nuclear power even if Skybolt were scrapped.

Five days later, on television, Kennedy warned Western Europe that it ought to do more to strengthen its conventional forces, and added: 'we don't want six or seven powers in Europe diverting their funds into nuclear power, when the United States has got this tremendous arsenal.' The question, he said, was 'whether the United States should join in helping to make France a nuclear power, then Italy, then West Germany, then Belgium. . . . Why duplicate what we have already done, and are doing in Western Europe, so long as our guarantees are good?' He said nothing of Britain, which he obviously placed in a different category from the other West Europeans. He went on to say that he was not threatening to withdraw American forces and 'leave Europe naked'. But there seemed to be an implied warning.

This was not a way of talking which was likely to please the West Europeans (other than the British), least of all de Gaulle. The apparent discrimination in favour of Britain was unlucky just at a time when the British negotiations for entry into the EEC were at a crucial point and there was almost open French antagonism to the British. But Kennedy was talking only a few weeks after the Cuba missiles crisis. To Kennedy this had shown clearly, first, how effectively American nuclear power could be used for political ends, and next, how important it was that when there was a real danger of nuclear war, there should be only one centre of 'crisis management' and decision. To the West Europeans, on the other hand, Cuba had shown that in a major world crisis, where the flashpoint was outside the European area, they could not expect to be consulted by Washington, only informed and asked for support. They did not find this pleasant.

Kennedy had obviously come to the conclusion that something ought to be done about the Western alliance, even if he was not quite clear what. On the American side, there was a feeling that the Europeans were not carrying their due share of the military and financial burden, and that this was particularly unfair at a time when the 'dollar gap' had been replaced by an American balance-of-payments deficit. On the other side, Washington knew that de Gaulle's more or less open feeling of distaste for America, and for American intervention in Europe, was not an isolated phenomenon; similar feelings existed elsewhere in Western Europe, though they were often mixed up with the opposite feeling that American protection was very useful. Yet this feeling in turn, since the Soviet Union had acquired the hydrogen bomb and the power to destroy American cities, had been mixed with fear that the West Europeans could no longer count on nuclear protection from the Americans, who might be unwilling to risk nuclear attack unless their own national survival was at stake. From this, again, sprang a feeling among some West European politicians that the European allies in NATO should break down American exclusiveness and obtain some share in the control of nuclear strategy.

To advise him on this tangled situation, Kennedy had George Ball, a passionate enthusiast for Monnet-type integration of Western Europe. It was therefore natural that the solution to the problems of the Western alliance should be sought in encouraging the West Europeans to widen and deepen the Monnet-type integration which had already been begun; Western Europe would then become a stronger, more satisfied and therefore more independent 'second pillar' of the alliance. It might also begin to pay its own way in the defence field.

De Gaulle obviously saw, and resented, Washington's eagerness to push supranationalism or federation on Western Europe; he suspected that the aim was to strengthen American domination. At his press conference on 15 May 1962, he condemned supranationalism harshly and said: 'there could perhaps be a federator, but the federator would not be European.' In December 1962, however, Kennedy did not seem to realise that American enthusiasm for European supranationalism could easily misfire, nor that nuclear defence was the last place where supranationalism was likely to work.

When Macmillan met Kennedy in Nassau on 18 December 1962, he was much less worried about Kennedy's problems than about his own problem of the British nuclear deterrent and his political critics at home. It was surprising that there was any meeting of minds. But, according to the account of George Ball, 'above and beyond the logic of the situation was the atmosphere of the Nassau conference itself, the overwhelming circumstance that the participants liked one another. President Kennedy was fond of Prime Minister Macmillan and he had a relationship of extraordinary confidence and intimacy with the able British Ambassador, David Ormsby-Gore. . . . They were nice people and we should try, if we could, to help them out . . .'. (Ball himself believed that Kennedy should have refused help to Macmillan, so ending British pretensions to an independent deterrent.)[15]

Out of this atmosphere came the Nassau agreement, from which both sides got something. Macmillan got the promise of Polaris missiles, to be fitted with British nuclear warheads and launched from British-built nuclear-powered submarines. In return he agreed with Kennedy that this issue 'created an opportunity' for new and closer arrangements for the organisation and control of strategic Western defence, which in turn 'could make a major contribution to political cohesion among the nations of the Alliance.' In other words,

Kennedy thought – as it turned out, wrongly – that the Polaris question could be used to solve at least some of the problems of the worsening relationship between the United States and the European NATO allies. He was wrong because the practical method of dealing with them proposed in the Nassau agreement – the 'development of a multilateral NATO nuclear force', centred around American and British Polaris-carrying submarines – proved to be a pipe-dream.

Just what Macmillan himself thought about the plan, at Nassau, is not clear. He may not have bothered about it very much. What was important for him was that he had got a firm promise of Polaris missiles, to replace the lost Skybolts, and so could go home and face Parliament with a look of success. 'In Polaris,' he said, 'we have got a weapon which should last for . . . a generation.' What was more, Kennedy had made it possible for him to say that the British deterrent was still independent: in the Nassau agreement, Macmillan undertook that British Polaris submarines would be used for the purposes of the Western alliance, 'except where the British Government may decide that supreme national interests are at stake'. This was the crucial phrase which was held to preserve British independence intact. A group of Conservative MPs asked for assurances that Nassau would not mean that Britain would be left without an independent deterrent; Macmillan felt able to satisfy them.

In the House of Commons on 31 January 1963, he reaffirmed his arguments in favour of keeping an independent deterrent: it would enable the British to contribute 'within our power' to the Western alliance; 'the alliance would be healthier and better if sole power did not rest with one country however great'; finally, there was 'the contribution we can make to international influence'. He quoted in particular the part which Britain had played as a nuclear power in the test ban negotiations; and he hinted strongly that Kennedy had in fact kept in close touch with him throughout the Cuba crisis, although the official version had not suggested that Britain was treated any differently from other NATO allies.

Macmillan's reasons for maintaining the independent deterrent were therefore mainly political, almost as political as de Gaulle's reasons for building a French deterrent, and were in many ways like them, except that Macmillan's lacked the anti-American twist of de Gaulle's. Macmillan in fact went out of his way to express sympathy for French aims.

For further proof of the British deterrent's independence, Macmillan

195

said that he had agreed with Kennedy to continue 'the moral understanding which we and the United States already have, that is, not to use nuclear weapons anywhere in the world without prior consultation with each other, if circumstances permit'. (In December 1950, Acheson had stopped President Truman from giving Attlee any such undertaking on the grounds that it would have caused an uproar in the Congress. But perhaps a 'moral understanding' was something different from an undertaking.) Macmillan went on to say that he had assured Kennedy that, if the British Government wanted to operate the 'independent' clause of the Nassau agreement, it would give notice of its intention. This, Macmillan suggested, showed how independent the British deterrent really was.

In the same debate Harold Wilson (who was shortly to be elected Labour Party leader in succession to Gaitskell, who had died in January) poured scorn on Nassau. It 'was not a willing agreement between partners; it was a reluctant sop thrown by the Americans to a Prime Minister who knew in his heart that what he was asking had no defence relevance, but who knew that he dare not return and face some of his more atavistic supporters without it'. Wilson accused the Conservative leaders of nostalgia, and of striving to relive Britain's imperial greatness. He reaffirmed the Labour Party's current policy, that Britain should cease the attempt to remain an independent nuclear power, and should concentrate on strengthening the British contribution to NATO, in particular, British forces in Germany.

Under two years later, Wilson fought an election campaign on a manifesto which contained an undertaking to 'propose the re-negotiation of the Nassau agreement', and condemned it as adding nothing to the deterrent strength of the Western alliance. 'Nor is it true,' the manifesto said, 'that all this costly defence expenditure will produce an "independent British deterrent". It will not be independent, it will not be British, and it will not deter.'

After Wilson had become Prime Minister, the undertaking to 're-negotiate' Nassau was somehow lost from view; so also was the question whether or not the British nuclear deterrent should be – or actually was – independent. It was to be (almost completely) committed to NATO; this commitment was held to answer all awkward questions. The construction of the Polaris-carrying submarines went ahead; so also did the purchase of American Polaris missiles. When the Conservatives returned to power in 1970, they found that the programme had been carried through.

British nuclear deterrent and the defence of Western Europe

Nassau and French Nuclear Strategy

In January 1962, the most immediately striking impact of Nassau was its repercussion on Britain's effort to join the Common Market. According to George Ball's account of the Nassau meeting, it was realised that 'we were stirring up possible trouble with the General'. It was, he wrote, Kennedy himself who suggested that he should send a letter to de Gaulle offering the same deal to France as to Britain; 'concern about a possible adverse French reaction was not, as I recall, shared with the same intensity by the British, even though they had the most to lose if the French shut them out of Europe.'[16] Kennedy sent his letter. 'It did not temper the violence of the General's reactions . . . it had too much the flavour of a compassionate letter from a honeymooning couple to a jilted suitor . . .'. In any case, George Ball remarked, the idea of a mixed-manned multilateral force was unlikely to attract a leader who had already withdrawn units of the French fleet from NATO.[17]

Even if de Gaulle had taken his decision to keep Britain out of the Common Market long before, Nassau obviously angered him – in part because it highlighted French nuclear weakness. During his press conference on 14 January 1963, at which he delivered his veto on Britain, he said that France could not subscribe to the Nassau agreement: 'It would be truly useless for us to buy Polaris missiles when we have neither the submarines to launch them nor the thermonuclear warheads to arm them.' Moreover, de Gaulle said, it would not serve the principle that France must have its own deterrent force under its own command. He also stressed his distrust of American protection. The Russians, he said, had developed a nuclear armament sufficient to put the life of America in peril; the defence of Europe had therefore become, for the United States, of secondary importance; 'in these conditions, no one in the world, especially in America, could say if, where, when, how and in what measure, American nuclear weapons would be used to defend Europe.'

De Gaulle's argument for a French independent deterrent was forceful. However, so also was the counter-argument that the French *force de dissuasion* could never be powerful enough, in military terms, to deter the Soviet Union from attacking France if it so wished. To counter this in turn, various theories were propounded by French strategists during the 1960s; for instance, that if the Americans were unwilling to use nuclear weapons to stop a Soviet invasion of Western Europe, the French deterrent, by triggering off nuclear warfare, could force the Americans to bring their nuclear armoury into play.

This sort of argument was lent force by the doctrine – sponsored by Kennedy's Defence Secretary, Robert McNamara – that NATO should be capable of 'flexible response' to any Soviet attack, ranging from resistance with conventional forces through the graduated use of tactical nuclear weapons to full-scale nuclear attack. This, according to McNamara, should replace the American doctrine of the 1950s, usually identified with Dulles, of immediate 'massive retaliation' as the best way of deterring any Soviet attack. The American argument of the 1960s was that in the new circumstances the Soviet Union might no longer find it credible that, in answer to a Soviet attack in Europe with conventional forces, the United States would let loose its full nuclear armoury; therefore 'massive retaliation' had ceased to be an effective deterrent. 'Flexible response' would be more convincing; it would also give more time for 'crisis-management' (as in the Cuba crisis) and for second thoughts on the part of the enemy.

This American argument, sensible though it was, aroused old fears in West Germans and other West Europeans that the Americans would allow their territory to be fought over and devastated, eventually re-conquering it as 'liberators'. But slowly, during the 1960s, it gained ground. Strongly supported by Britain, a strategy for 'a wider and more flexible range of response' was finally approved by NATO Ministers in 1967.

To de Gaulle, however, 'flexible response' had no appeal. Having pinned his faith on a French nuclear armoury, he favoured massive retaliation as a strategic doctrine. Moreover, more and more openly he let it be seen that he regarded the French deterrent as a political weapon which would increase the world status of France and give it freedom of action in dealing with its allies, especially the United States. One of his strategists, General Ailleret, in the late 1960s propounded the theory of a nuclear defence 'tous azimuths' – facing all points of the compass. This presumably meant that it could be directed westwards against the United States, as well as eastwards against the Soviet Union – and, conceivably, Germany.

This strategic concept, however impracticable, may have had a certain appeal for sections of the French public (though probably not for de Gaulle's more down-to-earth successor, Pompidou). But the Gaullist independent deterrent had very little appeal for the other West European allies, and did not help them to solve the problem of

198

the American near-monopoly of the nuclear armoury of the Western alliance.

'Nuclear Sharing': from the MLF to the Nuclear Planning Group
Two ways of solving this problem were considered during the 1960s: some form of 'nuclear sharing' with the United States; or some form of 'European' deterrent. Both involved Britain. The first form of 'nuclear sharing' discussed was the NATO multilateral nuclear force forecast in the Nassau agreement. If this displeased France, it pleased West Germany, which officially welcomed it. Early in 1963 George Ball visited Bonn, and had a very satisfactory talk with Adenauer. Other allies were less enthusiastic; the more closely the British looked at it, the more they disliked it, though they remained bound by the terms of the Nassau agreement The feelings of the defence experts seemed rather like Churchill's towards the EDC (see p. 107 above). Language, technical and morale problems loomed large – particularly in the context of nuclear-powered submarines.

However, before the end of February the Americans had switched from the Nassau idea of a multilateral fleet of Polaris-carrying submarines to a fleet of mixed-manned surface vessels, as better suited to multinational ownership and multinational crews. Although surface vessels would have raised fewer technical and purely human problems than submarines, there was still the difficulty that they would be highly vulnerable – unless disguised as merchant ships, and any maritime nation could be expected to object very strongly to that solution. Livingston Merchant, Kennedy's special representative for the MLF project, was in London in mid-March; it was said publicly that he had been assured of the British Government's 'continuing support for the idea and their hope of finding ways to participate'. A fortnight later Heath told the House of Commons that the Government was examining ways and means, but had made no commitment.

By October 1963, the Americans had settled for a force of twenty-five surface ships with eight Polaris missiles each, all with mixed crews. Britain was supporting the idea though still keeping as aloof from it as was reasonably possible; it had also agreed to take part – again without commitment – in an experiment in 'mixed-manning' in an American battleship – which actually took place. But the Conservative Government made it quite clear that its real interest was in the Polaris submarines which would in due course take over from the V-bombers, whose estimated life-span had been prolonged to avoid a gap. The 1964 Defence White Paper said that Britain, in addition to contributing forces to 'the main strategic deterrent' would also maintain 'an independent British deterrent'. Even a small number of Polaris submarines, it said, would possess 'immense destructive capacity'. The White Paper then declared a strategic doctrine which was close to de Gaulle's 1963 model: 'if there were no power in Europe capable of inflicting unacceptable damage on a potential enemy he might be tempted – if not now, then perhaps at some time in the future – to attack in the mistaken belief that the United States would not act unless America herself were attacked.' This, however, was not put forward as a solution of the problems of the non-nuclear European allies.

In the autumn of 1964, the Labour Government came to power. If Wilson did not bother about 're-negotiating' Nassau, he did in effect scuttle the MLF. He saw President Johnson in Washington in December, and put forward an alternative plan for an 'Atlantic Nuclear Force'. This was a mixture of earlier ideas: it was to consist of the existing British V-bomber force except for aircraft needed 'outside the NATO area'; all British Polaris submarines (when in service); an equal number of American Polaris submarines; and some form of 'mixed-manned' contribution in which non-nuclear allies would take part. Britain remained uncommitted to the MLF surface fleet. Johnson and Wilson agreed that both plans should be discussed by the NATO allies.

It was not clear how seriously Wilson intended to push the ANF plan. It had the immediate political advantage of providing a home for the British nuclear deterrent and burying the argument about whether it was or was not independent. Both plans in fact sank leaving little trace. There were too many doubts about the whole MLF project, and in particular about the money the European allies would have to put into it while still leaving the United States with an ultimate power of veto over its use, for there to be much ill will in other West European countries about Britain's embarrassed aloofness.

In May 1965 a new start was made when the American Defence Secretary, McNamara, proposed a small select committee on ways of extending nuclear consultation among the allies. The British, heaving a sigh of relief, welcomed this proposal. From then on it gained more and more support from the NATO allies. They came to feel that, while there could be no fully satisfactory solution for the problem of 'nuclear sharing', the best way out would be for the United States (and Britain) to give much more information to the allies on nuclear defence questions, including planning and targeting, and to institute some form of joint nuclear planning for the NATO area.

In December 1966, the NATO Ministers (still meeting in Paris, although de Gaulle had announced the withdrawal of France from the NATO integrated structure earlier in the year) formally decided to set up two committees: a Nuclear Defence Affairs Committee consisting of all NATO members (except France) and a smaller Nuclear Planning Group for detailed work. These proceeded to meet regularly and seemed to give reasonable satisfaction to the non-nuclear allies. Britain fully supported them, and was a permanent member of the Nuclear Planning Group, since the British nuclear contribution to the alliance was naturally involved in the joint planning and targeting.

This practical, if undramatic, attempt to establish a healthier relationship between the Americans and the non-nuclear allies probably helped the Western alliance to survive without difficulty the shock of de Gaulle's decision on military withdrawal (though at considerable cost in money), and to celebrate its twentieth birthday in a reasonably cheerful spirit. France remained a member of the Atlantic alliance created in 1949 but did not re-join the NATO integrated military structure created in 1951.

NATO and European–American Relations

At the end of the 1960s, however, the basic question of American–European relations within the alliance still remained open. On the American side there was pressure (notably from Senator Mansfield) for withdrawal of American troops from Europe; the 1968 Soviet invasion of Czechoslovakia damped this down for a time but it soon revived. The Americans continued to feel that they should spend less money on the defence of Western Europe and the rich and prosperous West Europeans should spend more. The West Europeans, enjoying their prosperity, were most unwilling to spend more; even if they resented American overlordship, they were (mostly) reluctant to agree to more than small-scale American withdrawals, and they (mostly) wanted to keep the protection of the American nuclear deterrent.

Richard Nixon, with the eagerness of a new President, tried to tackle the problem both in an address to the NATO Council in

February 1969 and in his report to the Congress on policy in the 1970s, in February 1970. He told NATO that he knew there had been rumblings of discontent in Europe and that the United States was determined to listen with new attentiveness to its NATO partners. He went on to say that America was about to enter a period of negotiations with the Soviet Union on a wide range of issues, some of which would directly affect the European allies. He promised full consultation and cooperation. To the Congress, too, he said that for too long the United States had led without listening, talked to its allies instead of with them. A more balanced association and a more genuine partnership would be in America's interest. But he did not reveal quite how this was to be achieved, for he could see no new development in the nuclear field and stated that the American contribution in maintaining the nuclear deterrent would continue to be 'unique'.

In fact, the logic of the nuclear arms race, which pushed the United States and the Soviet Union into the strategic arms limitation (SALT) talks at the end of the 1960s, was steadily widening the power-gap between America and the West European allies in the field of defence. The American–West European partnership would inevitably remain unequal, and mutual grumbling would continue. But to both sides the partnership was quite tolerable, even if the Americans were sometimes frustrated by the obstinacy or short-comings of their allies, and the West Europeans sometimes found it difficult to maintain self-respect and independent-mindedness in the face of American military and economic superiority. The British in general, having an unexhausted stock of self-confidence and fairly thick skins, adapted themselves to the relationship without much trouble.

18 The politics of a European or Anglo-French deterrent

The 'European deterrent' and the 'Anglo-French deterrent' flitted on and off the West European stage during the 1960s like will-o'-the-wisps. Whenever a West European politician tried to clasp one of them to his bosom, it tended to melt into a cloud of mist. In Britain, Conservative 'Europeans' such as Duncan Sandys were more apt to pursue them than Labour politicians, who mistrusted them as sinister sprites which could lure the unsuspecting into the quagmire of betrayal of NATO, towards which they had paternal, protective feelings. No British political leader put forward any firm public proposal about either of them.

When Heath, during the Common Market negotiation, on 17 April 1962, spoke in the WEU Council about a possible European political union, he made clear the British Government's loyalties to the wider Atlantic alliance. A European political union, he said, would inevitably concern itself with defence, but European defence arrangements must be within an Atlantic context. There was no mention of nuclear matters. Nevertheless, there was unofficial talk during 1962 about the desirability of British support for the idea of a European deterrent, as something which would help to get Britain into the Common Market. But what Macmillan did or did not say to de Gaulle on the subject at the Château de Champs in the summer remained obscure. Wilson, in the House of Commons at the end of January 1963, accused him of 'conniving' at French insistence on a French deterrent, in a vain attempt to buy British entry into the Common Market; but that was a rather different charge.

With more precision, Wilson demanded a clear statement from the Government on its stand towards a European deterrent. Labour, he said, rejected it, because it would distract urgently needed resources from NATO, would cause strains within the Western alliance, and would strengthen the danger of a 'narrow, nationalistic, . . . revanchiste' third force in Europe. In particular, Labour opposed any proposal which would mean a German finger on the nuclear trigger.

Macmillan, replying to Wilson, did not provide the requested statement. All he said was that the best way of making sure that Germany remained non-nuclear would be to find a way, 'somehow or other', of associating the great European powers in 'some form of responsibility'; 'that is what we have tried to do.'

It was not at all clear how many West Germans did want a finger on the nuclear trigger. In the mid-1960s the idea of a European deterrent, independent of the American deterrent, was being urged by some West Germans, notably Franz Josef Strauss, who had been Defence Minister under Adenauer until 1962, and then spent several years out of office. He was important because he was the leader of the Christian Social Union (the Bavarian wing of the Christian Democratic Party), because he was extremely energetic and because he was regarded as the most nationalist of the West German politicians close to the Government. He shared the Gaullist view that the West Europeans could no longer depend on unconditional American nuclear protection, and thought that the European allies should therefore form a European nuclear force, with which the United States might cooperate. He regarded this as a realistic alternative to the American-sponsored M L F and the British-sponsored A N F. At one stage he said that there should be a European nuclear arsenal, based on the French and British nuclear deterrents (if the British were willing); this should be under the control of a European nuclear council, formed by the Defence Ministers of member countries.[18]

The idea had obvious attractions for those West Germans seeking even fuller equality of status with other Western allies, this time in the nuclear field. It could be combined with the pledge given by Adenauer at the time of the Paris agreements of 1954, that West Germany would not manufacture nuclear weapons, and with a general renunciation of all aspirations to becoming a 'national' nuclear power. (The West German 'peace proposals' put forward by the Bonn Government in March 1966 suggested that all non-nuclear NATO and Warsaw Pact countries should renounce production of nuclear weapons and submit to international control.)

The Christian Democratic Party leaders took the 'European deterrent' sufficiently seriously to insist that when the United States was negotiating with the Soviet Union on the treaty to stop the spread of nuclear weapons, this should be so phrased as to allow for the eventual emergence of a European union or state possessing nuclear weapons.

The politics of a European or Anglo-French deterrent

For the France of de Gaulle, the idea had little attraction. One of the political purposes of the French deterrent was to serve as a counterweight to German economic strength within the Community of the Six. If France had to give up national control of its nuclear arm, this advantage would be lost. De Gaulle was ready to use it on behalf of Western Europe, thereby demonstrating the leadership of France, but not to share control with any other state. Because of this reluctance to water down national control, he also probably thought of an Anglo-French nuclear partnership – if he did seriously think of it – only in terms of an exchange of information and perhaps mutual aid on the production of weapons and delivery vehicles, rather than shared nuclear strategy and targeting.

For the British, both a 'European deterrent' and an 'Anglo-French deterrent' should perhaps have been politically attractive ideas. In the 1960s Britain was a much stronger nuclear power than France. Leaving aside the V-bombers, by the end of 1969 Britain had three Polaris submarines in operation and a fourth 'coming into service', carrying missiles equipped with H-bomb warheads. The first French missile-carrying submarine was due to become operational at the end of 1971, the second in 1972, the third in 1974 and a fourth 'later'. Moreover, until the mid-1970s, France would have atomic warheads only; not until then would French H-bombs, or thermonuclear warheads, become available.

Theoretically, the British nuclear arm could have been used either to purchase de Gaulle's good will in getting Britain into the Common Market, or to outflank and outbid de Gaulle and purchase the leadership of Western Europe, leaving France out in the cold. However, realism prevented any British leader from seriously attempting either course. It was always regarded as unlikely that de Gaulle would want any real form of nuclear partnership with Britain; to Britain, because of the British nuclear lead, France had little to offer. Moreover, Britain would have been debarred by its 1958 agreements with the United States – which it regarded as most important – from giving to France nuclear information which could be said to be derived from American sources; and it would have been difficult to disentangle what was or was not American-derived information.

As for a European deterrent, British defence experts did not think this credible enough to prevent a Soviet attack; they continued to believe that the American deterrent was essential for the defence of Western Europe. Whatever the eagerness with which Conservative or

Labour leaders tried to 'enter Europe', economically or politically, in the defence field most of them remained at bottom incorrigibly 'Atlantic-minded'. (Fortunately, so too were most other West European leaders, including probably the French.)

There was however a clear difference of approach between Labour and the Conservatives. Labour, both out of power and, from 1964 to 1970, in power, openly opposed the idea of a European or Anglo-French deterrent unless it could be firmly placed inside the NATO framework. The Labour Government, on taking office in 1964, got over the difficulty of its proclaimed opposition to an independent British deterrent by 'committing' the British nuclear arm to NATO and so making it respectable, and by offering to put it into any eventual Atlantic nuclear force. Denis Healey, who was Defence Minister throughout the period, was a strong believer in NATO, and in the American deterrent as essential to the security of Western Europe. This was re-stated in every Defence White Paper that appeared during his period of office. He suspected anything which might undermine NATO nuclear strategy. After the Labour Government's decision to try to enter the Common Market in 1967 and even more after the Soviet invasion of Czechoslovakia in 1968, Healey urged the need for the European allies to develop cooperation among themselves in various fields and to establish what he called a 'European identity' within the Western alliance. But this obviously had nothing to do with a European or Anglo-French deterrent.

A further reason for Labour hostility to the idea of a European deterrent was the fear (which turned out to be exaggerated) that it could complicate dangerously the negotiation of a non-proliferation treaty, because of Soviet hostility to anything which could possibly place a German finger on the nuclear trigger. (This feeling was shared by a good many Labour supporters.) Strong support for this treaty by the British Labour Government did not please the Christian Democratic leaders in Bonn, who fought a long rear-guard action against certain aspects of it. This did not help the Labour Government in its fresh approach to the Common Market during 1966 and 1967.

However, Wilson was not willing to compromise on the matter. He wanted to bring Britain together with the Six; but he also wanted to improve relations with the Soviet Union, and regarded the non-proliferation treaty as an important step on the way. After he had put his plan for an Atlantic Nuclear Force to President Johnson in

December 1964, he told the House of Commons that any form of majority vote, in the control of a NATO nuclear force, would involve proliferation and would be regarded as highly provocative 'by those with whom we hope to negotiate with a view to easing East–West tension'. During 1965 and early 1966 the British were openly critical of American drafts for a non-proliferation treaty which were specifically phrased to leave open the possibility of an eventual European nuclear force which might develop out of either the MLF or the ANF (if either came into existence). At this period, the Soviet Union strongly criticised the American drafts on the grounds that they left 'gaping loopholes' for proliferation of nuclear weapons, and an accusing finger was pointed at the West Germans. The British showed understanding for the Soviet stand.

However, in the course of 1966, both the MLF and the ANF quietly sank; instead the NATO allies adopted the McNamara solution of nuclear consultation and set up new organs for this purpose. The Soviet Union seemed to find these unobjectionable, and presumably thought the prospect of a West European state possessing its own nuclear force so very remote as to be not worth worrying about.

In any case, following the meeting between Johnson and Kosygin at Glassboro in July 1967, the Soviet Union decided to conclude a non-proliferation treaty and the two superpowers presented identical texts at the end of August. Britain could not criticise what the Soviet Union had accepted. The interpretation placed both by the American Government and by the British Government on the final text was that it left open the possibility of a federated European state taking over an already existing European national deterrent – that meant, either the British or the French or, of course, a joint Anglo-French deterrent if such a thing ever came into existence.

Britain was one of the three nuclear powers which signed the treaty on 1 July 1968; the ceremony of signature took place on the same day in London, Washington and Moscow. (China and France refused to sign.) It looked as though this would probably be the last occasion on which Britain could play the role of a sort of privileged junior partner to the two superpowers. However, the Labour Party as a whole was inspired, not by status-seeking, but by a simple straightforward wish to stop the spread of nuclear weapons and by the remnants of a long-standing fear of Germany.

The Conservative Party's attitude to a European or Anglo-French deterrent was, at least in appearance, different from Labour's during the second half of the 1960s. They were more kindly disposed towards the idea and did not show the sort of moral distaste for it displayed by the Labour leaders, in spite of their effort to get Britain into the Common Market. But while Heath was obviously very interested in a European or Anglo-French deterrent, some of his colleagues seemed more dubious.

Just for this reason, perhaps, the Labour leaders turned it into a matter of party warfare when Wilson decided to make a new bid for Common Market membership. In the House of Commons debate on 16 and 17 November 1966, after Wilson had announced that his government was considering a fresh approach, his Foreign Secretary, George Brown, went out of his way to stress that the Rome Treaty did not involve any supranational authority for defence, and that the Government was 'resolutely opposed' to any change in Britain's relationship with the United States as a result of joining the EEC, particularly in defence. Wilson was more explicit. He referred to suggestions 'coming from Conservative quarters' that a major change in international nuclear policy would be required and that Britain should move from its existing nuclear relationship with the United States to a position of closer nuclear relationship with France or even of an Anglo-French nuclear deterrent. But, Wilson said, a separate nuclear deterrent in Europe would be a fundamental danger to any hope of understanding with the East and a divisive and weakening factor within NATO. In support of this view, he quoted what Reginald Maudling, one of Heath's closest colleagues, had said in the debate.

What Maudling had actually said was that it would clearly be a mistake to try to build up a European deterrent to duplicate that of the United States. The Conservative elder statesman and spokesman on foreign affairs, Sir Alec Douglas-Home, trod a middle path. On the one hand, he pointed out that there was little sign that de Gaulle was interested in an integrated European defence command and that the French nuclear force would certainly be kept under French control. On the other hand, there might be an opportunity to 'explore the ground' with the French and the Germans, so as to start the process of Europe's carrying a greater share of responsibility for its own defence.

Heath, as Conservative leader, admitted that de Gaulle's intentions were unclear. But he seemed to have in mind a possible major shift in British nuclear policy. Urging Wilson to 'thrash things out in Paris', he said that this would involve 'the relationship between our own nuclear power and that of France, and the relationship of this with American nuclear power'.

Wilson met de Gaulle in Paris the following January but there was no sign that he had followed Heath's advice. However, Heath went on to make a more precise proposal. In March 1967 he delivered the Godkin lectures at Harvard University, and suggested that the British and French nuclear forces should be pooled to form a joint deterrent which would be 'held in trust' for Europe.

In the debate in the House of Commons on the Government's decision to apply for EEC membership, from 8 to 10 May 1967, Wilson pressed Heath on this proposal, asking him whether it was his policy to share the British deterrent with other European countries. Heath said that France and Britain, each with its nuclear deterrent, should say that they were prepared to have 'some sort of committee as there is in NATO – the McNamara Committee or something of the sort – in which members of the enlarged Community can deal with these matters'. The Foreign Secretary, George Brown, called Heath's proposal 'dangerous, unwise, and not well informed'.

Heath's proposal produced no visible response from France. However, de Gaulle may have had it in mind when, at his press conference a week after the debate, he spoke of the impossibility of intermingling the policies of Britain and the Six 'unless the British changed, notably in the field of defence, their entire outlook, or unless the continentals renounced forever a Europe that would be truly European'. He said nothing to suggest he was ready to change his outlook on the independence of the French deterrent.

The departure of President de Gaulle in 1969, and his replacement by the reputedly pragmatic Pompidou, raised the question whether France might re-consider its attitude to NATO. The appointment as Defence Minister of Michel Debré, a fervent Gaullist, made this seem most unlikely. However, in March 1970, the British Defence Minister, Healey, told a West German newspaper that nothing would please Britain better than a French decision to draw closer to the NATO structure. On 12 April both Healey and Debré appeared on BBC television; Debré, speaking of nuclear defence, said that Anglo-French technical cooperation could reduce costs and perhaps lead to eventual pooling of research; but he ruled out the integration of the French nuclear force with others on the ground that it would make it impossible for France to have a policy independent of the United States. Healey, on his side, thought an Anglo-French force might disturb other allies and make them want their own nuclear weapons; it might also put in question the American nuclear guarantee of Western Europe, and could therefore be 'de-stabilising and dangerous to peace'. But Healey implied that if Britain joined the Common Market, the problem might become easier.

Debré's attitude was reaffirmed by President Pompidou himself, at a press conference in July 1970: there could possibly be agreements on nuclear matters between France and Britain, he said, but France could not be expected to go beyond certain limits: in particular, it could not be forced to re-enter NATO.

Between the British Labour Government and the Pompidou Government there seemed very little chance of agreement on an Anglo-French force. When Heath became Prime Minister in June 1970, he refused to abandon hope. In an introduction which he wrote to a book containing his 1967 Godkin lectures, he suggested that a pooling of the British and French deterrents would not mean a break with America or with NATO, but could be a means of healing the breach between France and its NATO allies. When his Foreign Secretary Sir Alec Douglas-Home, visited Paris for talks with his opposite number, Maurice Schumann, the question of Anglo-French nuclear cooperation was apparently touched on in gingerly fashion; but both sides seemed willing to leave it over for discussion at some remote future time. However, Heath, when pressed by Wilson in the House of Commons, said that he saw no reason why joint Anglo-French nuclear arrangements, whether inside or outside NATO, should not be discussed with the French Government. The Prime Minister added: 'my hope remains that they can be done in NATO.'

Heath might well hope this. The basic dilemma was that if an Anglo-French nuclear force were to be truly 'European' in the current French sense of the word, Britain would presumably have to give up its joint targeting arrangements with the United States inside NATO. But that, for the most important military and political reasons, any British government would be extremely unwilling to do. The other European allies might also feel they were getting a very bad bargain: an Anglo-French force would be no fair exchange for the protection of the United States deterrent.

It also seemed doubtful whether by the end of the 1970s the

question of an Anglo-French nuclear deterrent would still seem a real one. During the 1970s the British would have their Polaris submarines, the French their submarines and their fixed-site missiles in northern Provence. But the new and immensely costly complexities of the anti-missile missiles and MIRVS (multi-targeted missiles), which the two superpowers had developed, raised the whole business of being a nuclear power to a level of effort and expenditure which Britain and France could hardly hope to reach, whether jointly or separately. Particularly if a firm nuclear understanding were reached between the superpowers at the SALT talks, it would become more and more dubious whether a purely European deterrent would have any real practical significance, either for the defence of Western Europe or for the exercise of political influence in the world. However, for a country to divest itself of a nuclear deterrent gracefully, once it possessed it, presented awkward problems of domestic politics and international face-saving. No British or French government would hurry to tackle them.

19 Britain and a 'European defence identity'

Since the nuclear weapon seemed ill-fitted to be the kernel of West European unity, there remained the possibility of what Healey had called a 'European defence identity'. The Labour Government's defence policy, when it took office in 1964, did not show the concentration on Western Europe which it developed later. The 1965 White Paper laid more stress on commitments elsewhere. Britain, it said, had a major interest in the stability of the world outside Europe; the British contribution was 'paramount' in many areas East of Suez (in particular Aden and Singapore). It would be politically irresponsible and economically wasteful if these bases were abandoned. In Europe, on the other hand, there was much less likelihood of war than in the past; British forces in Germany, which imposed a heavy burden on the balance of payments, must always be 'subject to review'. (At that moment there were about 51,000 British troops in West Germany, about 4000 below the agreed target figure.)

By 1966 the balance was already changing – mainly because the balance-of-payments problem had become even more acute and the need to cut government spending overseas even more pressing. The White Paper issued in February declared the aim of reducing overall defence spending from over 7 per cent of the Gross National Product to a stable level of around 6 per cent. It forecast withdrawal from Aden by 1968. From then on the Labour policy of withdrawal from East of Suez gathered speed until it culminated in the firm statement that withdrawal from the Persian Gulf would be carried out by the end of 1971, and from Singapore not long after.

This bold decision – which was strongly contested by the Conservatives – stemmed partly from the shift in the Labour Government's attitude towards the Common Market which took place during 1966 and led to the second British application for membership in May 1967. Healey (not previously a 'European') backed up this move fully in his defence policy; de Gaulle's second veto towards the end of 1967 made no difference. The White Paper of February 1968 said that Britain's first priority must still be to give the fullest possible support to NATO, 'on a scale corresponding with our efforts to forge closer political and economic links with Europe.' A further policy statement of July 1968 said that the planned withdrawal from East of Suez made it possible for Britain to offer immediate increases of availability of some of its forces to NATO. Looking forward to the 1970s, the statement said that it would conflict with Britain's new political priorities to deploy more than a relatively small part of its total strength outside Europe, though it would be possible to supply 'appropriate forces for overseas needs', for instance, for the Commonwealth five-power exercise in the Far East planned for 1970.

In the following August, the Soviet invasion of Czechoslovakia gave a fresh impulse to British concentration on the defence of Europe. At the same time Soviet naval activity in the Mediterranean, which had greatly increased after the six-day war between Israel and the Arab states in 1967, was worrying Britain and other NATO countries. In consequence Britain 'improved its contribution' to NATO in both areas. The 1969 Defence White paper pointed out the danger that another crisis like the Czechoslovak crisis might present 'a more urgent and immediate threat to the stability of Europe'; moreover, changes within the Communist world might produce new policies in Russia which could bring fresh dangers to world peace. NATO must therefore maintain political unity and also the American commitment to the defence of Western Europe. Britain, the White Paper said, had a 'central role' to play in supporting the solidarity, strength and strategy of NATO. The decision to concentrate British efforts in the NATO area made Britain better able to do this, as the only European Power with a role and military capabilities covering 'the three main NATO fronts from the Arctic to the Caucasus on land, sea and air'.

So if Britain was laying down a 'world role', East of Suez, it was hoping to fill a 'central role' among the European allies of NATO. In this, it would not have to contend with France, since France had withdrawn in 1966 from the military activities of the alliance, keeping its troops in West Germany under a separate bilateral agreement with the Bonn Government; and French efforts during the 1960s to start up defence cooperation among the Six had always come up against either loyalty to NATO or a desire to bring in Britain. On the other hand West Germany, since the 1950s, had had the reputation of the 'favourite ally' of the United States, and had far bigger ground forces on NATO's central European front than Britain. However, in the second half of the 1960s, Britain fortunately managed to establish with the West Germans a relationship which was not based on competition but on a shared interest in making NATO as efficient as possible from the point of view of the European allies.

Cooperation between the two was close when they joined in working out the practical implications of the policy of 'flexible response' adopted by NATO in 1967. (This was warmly backed by Britain provided that it did not demand an increase in British defence expenditure.) The British and West Germans together prepared political guidelines for the use of NATO nuclear weapons in Europe which were finally approved by the other allies in 1969.

A close and equal partnership between Britain and West Germany was – in the absence of France – essential for the development of a 'European defence identity'. Another move which Healey made was to institute regular informal meetings of European Defence Ministers, usually during NATO ministerial meetings, with the idea of developing a European standpoint on strategic problems. By the end of the 1960s, this practice was well-established. There was also a renewed and intensified effort by Britain to get cooperation with other NATO countries in the manufacture of defence equipment, especially aircraft, so as to save money and become less dependent on the United States for supplies. British hopes in this field had repeatedly been disappointed in the past, but in the late 1960s there seemed a better chance of success.

All these were moves in the direction of creating Healey's 'European defence identity'. They were made without upsetting the Americans; Nixon in fact welcomed them when NATO was celebrating its twentieth birthday in April 1969. In his report to the Congress of February 1970, he said that the United States favoured 'a definition by Western Europe of a distinct identity, for the sake of its own continued vitality and independence of spirit'. At the same time he reaffirmed the American involvement in Europe: 'as we move from dominance to partnership, there is the possibility that some will see this as a step towards disengagement. But . . . we can no more disengage from Europe than from Alaska.'

The 1970 Defence White Paper – as it turned out, Healey's last – developed further the idea of 'a closer European defence identity within NATO'. One purpose would be to enable the European members of NATO to speak with a common voice in the expected negotiations with the Warsaw Pact countries on European security. Another would be to face the likelihood of some 'redistribution of the common burden of Europe defence' – that meant, some reduction of American forces and of the overall American contribution – during the 1970s. The European allies, the White Paper argued, could only take on a 'fairer share' without an unacceptable increase in their defence expenditure by cooperating more closely together. This would be particularly important in the production and use of common defence equipment, as in the British–West German–Italian plan for a multi-role combat aircraft. There should be closer collaboration between the European military staffs in developing their tactical doctrines. All this, the White Paper said, would 'give an impetus to the developing political unity of Western Europe'; it would extend Europe's capability in many fields of advanced technology. It added the hope that during the 1970s France would find it possible to take a fuller part.

So long as the 'European defence identity' was to grow up inside NATO, it was certain to be rejected by de Gaulle's more devoted followers, who still wielded influence on the post-de Gaulle Government both from inside and from outside – though this seemed likely to decline after de Gaulle's death in November. Britain's claim, as stated in the 1970 White Paper, to 'take the lead in cooperation' was also bound to annoy them. However, even if there was a certain amount of 'boosting Britain' in its presentation, the Healey policy seemed an honest and useful attempt to combine the need for an American-backed alliance with a more self-reliant, self-assertive and united stand by the European allies. The British failure to propose an institutional structure for the 'European defence identity' could be seen as a defect. But if the EEC were widened to take in new members and deepened by acquiring a political content, the necessary structure for defence cooperation might emerge.

When the Conservatives took office in June 1970, they were pledged to review and perhaps revoke the Labour Government's decision on withdrawal from East of Suez. They did in fact revise it, to the extent of promising a modest 'military contribution' to five-power defence arrangements in south-east Asia. But it was obvious that a government headed by Heath would not divert Britain's energies and resources away from Western Europe, particularly at a time when negotiations with the Common Market at last seemed to have some chance of success. The Labour Government had made a strenuous

effort to fit its defence policy both to the realities of Britain's economic position and to the aim of anchoring Britain firmly to mainland Europe. In broad effect, this policy was reaffirmed in the
Conservative Government's supplementary Defence White Paper of
28 October 1970. This once again declared that Britain's security
rested on the strength of NATO, and that the maintenance and
improvement of the British contribution to NATO remained the
first priority. It also said that Britain would continue to work with
the European members of NATO to take a fuller share of the
common defence burden.

Towards the end of 1970, there was renewed pressure in the US
Congress for American troop withdrawals from Europe. In response
to these pressures, the European allies promised in December to
increase their military and financial contributions to the alliance.
President Nixon in his turn responded with a pledge to NATO not
to reduce American forces in Europe unless matching reductions
were made by the other side. This pleased the European allies, but
they knew that sooner or later there would be fresh demands in the
United States for withdrawals from Europe. In any case, given the
prospect that there might soon be a wider European community of
ten countries, they were coming to feel that a 'European defence
identity' would be natural and desirable for its own sake.

20 Britain and the EEC, 1966–70

The Labour Government turns to the EEC
In the House of Commons on 31 January 1963 Harold Wilson had spoken harshly about the Conservative Government's failure in its attempt to negotiate with the Common Market. He said: 'naked in the conference room is one thing; naked and shivering in the cold outside, while others decide our fate, is an intolerable humiliation.' He added that the Macmillan administration was too tired and too stale; the task of governing must pass into the hands of a party which was ready to face the challenge of the future.

The same note was struck in the manifesto on which the Labour Party successfully fought the general election of 1964. The Conservatives, it said, had been driven by economic failure, had lost their nerve, and had been prepared to accept humiliating terms for entry into the Common Market. The manifesto did not suggest that a Labour Government would try again. Instead, it accused the Tories of having allowed the Commonwealth share of Britain's trade to drop from 44 per cent to 30 per cent; Labour, in power, would make a drive to step up exports to the Commonwealth.

A relatively short period in office, grappling with a monetary crisis and a bigger than usual balance-of-payments deficit, produced a change in the Labour Government's attitude. It fought the election of March 1966 on a manifesto saying that Labour believed that Britain, in consultation with the EFTA partners, should be ready to enter the EEC, provided that essential British and Commonwealth interests were met. When the new Parliament met in April, there was a statement of the same kind in the Queen's Speech. From then on, the Labour Government's advance towards the Common Market gathered momentum until the formal application for membership was made in May 1967.

The change in Wilson's attitude seemed surprising. In his earlier career in the party he had been regarded as close to its Left wing; his personal associates had been against joining the Common Market. He himself, in the earlier negotiations, had insisted so strongly on

217

the need for cast-iron safeguards that he was usually reckoned an opponent of British entry.

Within the Cabinet which he formed after the 1964 election there were two outstanding and influential 'Europeans': George Brown, who had once fought Wilson for the party leadership, and Roy Jenkins, who had been a close friend of Hugh Gaitskell. There was also a prominent anti-marketeer, Douglas Jay. Wilson's first Foreign Secretary, Patrick Gordon-Walker, was also reckoned an anti-marketeer, and was certainly very much of a Commonwealth man. His second Foreign Secretary, Michael Stewart, had not been one of the original 'Europeans' but soon became one. Possibly Wilson thought the most satisfactory balance of forces inside the Cabinet could be struck by taking up the cause of Common Market membership. However, inside the Parliamentary Labour Party there was strong feeling against the Common Market, and Wilson had to make a special effort early in 1967 to win over the doubters or at least keep them quiet. In the country as a whole, the Common Market was certainly not a popular or attractive cause in the mid-1960s.

When Wilson was asked by a Conservative in the House of Commons on 2 May 1967 why he had changed his mind about the Common Market, the reason he gave was that 'my experience of the working of the Community, the actual practical working, . . . renders unfounded the fears and anxieties which I certainly had, . . . based on a literal reading of the Treaty of Rome and the regulations made under it'.

Wilson may have had two things in mind. One was the big crisis inside the Common Market in 1965 during which France imposed a partial boycott for a period of seven months. In this de Gaulle showed clearly that he was not going to let the EEC Commission exercise the supranational authority foreseen in the Rome Treaty. Couve de Murville went so far as to say in the French Assembly: 'no member of a responsible government talks seriously of supranationalism, which is a myth, except in order to fight out-of-date battles.' The compromise which ended the French boycott was an understanding among the Six that on a matter of very great importance to a member country, an effort would be made to try to reach unanimity; in practical terms, this was taken to mean that France would retain a veto rather than proceeding to the form of majority voting foreseen in the Rome Treaty. All this seemed to show that British fears of supranationalism would be misplaced; moreover, friendly Common

Market governments assured the British that the way in which things actually worked inside it was much less rigid and inflexible than might appear from outside it.

There was little sign of any American pressure on the Labour Government to make a new approach to the Six; relations between Wilson and President Johnson were not like those between Macmillan and Kennedy and the Americans had lost their first enthusiasm for the Common Market, which showed little sign of turning into the political union for which they had hoped. However, de Gaulle's decision to withdraw France from the NATO military structure in 1966 inevitably re-awakened old American worries about the European allies, and revived the old idea that British entry into the European Community would be a stabilising factor. In July 1966 Wilson was in Washington and had a seventy-minute talk alone with Johnson; this subject must almost certainly have come up. On 7 October 1966, Johnson made a speech on Europe and the 'two-pillars' concept. A united Western Europe, he said, could be America's equal partner; it could move more confidently in peaceful initiatives towards the East. The United States therefore looked forward to the expansion and further strengthening of the Community: 'the outlines of the new Europe are clearly discernible; it is a stronger, increasingly united, but open Europe, with Great Britain a part of it, and with close ties with America.'

Perhaps, however, the decisive factor for Wilson was that he became intellectually convinced by the arguments showing that Britain sooner or later would have to make a fresh effort to join the Common Market, in order to avoid finding itself both economically and politically on the outer fringe of West European affairs, with a static standard of living while standards in the Common Market countries were rising rapidly. Moreover, if the attempt was to be made, there were advantages in making it quickly before the Six made further important decisions in which Britain had no part – in particular, before they completed their agricultural and financial policies; the target date for this was the beginning of 1970. In any case, the job of storming the Common Market citadel, and succeeding where his predecessor had failed, had obvious attractions for a man of Wilson's self-confident, optimistic and active temperament.

When the Labour Government was first looking at the venture in the spring of 1966, its members may have been over-optimistic about the chances of success, for two reasons. For one thing, they were

H   219 taking a confident view of the outlook for the British economy. They obviously did not foresee the crisis of the summer of 1967 and the devaluation of the pound in the following November. As late as May 1967 Callaghan, as Chancellor of the Exchequer, was forecasting that the 1966–7 deficit of £189 million on the balance of payments would be turned into a surplus in the year 1967–8, and that the cuts in overseas defence expenditure would be achieving their maximum effect at the end of the 1960s. The Labour leaders therefore presumably thought that they would be able to go into negotiations with the economy in a promising condition and that it would be in good health by the time Britain actually entered the EEC.

They may also have taken too rosy a view of the French attitude to Britain, or at least of the chances that de Gaulle would refrain from a second veto. At a meeting of the WEU Council in London on 15 March 1966 the French representative, the State Secretary for Foreign Affairs, M. Jean de Broglie, said courteously that France would welcome Britain in the EEC 'in the spirit of the Treaty of Rome'. This remark probably had little political significance, but was taken at the time as a hint that France was taking a kindlier view of British entry. At a press conference the next day, Stewart, the Foreign Secretary, said that the situation now seemed 'healthier' than it had been at the time of the 1963 veto; the considerable difficulties in the way of British entry might not be insuperable.

In any case, the Labour Government went ahead. A speech by Wilson at Bristol on 18 March revived Labour's old conditions for entry and sounded unenthusiastic; but at a meeting of the WEU Assembly in June, George Thomson, the Minister with special responsibility for European affairs, said that in Britain there now existed 'the political will' to join the Common Market: the general debate on whether or not Britain should join was finished. He added that some of the difficulties, for instance over the Commonwealth, appeared less formidable than in 1962.

Very soon a chill wind started blowing from France. Early in July Georges Pompidou, de Gaulle's Prime Minister, visited London. The atmosphere of the visit was marred by the fact that Healey, the Defence Minister, had just had to make a public apology in the House of Commons for having said that de Gaulle was regarded as a bad ally in NATO and a bad partner in the EEC. The communiqué on the Pompidou–Wilson talks showed marked lack of enthusiasm on the French side. It said that Pompidou 'recalled that nothing prevented the entry of Britain into the Common Market provided that it accepted the Treaty of Rome and the arrangements subsequently agreed'. The two governments were to keep in touch. On 30 September, after a WEU Council meeting in Paris, the unfortunate M. de Broglie gave a press conference in a discouraging tone. He said that France was not doctrinally opposed to British entry but many difficulties remained and things could not be solved quickly. This was perhaps intended to correct his undue amiability of the previous March.

The British Government pressed on. On 10 November, Wilson told the House of Commons that, following a deep and searching review of the whole problem, the Government had decided to make a new high-level approach to see whether conditions did or did not exist for fruitful negotiation. He and the Foreign Secretary (George Brown) intended to engage in discussions with each of the Heads of Government of the Six. Four days later, in his Guildhall speech, Wilson spoke with some enthusiasm about the prospect of British entry: one of his main themes was the need for European technological cooperation, to enable Europe to become more self-reliant, 'neither dependent on imports nor dominated from outside'. This theme, with its open appeal to West Europeans to unite to prevent American industrial penetration and domination, became one of his key arguments during the following year. In his Guildhall speech, as often later, he stressed that Britain had much to give; and he said he would like to see a drive to create a 'new technological community' in Europe.

(Wilson's enthusiasm for European technological cooperation was counterbalanced by British refusal to carry through joint projects which were proving over-costly or unlikely to give worthwhile results. One of the Labour Government's early moves had been to express public doubts about the Anglo-French project for the Concorde supersonic airliner; in April 1968 Britain announced withdrawal from the European Launcher Development Organisation (though not from the European Space Research Organisation); in May 1969 it withdrew from the French–German–British project for a European air-bus. However, Wilson's argument had a good deal of appeal in the Common Market countries, even in France.)

On 16 November 1966 the House of Commons debated the subject. George Brown naturally spoke with enthusiasm. He said that the issue was whether Britain could play such a role that in future it could effectively be a leader of a unified Europe. He spoke of the economic advantages of a market of around 280 million people, potentially a very prosperous one, compared with the EFTA market of just under 100 million. Britain, he went on, could help, through its industrial and technological competence, to redress the imbalance existing between Europe and America. 'We could clearly play a much greater role from within the Community than we can play from outside.' George Brown also spoke of the French problem, admitting that Britain and France did not see eye to eye on all points of their European, Atlantic or defence policies. But if France was indispensable to Europe, so also was Britain. 'Therefore we must not enter upon our discussion on the assumption that France would want to be an obstacle to the establishment of a wider and more influential Europe.'

Heath, as Opposition leader and as the chief British negotiator in the 1961–3 attempt, made a speech remarkable for its sympathetic presentation of de Gaulle's views. These were, he said, that 'there must not be what he terms an allegiance foreign to Europe'. 'What Europe is all about', Heath went on, was redressing the balance on the two sides of the Atlantic – in trade, finance, defence and political influence. For far too long, 'the prairies, whether of North America or Australasia', had been able to ship their food to Europe, and European (he clearly meant, French) agriculture had been unable to compete. In monetary policy, Heath went on, the whole purpose of French policy was to 'redress the balance against the two reserve currencies and, in particular against the dollar.' (The other reserve currency was of course the pound sterling.) The same applied to defence; and Heath urged Wilson to go and thrash out the whole question in Paris. But he did not say just how far he thought Wilson ought to go in meeting de Gaulle's policy of 'redressing the balance'. However, Heath said at one point, 'I believe that these changes are really necessary'.

De Gaulle's Gold Campaign, Britain and the EEC
When Heath spoke of French monetary policy, he was touching on a key factor in the whole complex situation surrounding the new British approach to the Common Market. There was no real reason to suppose that de Gaulle felt any more kindly towards 'les Anglo-Saxons' than he had done in 1962 and 1963. In fact, his break with NATO in March 1966 showed determination to loosen his ties with

them, in particular the Americans, to the furthest limit short of a definite rupture. But during 1966 he had turned his attention from defence to a new field – the monetary field. This was especially interesting for him because both the United States and Britain were in difficulties; Britain's were far more serious. Both had large balance-of-payments deficits and seemed unable to cure them. Both had currencies widely used in world trade and as reserve currencies. The dollar was much stronger than the pound, but even the dollar was vulnerable. This weak spot in the Anglo-Saxon armour offered an opening to France; or at least de Gaulle believed that it could be used to 'redress the balance' between Europe and America.

During 1966, France started selling dollars and buying gold with them, nearly 700 million dollars' worth, from the United States. By the end of the year, the Finance Minister, Michel Debré, said that France's gold stocks were back to the 1938 level when they had formed one quarter of the world total. (In 1966, the French share was one-eighth.) In addition, measures were announced in Paris in November which were designed to develop Paris as a major international financial centre. Among other things, gold could be freely bought or sold, and imported and exported.

At the same time, French financial experts praised the virtues of gold as the only solid basis for the world monetary system, far more reliable than the dollar. In June 1967 France withdrew from the informal international group of central bankers known as the gold pool – though that fact was not publicised until the big 'gold rush' at the time of the devaluation of the pound in the following November.

De Gaulle cannot have aimed to force Britain to devalue the pound: France could not want this since it was bound to make British exports more competitive in European markets. His real target was the dollar; if France was able to go on buying gold for long enough, stimulating others by example to do the same, it was conceivable that the United States might at last be forced to devalue the dollar, in the sense of raising the price of gold from its long-standing level of 35 dollars an ounce. The dollar might then cease to be the main base of the world monetary system – and the value of France's gold reserves might be doubled. As de Gaulle himself put it on 27 November 1967: 'it is possible that the squalls at present raging, without France having any responsibility for them, which brought down the rate of the pound and threaten the dollar, may ultimately lead to the restoration of a monetary system based on the immutability, the impartiality, and the universality that are the characteristics of gold.'

Even if de Gaulle had no particular interest in the pound, except in so far as the weakness of the pound further weakened the dollar, the general atmosphere of uncertainty and speculation on the money markets during 1967 added to the other very much more real difficulties – such as the dock strike and the closing of the Suez Canal after the Arab–Israel war – which thwarted all the Labour Government's hopes of curing the balance-of-payments malady and making the pound and the economy healthy. The belated and enforced devaluation of the pound, in November 1967, weakened Britain's position in its approach to the Six and provided de Gaulle with a new argument for declaring that Britain was not ready for membership of the Common Market nor even for negotiations.

However, at no time can Wilson have thought of joining de Gaulle in his monetary policy of 'redressing the balance' with America, as Heath had given the appearance of recommending. Throughout the difficulties of 1967 he showed that he had an almost over-scrupulous respect for the stability of the international monetary system and the close international cooperation on which it was based. In any case, the British economy was too weak for any indulgence in Gaullist tactics.

If an alliance with de Gaulle over monetary policy was ruled out, Wilson may well have hoped that he could win de Gaulle's sympathy by his insistence on the need to defend Western Europe against an American industrial and technological take-over. The penetration of American industry into France, especially in advanced science-based sectors such as computers, was worrying some French politicians and journalists (notably Jean-Jacques Servan-Schreiber, who wrote a widely-read book, *Le Défi Americain*, on the subject). It could be expected to worry de Gaulle too.

Probably it did. However, he found a different solution to the problem from Wilson's European technological cooperation. In his press conference of 27 November 1967, he said it was true that there was 'an American hold over some of our enterprises'. This however was not due to the 'organic superiority' of the United States but to the dollar inflation which it exported to others. De Gaulle said that the total of the American balance-of-payments deficit of the last eight years was just the same as the total of American investment in Western Europe. 'It is well known that France would like to see an end of this abuse,' he went on; he then urged a return to gold as the basis of the international system. In other words, he thought the monetary weapon superior to Wilson's technological cooperation as a means of stopping American penetration.

From the Labour Government's Application to de Gaulle's Second Veto
The lack of any common ground with de Gaulle must have become more and more obvious to the Labour Government as it took one step after another towards the Common Market in a carefully-planned and energetic advance, pinning its faith on the power of the five friendly members to dissuade the ageing French President from exercising a second veto. On 5 December, Wilson explained his approach to EFTA heads of government at a special meeting in London. EFTA had been badly shaken by one of the very first acts of the Labour Government in October 1964 – the imposition of a 15 per cent import surcharge, applying to EFTA just as much as to the rest of the world, and reduced to 10 per cent, largely because of loud EFTA protests, in April 1965. However, the other EFTA countries had gradually recovered confidence in Britain and they were prepared to back the new move towards the EEC on the assumption that they would all be able to participate 'in an appropriate manner' in European economic integration. (The manner appropriate to the neutrals, Austria, Switzerland and Sweden, and to the economically backward Portugal, was bound to be different from the full membership sought by Britain, Norway and Denmark.)

Early in 1967, Wilson and George Brown visited Rome, Paris, Brussels, Bonn, The Hague and Luxemburg. In Paris de Gaulle was polite; Wilson delivered a seventy-five minute explanation of the international role of sterling, promising that Britain would not land the Six in embarrassing financial obligations. (Couve de Murville had just been saying that sterling was an extra-European institution and would create risks for the Six.) During this diplomatic campaign, Wilson addressed the Council of Europe Consultative Assembly in Strasbourg, on 23 January, stressing the need for Europe to be technologically and industrially independent, and speaking of British pre-eminence in such fields as jet aircraft, antibiotics, radar and basic nuclear research.

At the same time Wilson and George Brown dealt methodically with unrest inside the Parliamentary Labour Party over the Common Market. A warning shot was fired on 21 February by 107 Labour

M Ps who tabled a motion recalling the Party's earlier stiff conditions for entry and saying that Britain should only be ready to go in if essential British and Commonwealth interests were safeguarded. Three meetings of the Parliamentary Labour Party were held early in 1967 to discuss the Common Market. At one George Brown said he did not think it would be an easy thing for the President of France to deliver a veto, adding that French farmers had a great interest in seeing Britain in the EEC, since they stood to gain a good deal from it. Wilson told the last meeting that although Britain was a loyal ally of the United States and sought a most friendly relationship with the Soviet Union, it could not accept the idea that all great issues should be settled by these two powers 'because we in Europe are not sufficiently powerful, economically and therefore politically, to make ... our own influence felt'. This, he said, was the broad philosophy underlying the Government's approach. The hard-line anti-marketeers were unmoved but the Parliamentary Party as a whole was rallied.

On 2 May 1967 Wilson announced to the House of Commons the Government's decision to make a formal application to the EEC for full membership. He spoke of 'the long-term potential for Europe, and therefore for Britain, of the creation of a single market of approaching 300 million people, with all the scope and incentive which this will provide for British industry, and the enormous possibilities which an integrated strategy for technology, on a truly continental scale, can create ...'.

From 8 to 10 May, there was a full-scale debate. Wilson, dealing with the economic aspect, said that Britain must recognise that the EEC's common agricultural policy was an integral part of the Community and was not negotiable. This would mean that British food prices would rise by 10 per cent to 14 per cent, which would mean a rise in the cost of living of $2\frac{1}{2}$ per cent to $3\frac{1}{2}$ per cent. It would also result in a new burden on the British balance of payments. On the other hand, Britain could expect a higher rate of industrial growth as a result of joining, which would help it to increase exports.

On the political aspect, Wilson said, as Gaitskell had said five years earlier, that British public opinion was not ready to contemplate any rapid move into a federal Europe. But, he added, the federal momentum towards a supranational Europe, where issues of foreign policy and defence would be settled by majority voting, had died away, for the time at least. All the same, a strong, united and independent Europe would be able to exert more influence in world affairs 'than at any time in our generation' and would be better able to heal the East–West division in Europe. Callaghan, as Chancellor of the Exchequer, forecast that Britain should be able to join the Community with a strong balance of payments. The Government's decision was approved by 488 votes to 62 – an impressive display of the unity of the big majority of members of all three political parties.

By this time the arguments in favour of joining the EEC were becoming reasonably familiar and to many sounded reasonably convincing. The 1967 forecasts of the economic effect on British food prices and the balance of payments were much less alarming than those made three years later. For the moment the prospect of a French veto did not loom very large.

However, de Gaulle gave a press conference on 16 May 1967 full of warnings and gloomy predictions. He noted 'with sympathy' the movement which seemed to be leading Britain to link itself with Europe, instead of keeping itself apart: 'for our part there is no question of a veto, and there has never been one.' But he then talked about the danger of 'destructive upheavals' in the Common Market as a result of British entry, or of the 'complete overthrow of its equilibrium', which would take away from France one of its principal reasons for being part of it. De Gaulle also spoke gloomily about the pound: 'while one does not despair of the pound holding its own . . . it will be a long time before one is certain about this. . . . Parity and monetary solidarity are essential conditions of the Common Market and could not possibly be extended to our neighbours across the channel unless some day the pound sterling shows itself in a completely new position.' He seemed to mean that sterling must cease to be a world trading and reserve currency before Britain could join.

The alternatives to admitting Britain and thereby razing the edifice of the Common Market, as de Gaulle saw them, were either some sort of associate membership, or to wait until 'this great people, so magnificently gifted with courage and ability, should on their own behalf, and for themselves, achieve the profound economic and political transformation which would allow them to join the six continental countries.'

From this it was obvious that the old struggle between France and Britain was on. Wilson – both before and after the second French veto – ruled out associate membership on the ground that it would lay obligations on Britain without giving it any share in the decisions which would shape the future of the European Community. As for the profound transformation which de Gaulle required, Britain was trying painfully to achieve economic change but was unwilling to cut links with the Commonwealth and the United States which, de Gaulle said, would debar it from 'merging in a community of fixed dimensions and rigid rules'.

On 18 June Wilson visited Paris and saw de Gaulle. He told the House of Commons afterwards that he did not want to suggest that de Gaulle was more enthusiastic about British entry than before. However, he had told de Gaulle why the British did not believe that any of the problems were insoluble and 'why we do not intend to take "no" for an answer'. He had talked once again about technological cooperation in electronics, computers and peaceful nuclear energy. The meeting clearly left de Gaulle unmoved, except that he may have begun to think that given the Labour Government's doggedness and drive, it might be a mistake even to allow negotiations to begin.

The British tried hard to keep up the momentum. On 4 July George Brown made a speech at the WEU Council in which he sketched in broad outline the British negotiating position on agriculture, the common external tariff, New Zealand dairy produce, the Commonwealth Sugar Agreement and association for those African Commonwealth countries which wanted it. He looked forward to a Community expressing its own point of view in the political and defence fields, as well as the economic field: 'we shall join eagerly with other members in creating new opportunities for the expression of European unity.' A few weeks earlier the WEU Assembly had passed a resolution supporting the British application by 55 votes to none, with six French Gaullist deputies abstaining.

On 6 October, speaking at the Mansion House, Callaghan tackled the problem of sterling. He said that sterling, as a world currency, coupled with the experience of the City of London, would give Europe new opportunities for financial expansion; it could be an instrument at the service of Europe. Nobody had planned or created the sterling area; it had grown by an impersonal process. As for the sterling balances, various solutions were possible; one of them would be that the EEC should play an 'enlarged role'. (A year later, in September 1968, arrangements to deal with fluctuations in the sterling balances, and to enable Britain to guarantee their dollar value, were agreed by the 'Basle group', in which the Common Market countries, except for France and Luxemburg, took part.)

On their side, the Common Market ministers and the EEC Commission had started the slow process of considering the applications of Britain, Denmark, Norway and Ireland. In June the ministers had instructed the Commission to prepare a report. In July the French Foreign Minister presented his Common Market colleagues with a long list of objections to British entry, ranging from the danger that it would complicate the German problem and jeopardise relations with Eastern Europe to the menace of Britain's sterling balances and the impossibility of giving privileged treatment to Commonwealth sugar or New Zealand dairy produce.

In September the Brussels Commission unanimously recommended to the ministers that negotiations with Britain and the other applicants should start. 'Unquestionably,' it said, 'the Community must accept certain risks where an undertaking of this importance, the achievement of European unification, is to be attempted.' The report examined in detail the risks and problems involved, including the weakness of the British economy and the position of sterling. It would be hard, it said, to see how, after Britain's entry, sterling could continue to hold a position in the international monetary system different from that of the currencies of other member countries. A condition of entry would therefore be a restoration of lasting equilibrium to the British economy and its balance of payments, entailing 'concerted action' between Britain and the member countries, together with examination of ways of adjusting the existing international role of sterling so that it could be fitted into a Community monetary system. The Commission's suggestion of 'concerted action' was of course very different from de Gaulle's requirement that Britain should alone and unaided carry out a 'profound transformation'.

During October the Common Market Ministers met twice; the French Foreign Minister argued first that the Community should settle its own internal problems before admitting new members, next that negotiations with Britain should not start before Britain had a stable balance of payments and a solid pound. Italy and the three Benelux countries pressed for an early start to negotiations.

West Germany was more cautious. Since December 1966, when the Erhard Government had been replaced by the 'grand coalition' of Christian Democrats and Social Democrats, there had been an uneasy balance and underlying antagonism between the two parties on a number of issues. In particular, the Christian Democratic Chancellor, Dr Kiesinger, wanted to keep close to France, giving this priority over relations with Britain or British entry into the Common Market; the Social Democratic Foreign Minister, Willy Brandt, attached rather more importance to Britain and good relations with the Labour Government. Kiesinger visited London on 23 October for talks with Wilson; he was sympathetic over the British approach to the Common Market but said, with some reason, that it was futile to exert pressure on de Gaulle to do what he did not want to do. At a Foreign Press Association lunch, Kiesinger told journalists that it was not true that he himself was lukewarm about British entry; but since he wanted to avoid a French veto, he had agreed to discuss French anxieties before attempting to start negotiations.

At the time, there was a rather sour and critical attitude in Britain towards the Bonn Government because of its supposed half-heartedness. It was very doubtful whether a tougher West German attitude would have had any effect except to make de Gaulle deliver his second veto still earlier. Nevertheless, so far as British opinion was concerned, Bonn's apparent lack of enthusiasm for the British effort helped to revive old feelings of distaste for the Common Market.

During November 1967, people in Britain were preoccupied with the monetary crisis and the eventual devaluation of the pound. In this, some people had a vague and probably unfair feeling that France had played an unfriendly role, in spite of French participation in international support for the pound following devaluation. These confused suspicions of France added to the growing mood of sourness towards the Common Market.

People in Britain therefore felt no great shock or pain when on 27 November de Gaulle, at one of his press conferences, dealt the final blow to the Labour Government's approach. Devaluation had given him his immediate reason for rejecting Britain, as the Nassau agreement had done four years before. But it was obvious that much deeper reasons – and emotions – were at work. His attitude towards Britain was near-scornful. Britain, he said, had proposed opening negotiations 'with truly extraordinary haste, some of the reasons for which may have been made clear by recent monetary events'. (It was perhaps true that the opening of negotiations with the Six would have strengthened the position of the pound in the international money market; but it was also possible that French resistance to negotiations, combined with repeated French comments on the weakness of the British economy and the pound, encouraged the flight from sterling which led up to devaluation.)

There was, de Gaulle said, a tendency for Britain to look for a framework, 'even a European one', which would help it to save and safeguard its own substance, allow it to play a leading role again, and relieve it of part of its burden. However, he went on, Britain would have to undergo a radical transformation before it could join 'the continentals'. What France could not do was to enter into any negotiations with Britain and 'its associate countries' which would lead to the destruction of the European Community. France would consider association or any similar arrangement; but 'in order that the British Isles can really make fast to the continent, there is still a very vast and deep mutation to be effected'.

After de Gaulle's Veto: the WEU Row and the Soames Affair

The second veto was delivered. Wilson refused to accept it as the end. He told the House of Commons the next day that the British Government had no intention of withdrawing its application for Common Market membership. His most critical remark about de Gaulle was a reference to 'mis-statements of fact or wrong deductions, based on a rather out-of-date approach'. On the day after, he gave parliamentary correspondents a sixteen-point reply to points made by de Gaulle. One obvious distortion was that de Gaulle, in support of his own refusal to negotiate, had quoted the Brussels Commission's report of September 1967 as 'showing with the greatest clarity that the Common Market is incompatible with the economy, as it is today, of Britain.' The Commission had in fact recommended the opening of negotiations. The conclusion of Wilson's reply was that the British application remained in: 'the great debate will continue, not only in Britain, but throughout Europe.'

On 18 and 19 December, the ministers of the Six met; for France, Couve de Murville said formally that the British economy must be completely re-established (and sterling must cease to be a reserve currency) before negotiations could begin. The other five wanted negotiations to begin 'immediately'. On 20 December George Brown told the House of Commons that the Government would now enter into consultations with those five members of the European Community who supported the opening of negotiations. Soon after Christmas he set off on a round of visits.

Britain in a divided Europe

The five governments remained friendly to Britain and anxious to help, but accepted the fact that so long as de Gaulle was at the head of affairs in France, it was impossible to change the French attitude. So throughout 1968, various plans for interim arrangements between Britain and the Community were put forward by one or other of the five governments – or France. The British Government was uninterested in such plans, preferring to keep up the demand for full membership or nothing. But, not wishing to rebuff the five, Britain told the WEU Council that it would consider any proposal, provided that it was put forward by the Six as a whole, and provided it was clearly and inextricably linked to eventual full membership.

This insistence on a firm link with full membership was exactly what France would not accept. The furthest France would go was some form of commercial arrangement or tariff-cutting agreement with Britain and the three other applicants, on the condition that it was completely divorced from the question of membership of the Community. In consequence of this clash, there was never agreement among the Six on any specific plan, so Britain was never faced with a joint proposal. The West German attitude remained rather confusing, with the Social Democratic ministers showing a good deal more interest in Britain than their senior partners, the Christian Democrats. When de Gaulle visited Bonn in September 1968, Kiesinger said there could be no idea of West Germany's by-passing France to strengthen ties with other European countries; 'one cannot build Europe without France.'

One consequence of the second French veto was to give new importance to WEU as a place for discussion about relations between Britain and the Six. The Common Market question could always be raised in general terms under the heading of 'economic affairs', a regular item on the agenda at Ministers' meetings, and a subject on which the Brussels Commission was entitled to express a view. This did not suit France. At a WEU Council meeting in Rome on 21 October 1968, the Belgian Foreign Minister, M. Harmel, put forward a plan for cooperation between the Six and Britain within WEU, in foreign and defence policy, technology and monetary affairs. The five and Britain supported the idea; the French stalled. There was a private and informal meeting between the five and Stewart, the British Foreign Secretary (George Brown had resigned early in the year); a senior French official described this as 'diplomatic terrorism'. At a WEU Council meeting in Luxemburg in early

February 1969, Britain and the five agreed to an Italian proposal that before taking decisions on certain foreign policy questions, the governments would consult together through WEU; the French delegate reserved his position.

This was a situation which obviously could not last. Because a meeting of WEU permanent representatives (senior officials or diplomats) had been arranged to discuss Middle East affairs, on British initiative but without the approval of France, de Gaulle summoned his Ministers on 17 February 1969, and the withdrawal of France from WEU activities was announced. Three days earlier a very bitter 'press commentary' had been issued by the French Foreign Ministry saying that the WEU meeting had been 'one more step in the escalation, in which the British and their supporters have been indulging, to get round the French refusal to discuss among the seven [members of WEU] British membership of the Common Market'. Since 1968, it went on, the majority of the partners of France, aggrieved by continued French opposition to Britain's membership, and encouraged by Britain, had lent themselves to various manoeuvres aimed at forcing the hand of the French Government. If in future the unanimity principle were not respected in WEU, France would withdraw from it.

In the House of Commons Stewart said Britain had no desire to isolate the French but could not take the view that no progress could be made without the agreement of France. After some hesitation on the part of the Bonn Government, the WEU permanent council continued to hold meetings, without France; while France boycotted meetings, it did not withdraw from WEU altogether.

However, almost at the same time as the clash over WEU, a new incident made Anglo-French relations still worse. On 4 February, de Gaulle invited the British Ambassador, Christopher Soames, formerly a well-known Conservative politician, a noted 'European' and a son-in-law of Winston Churchill, to a private lunch, and expounded to him his ideas about the future of Europe. He also suggested that there should be talks between the two governments over economic, monetary, political and defence questions, aimed at solving their differences; the initiative should appear to come from Britain and he would then welcome it. An account of this talk was sent by the Ambassador to the Foreign Office; he also checked this account with the French Foreign Minister, Michel Debré, who had not been present; according to Soames, Debré, after showing the account to de Gaulle, raised no objection to it. (This was later contested by the French.)

De Gaulle, according to Soames, had said that Europe must be totally independent; once this had been achieved, NATO would not be needed. He would not object if the Common Market turned into a wider free trade area with special arrangements for agricultural products. There should be a small inner council of a European political association which would be formed by France, Germany, Italy and Britain.

For the British, it was difficult to interpret the purpose of this move. It was possible that the ageing French President sincerely wanted to prevent a complete estrangement, and was perhaps beginning to want an understanding with Britain, partly as a counterweight to the dominant economic position of West Germany. On the other hand, it might simply be a device by de Gaulle to split the front of Britain and the five and to enable France to break out of the isolation in which it found itself in Western Europe.

Ten days after the de Gaulle–Soames meeting, a British reply was delivered in Paris accepting the idea of Anglo-French talks, on the understanding that Britain did not share the French view of NATO and still wanted full Common Market membership, and on condition that the other members of WEU were kept informed. This could not please de Gaulle; but what angered him much more was that Wilson, who was in Bonn on 12 February, had told Kiesinger of the French approach, in the course of an unusually friendly meeting. Other WEU governments had also been informed – in some cases before the French Government had been told of Britain's intentions. The reason given for this, on the British side, was fear that de Gaulle might be trying to drive a wedge between Britain and the five. Still worse, after reports of the Soames–de Gaulle meeting had appeared in two Paris newspapers on 21 February, the story – including de Gaulle's ideas about Europe – was carried in London newspapers the next day, clearly on the basis of information supplied by the Foreign Office.

The Labour Government was criticised both in the British press and in the House of Commons for handling the affair clumsily and offending de Gaulle unnecessarily. There was an emergency debate on 25 February; the Conservatives attacked the Government for a breach of confidence contrary to normal diplomatic practice. Sir Alec Douglas-Home said that it had been too afraid of falling into a trap and had therefore reacted too hastily; this had led to real trouble. On the same day an official French protest was made against the British Government's behaviour. The Foreign Office went on saying that Britain was ready for talks with France; but there was very little hope that de Gaulle would agree.

De Gaulle's Withdrawal from Power; its Implications for Britain

By the spring of 1969, talks between de Gaulle and Britain could have had very little chance of success. He seemed to have become quite impervious to argument and the idea of compromise or concession was quite alien to him. He also seemed to be politically unsinkable. He had survived the storms of May and June 1968 – the violent and prolonged clashes with the students in Paris and elsewhere, and the countrywide strikes – apparently unscathed, perhaps even with increased prestige as the one man capable of saving France from chaos. When in November 1968, everyone from the West German Finance Minister, Strauss, to the Paris newspapers firmly believed that the French franc was about to be devalued, de Gaulle proved them all wrong by simply declaring that there would be no change, thereby delaying devaluation for nine months.

De Gaulle performed this act of monetary magic, defying the apparently inevitable, eight months after the failure of his campaign against the dollar. This had estranged him still further from his Common Market partners, as well as from Britain and America. None of the other Common Market countries belonging to the gold pool (West Germany, Italy, Holland and Belgium) had followed the French example in quitting it in 1967. When the international monetary crisis had reached its climax in mid-March 1968, it was not only Britain which worked very closely with the United States to prevent chaos; these four Common Market countries did too, along with Switzerland, which also belonged to the gold pool. After the British Government had shut the London gold market – still the main world market – at American request, the central bank governors of the gold pool countries met in Washington and agreed on the two-tier gold system, maintaining 35 dollars an ounce as the official gold price but freeing the central banks from the obligation to supply gold to the markets and allowing the unofficial gold price to fluctuate according to supply and demand. Three days later, de Gaulle once again publicly urged the need for a monetary system based on gold and an end to the system 'based on the privilege of the reserve currencies'. But after some months of uncertainty and doubt the two-tier system proved its strength, the gold rush gradually died away and the unofficial price of gold fell to somewhere near the official price. De Gaulle had lost a favourite weapon against American 'hegemony'.

This setback, the loss of French economic strength and the growing isolation of France in Western Europe, all had little visible effect on de Gaulle. Then unexpectedly, in the spring of 1969, he seemed deliberately to court defeat in a referendum on constitutional reform which he insisted on holding, and on making a vote of confidence in himself. When he lost, he resigned, on 28 April 1969.

At this moment, the question before Britain and other West European countries was whether the obstacles blocking progress towards unity would now be removed; or whether de Gaulle, with all his idiosyncracies, had expressed a fundamental French view of Europe and the world, so that everything would go on very much as before. For Britain, this was a particularly important question. Relations between Britain and France, already under some strain before de Gaulle came back to power in 1958, had become worse and worse during the ten years of his control of French affairs. The mutual distrust shown in the French boycott of W E U and the Soames affair had reached almost absurd lengths.

The British, for their part, showed considerable restraint and patience over two arbitrary French vetoes. But these vetoes left them in a painful dilemma. If, in pursuit of their long-term policy of working for West European economic and political unity, they kept as close as possible to the other five Common Market countries, they were suspected by de Gaulle of intrigue and manoeuvre and an attempt to isolate France. But if the British kept aloof from the five and sought agreement with de Gaulle, they could only hope for success if they were willing to take up an anti-American stand on defence and monetary matters which they knew to be unacceptable to the five – and to conflict with what they believed to be vital British interests. So if Britain could be accused of a series of psychological and diplomatic blunders in its dealings with France between 1956 and 1969, it was very doubtful whether these had more than superficial influence on Anglo-French relations. Nor, on the other side, were de Gaulle's deliberate attempts to wound British feelings likely to leave deep scars.

The real trouble seemed to lie deeper. What had to be discovered after de Gaulle's departure was whether or not there was a genuine and lasting conflict of interest between Britain and France which could not be resolved within the framework of the Common Market and the Western alliance. Politically, the two countries did not seem far apart. Both Britain and France, in the 1960s, wanted Western Europe to have greater independence and a stronger voice in world affairs; in the British view, it was to be independence alongside America; in de Gaulle's view, it was to be independence against America; but this anti-American bias did not seem rooted in French national policy or French history. In defence, Britain believed in military integration and close nuclear cooperation within the NATO framework as an effective and (in comparison with any possible alternative) relatively cheap method of insurance against war; at the same time Britain was interested in developing closer European cooperation and a European viewpoint, within NATO, especially in the field of research, development and the manufacture of weapons. Britain was also ready to prepare for a partial and gradual American withdrawal from Europe. France, under de Gaulle, had quit NATO, while remaining a member of the Atlantic alliance and in fact retaining the protection of the American nuclear umbrella. It had to be discovered whether this rejection of NATO was simply a matter of Gaullist doctrine or whether it had come to be accepted by the French as a whole as a real French national interest, even though it split France from its Common Market partners.

As for the struggle between France and Britain for the leadership of Western Europe, this seemed to have less and less meaning, as West Germany emerged towards the end of the 1960s as the strongest economic power in Western Europe, and also as a power with an active European policy of its own. The Anglo-French rivalry had in any case been mainly a sort of instinctive reflex of two countries which, when divesting themselves of vast empires, were looking for outlets and satisfactions nearer home. It had also been rather an undignified struggle, with de Gaulle trying to shut Britain out of Western Europe in order to secure French leadership, and Britain refusing to be shut out rather than seeking a dominant position. What remained to be seen was whether both sides were ready to recognise its futility and end it.

Britain, France and the Community Agricultural System
The immediate conflict of interest between France and Britain and the main real obstacle to British entry into the Common Market was

237

the agricultural system which, as a result of hard French bargaining during the negotiations for the Rome Treaty and later negotiations inside the EEC, had been shaped to meet the needs and protect the interests of French farmers. It ensured the exclusion of low-priced food from outside the Community; access for French agricultural produce to the wide Community market at stable prices satisfactory to French farmers; and shared Community financial responsibility both for the disposal (without loss to French farmers) of agricultural surpluses and for helping the modernisation of French agriculture. This system would of course also benefit farmers in other countries of the Six in varying degrees; but France, with its relatively big agricultural population and its vocal and politically important farmers, stood to benefit most and to lose least.

For Britain to fit into this system, without taking on a quite unfair burden, was obviously going to be difficult. As Wilson pointed out in the House of Commons in May 1967, Britain had a much smaller agricultural population ($3\frac{1}{2}$ per cent of the total, as compared with 16 per cent of the total population of the Six). Nor did Britain suffer from the splitting up of land holdings into small uneconomic parcels; about 40 per cent of Common Market farm holdings, Wilson said, were under fifteen acres. British agriculture was therefore relatively more efficient, and less in need of outside aid in modernisation. The other side of the picture was that Britain was traditionally a big food importer; in 1958 imports of food, drink and tobacco were 39 per cent of total imports, though the proportion had dropped to 25 per cent ten years later.

Under the EEC's common agricultural policy, therefore, Britain, which had traditionally imported its food at low prices, would have to pay more for its food imports. It would either buy at the Community price inside the Community (which would suit French farmers); or it would continue to buy from its traditional Commonwealth suppliers and pay the Community levy on agricultural imports from outside. These levies would go into the Community Fund and help to support the Community high food prices and finance the export of surpluses and the modernisation of agriculture, especially French and West German agriculture. In paying these levies, Britain would have to accept a new burden on its balance of payments; higher food prices would lead to higher wages and so to higher costs of production in industry and so again to less competitive industrial exports.

This whole prospect should in theory have been pleasing to France; As George Brown told Labour MPs in 1967, French farmers stood to do well out of it. But British willingness to face such a bleak prospect aroused French suspicions that in practice things would work out differently – that the other Common Market countries would want to find ways to ease Britain's difficulties, thereby undermining the whole tight complex structure designed to protect the interests of French farmers. Moreover Britain, once inside the Community, could be expected to press for lower food prices, since it would then pay lower levies on food imports from outside, and perhaps also for a general review of the uneconomic aspects of the EEC agricultural system. In France, it was privately admitted that some reform of the system would be needed during the 1970s, so as to check the overproduction caused by high farm prices and the consequent piling-up of agricultural surpluses; but it was feared that British influence inside the Community could make the reform needlessly painful to France.

Since any British government was bound to hope for some help over the problem of agriculture, whether transitional or long-term, there was a genuine clash of interest between Britain and France on this point. Without some practical good will on the part of the Six, no British government could hope to win the necessary political support at home for joining the Community. But for a French government to agree to concessions to Britain over agriculture would be politically damaging and unpopular in France.

After de Gaulle: Pompidou's Approach to West European Unity
The presidential election of June 1969 showed that although a majority of the French had rejected de Gaulle, they had not rejected the Gaullists – partly, probably, because the opposition parties were so disunited that they could not offer a convincing alternative to Gaullist Government. Moreover the Gaullist candidate, Pompidou, was regarded as a practical, level-headed man and a contrast to de Gaulle, whose favour he had lost. His main opponent, Alain Poher, a politician of the centre who was not widely known, called for a 'renovated' Atlantic alliance and for a summit conference of the Six to hasten and extend the building of a united Europe, including the opening of negotiations with Britain. On the first ballot, Poher got half as many votes as Pompidou; on the second ballot he automatically did better, getting nearly 42 per cent compared with Pompidou's

58 per cent. This did not suggest that there was any strong enthusiasm among French voters for British entry into the Common Market.

Pompidou, for his part, undertook to maintain both the independence of France and its alliances, and to work for the building of a Europe which would be 'mistress of its destiny'. This gave no clear notice of his intentions. However, in the formation of the Government, Pompidou chose as Foreign Minister Maurice Schumann, who had spent the war years in London as de Gaulle's spokesman in broadcasts to occupied France, but who was also known as a good 'European'. Valéry Giscard d'Estaing, not a member of the Gaullist Party though close to it, also reputed to be a 'European', became Finance Minister. On the other hand, Debré, an ardent Gaullist and close follower of de Gaulle's doctrines, became Defence Minister and soon showed that he was determined to press ahead with the French national nuclear deterrent and to keep France apart from NATO. President Pompidou personally backed this attitude (notably at his press conference of July 1970).

In his opening period in office, Pompidou, though introducing a new 'style' of government, clearly did not want to depart too far or fast from accepted Gaullist policies – whether through personal conviction or deference to de Gaulle's fervent personal following within the party, was not clear. But the quiet efficiency with which he conducted the devaluation of the franc in July 1969 (which aroused rather envious admiration in Britain) suggested that his approach to the Common Market problem would be based on economic interest rather than national prestige. Maurice Schumann, in the early months, conveyed an impression of sincere friendliness and good will towards the Common Market countries, also even towards Britain. In the autumn of 1969, an important new element in the West European situation was the change of government in Bonn: after the West German election, Willy Brandt became the first post-war Social Democratic Chancellor. He was expected to press more strongly than his Christian Democratic predecessor, Kiesinger, for negotiations with Britain. Pompidou was against any appearance of haste; but he agreed to a summit meeting of the Six at the Hague on 1 December 1969, at which British membership was to be discussed.

This meeting was personally dominated by Brandt rather than Pompidou, who had to tread delicately and gave the appearance of being more negative-minded towards Britain than he perhaps intended. He did not accept the wish of his partners to name a date for the opening of negotiations; but all the Six agreed that negotiations should be opened with Britain and the three other applicants, that the Community would do the essential preparatory work as quickly as possible and that they hoped to complete it by mid-1970.

However, France made an important condition. The Community members must first reach agreement among themselves on the further development of the agricultural system and Community finance, and undertake to work more quickly for economic and monetary unification. (The devaluation of the French franc and the upward revaluation of the West German mark had, in the past few months, badly shaken the existing agricultural system by upsetting the basis on which Community farm prices were calculated; and this had strengthened the argument that the agricultural system could not be completed satisfactorily unless there was progress towards some kind of monetary union, or even a common currency.) The French made it clear that negotiations with Britain could not start until the Six had settled these issues.

This gave France a powerful lever in the discussions among the Six which started later in December. Agreement was reached on agriculture and finance. There were to be transitional arrangements for the period 1970 to 1974; from 1975 onwards, all levies on agricultural imports from outside the Community were to be paid over directly to the Community Fund, together with all customs duties and a certain proportion of a value added tax. The Fund would be used to finance the agricultural system and also for certain other purposes. Three years later – in 1978 – the last vestiges of national payments to the Community Fund would vanish and the system would become entirely automatic. Member governments would no longer have any direct control. The existing system, by which the six governments made contributions on the basis of agreed fixed percentages, would cease completely. This would make it much more difficult for Britain to request, or be granted, special concessions over its contribution to the agricultural system.

With this agreement in hand, France could face the 1970s – and negotiations with Britain – in a powerful bargaining position. It was not surprising that the French Assembly approved the agreement at the end of June 1970, in advance of other Common Market parliaments, by an overwhelming majority of 420 to 34. Maurice Schumann said that the Government had kept its word in making the 'completion' of the Common Market, through this agreement, a prior condition of its enlargement: it had made the arrangements for financing the common agricultural policy 'final and irreversible', by giving the Community its own resources in place of contributions from member states. Any other course, Schumann said, would have damaged French farmers and destroyed 'the balance of the Common Market'.[19] A few days later, Schumann told the Senate that the negotiations with Britain would succeed to the extent that there was 'no further challenge' to the common agricultural policy 'based on Community preference and financial solidarity'.[20]

Wilson out: Heath in

Faced with the agreement of the Six on agriculture and Community finance, and pressed to produce some estimate of the cost of entering the Common Market, the Labour Government published a White Paper in February 1970 which caused some alarm and gloom in Britain, and led to accusations, both at home and abroad, that the Labour leaders had cooled off and were no longer eager for Common Market membership. Others (especially in France) suspected them of trying to put Britain in a good bargaining position.

The White Paper was in fact hedged around with reservations about the impossibility of making accurate predictions because of the complexity and uncertainty of the factors involved. Nevertheless, it gave a darker picture than the Government had given in 1967. In 1967 it had forecast a 10 to 14 per cent rise in food prices bringing about a $2\frac{1}{2}$ to $3\frac{1}{2}$ per cent rise in the cost of living; in 1970 it said that full application of the common agricultural policy might mean an 18 to 26 per cent rise in food prices, bringing a 4 to 5 per cent rise in the cost of living. In 1967 it had estimated the burden on the balance of payments at £175 million to £250 million. In 1970, in the light of the new Community agreement on agriculture and finance, it said that a 'theoretical upper limit' of what Britain might have to pay to the Community in agricultural levies, customs duties and value added tax was £670 million; taking this into account, the White Paper said that the overall burden on the balance of payments, resulting from entry into the Common Market, could be anything between £100 million and £1100 million.

At the same time, the White Paper argued once again the long-term benefits to British industry and to the British economy, and also the political benefits, of joining the Community. However, these positive arguments, being familiar, were hardly noticed. The probable steep rise in food prices and the cost of living hit ordinary people in Britain, especially housewives, much more forcefully; the top figure for the burden on the balance of payments gave new ammunition to the anti-marketeers of the two main political parties. Opinion polls began to show a strong swing against the Common Market, with as many as two-thirds opposing entry during April, even though a similar proportion thought that Britain would in fact join. However, British industrialists, apart from the shipbuilders, continued to support entry. On 19 May the Director General of the Confederation of British Industry, Campbell Adamson, said that Britain could afford an additional burden of £500 million (the usually accepted mid-way figure) on the balance of payments if there were a modest additional increase in the rate of economic growth: if the economy grew an extra one-half per cent faster, Britain could profit from the deal. However, the CBI criticised the 'restrictive' aspects of the Community's agricultural policy.

Abstract calculations about future riches had much less effect on the ordinary man and woman than an instinctive wish to safeguard a fairly satisfying and pleasant way of living which for most had become much easier and more comfortable over the past twenty years. However, the Labour Government continued to prepare for negotiations. George Thomson, the minister in charge of European affairs, visited Common Market countries in the spring. In mid-April he had a talk in Paris with Maurice Schumann in what was described as an exceptionally friendly atmosphere. The one concrete result was French agreement to end de Gaulle's boycott of WEU. This was formally announced in Brussels on 22 April. It seemed a good omen for Britain's coming negotiations with the Six.

When Wilson rather unexpectedly called for a general election on 18 June, both the main political parties realised that there was public apathy or opposition to the Common Market, and both said little about it during the election campaign. The Conservative manifesto was as cautious and reserved as the Labour Government's White Paper had been: 'if we can negotiate the right terms, we believe that it would be in the long-term interest of the British people for Britain to join. . . . The opportunities are immense. . . . But we must also recognise the obstacles. . . . Obviously there is a price we would not be prepared to pay. . . . Our sole commitment is to negotiate; no more, no less.' Some observers thought that one of the reasons for the Labour Party's defeat was housewives' fear of higher food prices, a prospect for which Labour was held responsible.

Heath's arrival in power as Conservative Prime Minister was welcomed in Paris and other Common Market capitals where he was remembered as a good 'European' who had worked hard and honestly in the 1961–3 negotiations and who tried valiantly to understand continental points of view. Heath moved cautiously. Reviewing foreign policy in the House of Commons on 3 July, he said – as any Prime Minister might have said over the past twenty-five years – that in Europe, it was a British interest 'that we should come together increasingly with our friends'. One of his first moves was to send his Foreign Secretary, Sir Alec Douglas-Home, to Paris for talks with Maurice Schumann; Heath had long believed that the way into the Common Market was through an understanding with France. The talks were friendly.

There was some speculation, after the Labour Party's electoral defeat, that Labour might swing over to opposition to the Common Market, or might at least hamper rather than help the new Conservative Government's efforts to negotiate. Certainly the veteran anti-marketeers, notably Lord Shinwell and Douglas Jay, became more vocal; Jay launched a campaign for a referendum on Common Market membership. However, when Roy Jenkins, one of the staunchest 'marketeers', was elected deputy leader of the Parliamentary Labour Party, it looked as though the party as a whole would maintain a steady course, and that the official policy of all three political parties would continue to be support for joining the Common Market. In both the Conservative and Labour parties there were active anti-market minorities (the former French Prime Minister, Couve de Murville, reckoned that the Conservative anti-marketeers equalled Heath's majority in Parliament); but they did not seem likely to play an important role.

Into the 1970 Negotiations

During the spring, the Community had been making its own preparations for the negotiations with Britain, Norway, Denmark and Ireland. In March the Commission submitted a paper on Britain to the ministers. It was reported to favour a very short transition period to ease British entry, with a fixed timetable for the alignment of British farm prices with Community prices. But the Commission had obviously been studying the British White Paper of February, and had noted two suggestions, or warnings, in it. One was that if Britain adopted the relatively high Community farm prices, British farmers might be stimulated to increase production rapidly. (In 1967 Wilson had said that British wheat production could easily be raised from 13 million tons to 20 million tons in a few years.) This would of course have the effect of increasing the Community's already fast-growing agricultural surpluses still further, laying an additional burden on the Community Fund which had to finance storage and subsidise export. The other warning in the White Paper was that if entry imposed too heavy a burden on the British balance of payments, the old problem would arise, that Britain would have to hold back economic growth in order to try to restore the balance of payments; and without economic growth, the cost of membership would be too great to be borne.

The Commission appeared to have decided that the best solution all round would be a sort of gigantic package deal. The Commission itself had been pressing for advance towards economic and monetary union, to which the governments of the Six had finally agreed in broad principle at the Hague summit in December 1969. The 'Barre plan' was ready at hand for the purpose. The Commission had also been pressing for action on the modernisation of agriculture on the basis of the 'Mansholt plan', since it realised that the existing system was subsidising inefficient farming at what would soon become a prohibitive cost to the Community, and was eating up the money which ought to be used for modernisation.

The Commission therefore thought that if a programme for advance to economic and monetary union, aiming at a single currency or system of closely interlocked national currencies within nine years, could be dove-tailed into a programme for bringing Britain fully into the Community, then several problems could be solved at one go. In particular, it was argued, a monetary union could overcome the problem of the burden on Britain's balance of payments; it would then be justifiable to apply to Britain the new agreement on finance and agriculture in full force, without special concessions – and without endangering Britain's economic growth; and a full British contribution to the Community Fund would help towards the realisation of the Mansholt plan for modernising agriculture.[21]

For the British, whatever the merits of the Commission's plan, it was bound to have the disadvantage of immensely complicating and lengthening the negotiations. The main British aim therefore was to persuade the Six to agree to some top limit to the contribution which Britain could be expected to make to the Community Fund through levies, customs duties and value added tax.

Among the Six, some were eager for full economic and monetary union, particularly because management of a single currency would inevitably mean a great strengthening of the supranational, federal-tending element in the Community. The Dutch Finance Minister, Dr Witteveen, talked on 26 May about the need for one European central bank and one supranational Department of Finance. Raymond Barre, the author of the 'Barre Plan' and Vice-President of the Commission, said that without union, an enlarged community would risk 'falling into the sterling area' and so indirectly into the dollar area.[22]

To many people in France, however, such ideas seemed quite unreal. President Pompidou, speaking in Strasbourg towards the end of June, saw Europe as a grouping together of sovereign States 'which agree freely to lower the barriers which separate them, progressively to harmonise their agricultural, monetary, industrial and social policies, so as to advance with realism, with precaution and step by step, towards a union which, when it has entered sufficiently into deeds and minds, but only then, will be able to have its own policy, its own independence . . .'.[23] (Bevin might have used almost the same words over twenty years earlier.) A few days later, at a press conference, Pompidou's comment on the idea of a European monetary union was that it took forty years to advance from the formation of the German Customs Union (the nineteenth-century Zollverein) to the appearance of the German mark, and another sixty years before the German Bank of Issue had the monopoly of issuing marks: 'you can see that we have quite a few decades ahead of us.'

It therefore seemed clear that the French did not want to face any real loss of national sovereignty in the economic or financial fields, even though they wanted to tie the Common Market currencies together so as to prevent disruption of the common agricultural policy through fluctuations in exchange rates. The other Common Market countries, especially West Germany, thought that little progress could be made in the monetary field without real advance towards economic union – that is, the merging of national economic policies in a common economic policy. But they had to take French resistance into account. So the 'Werner Report' was devised as a compromise, or watered-down version of the 'Barre Plan'. Even this went too far and too fast for the French, who found themselves at odds with the West Germans, while the British stood uncomfortably on the side-lines trying to avoid offending anybody and to suggest that in spite of appearances, the pound, as a weakened but still widely-used reserve currency, might yet prove an asset to the Common Market. This idea had little appeal for the French, who seemed to want to hold themselves free to make difficulties – as de Gaulle had done in 1967 – over the weaknesses of the British economy, the dangers of sterling's role as a reserve currency and the supposed threat to Common Market stability from the sterling balances. All in all, monetary union seemed most unlikely to provide the key by which Britain could enter the Common Market.

It was on 30 June 1970 that negotiations between Britain and the Six formally opened, in Luxemburg. The Belgian Foreign Minister, Harmel, speaking for the Community Council of Ministers, made only a passing reference to the monetary aspect. His main stress, in describing the Community's position, was on the need for Britain to accept the Rome Treaty 'and all the decisions of every type which have been taken since the treaties came into force'. Therefore problems of adjustment must be sought through transitional measures, not by changing the rules. As a general rule, there must be detailed timetables. The transitional measures must be conceived in such a way as 'to ensure an overall balance of reciprocal advantage'. All this sounded as though a French hand had written important parts of the statement and that, as in the past, French insistence on 'sticking to the rules' had provided a strong argument for bringing the five around to the viewpoint of France.

For Britain, Anthony Barber made a statement which some of the Six seemed to find tougher than expected. This was because he went to the heart of the matter: the impact of the new agreement of the Six on Community finance. He pointed out that the Labour Government had hoped to take part in negotiating it, in which case, no doubt, fair provision would have been made for Britain as for the other members. But Britain had not been there. In 1967 the Brussels Commission had said that the existing financial arrangements, if applied to Britain, would 'give rise to a problem of financial burdens'. The new decisions, Barber said, had made that problem of balance even more severe. Unless a joint solution could be found, the burden on Britain could not be sustained and 'no British Government could contemplate joining'.

So the new British effort to join the European Community started with a British appeal for fair play and insistence by the Six, notably France, on sticking strictly to the rules. By 1970 France did not seem to have any doctrinal objection to British entry or any political antagonism – still less after de Gaulle's death in November. In fact there seemed to be some French good will – but little readiness to accept anything which could upset the carefully built-in 'balance of advantage' in the Common Market. The final outcome seemed to depend on the willingness or unwillingness of all the political leaders concerned to take risks, including unpopularity at home, and to look more than two or three years ahead. If all were willing, then a solution to the very genuine problems could be found. If not, Britain could not simply turn its back on Western Europe: that would be economically, strategically and politically impossible. But the British would have the difficult job of trying to work out some different pattern of relations with the West European countries, less rigid, but also less 'dynamic' and in the long run less profitable. American economic penetration of Western Europe would automatically continue at a quicker and quicker pace, as industrial investment snowballed. In August 1970 the EEC Commission reported that 80 per cent of the big American corporations had branch establishments or subsidiaries in Western Europe – and, as the Commission pointed out, the policy of these enterprises was, in the final analysis, decided outside Europe.

21 Britain and the East–West split in Europe: The 1960s

The Dialogue of the Superpowers

Probably the most important development of the 1960s, for the world as a whole and more particularly for Europe, was the opening of the dialogue between the two superpowers, America and the Soviet Union. This became more and more exclusive. The West European countries found themselves more and more shut out, though the British could hope for a little more information than others from the Americans, at least in nuclear matters. When the Labour Government, making its fresh approach to the Common Market, talked repeatedly about the need to make a European voice heard in world affairs, this was much more than a political catch-phrase. It reflected a hard reality. By the end of the 1960s, no European country could feel that it had any real share in making the decisions which would shape world events in the 1970s.

The dialogue between Washington and Moscow developed in fits and starts, following a zig-zag course. In January 1960 Khrushchev announced cuts in Soviet conventional armed forces; there were no doubt sound economic reasons, but the announcement was also meant as a signal of peaceful intentions. In May 1960 the summit conference – which could perhaps have agreed on first steps towards a removal of European tensions – was wrecked by the U2 incident, which enabled hard-liners in Moscow to force a reluctant Khrushchev to try to impose unacceptable demands on Eisenhower. But there was no immediate Soviet attempt to hot up the Berlin crisis. The split between the Soviet Union and Communist China was already wide enough, in 1960, to exercise a restraining influence on Moscow in its dealings with the United States.

However, at the beginning of 1961 a new President took offce in the United States; Kennedy met Khrushchev in Vienna in June and emerged shaken after being mauled by the latter who could not resist the temptation to try to bully and frighten a young and inexperienced man. He led Kennedy to believe that there was a real possibility of war over Berlin. But Khrushchev miscalculated; Kennedy showed publicly that he was quite determined to stand firm over Berlin. Khrushchev was quick to accept the consequences: in August, Ulbricht was permitted to build the Berlin wall, cutting off the Eastern part of the city from the West, thereby stopping the flood of refugees from the East and restoring stability and economic viability to the East German State. Although this action produced a storm of protest in the West, including the United States, it was in fact a signal from Moscow that it did not intend to use force to reverse the *status quo*, as established at the end of the 1939–45 war.

In the following year, Khrushchev was tempted to try out Kennedy's nerve and resolution once again. Castro was afraid of an American invasion of Cuba; the Americans did not know how best to tackle Castro; so Khrushchev started installing Soviet missiles in Cuba which were capable of striking at the United States. The Kennedy administration's handling of the Cuba crisis in October 1962 was a model of firmness, patience and skill in rapid but wise decision-making. Once again Khrushchev saw that he had miscalculated and climbed down, saving face with the utmost cheerfulness. In the summer of the following year the 'hot line' between Washington and Moscow was established – a symbol of the determination of both sides to handle future crises without war, or at least without war-by-mistake. The 'hot line' – at least symbolically – excluded the European allies from the dialogue of the superpowers.

In August 1963, the partial nuclear test ban treaty was signed. The fact that the ceremony took place in Moscow was a fresh Soviet signal of peaceful intentions towards the West, in a situation where the Chinese-Soviet quarrel was in full spate. The apparently genuine regret in the Soviet Union over the assassination of Kennedy in November 1963 was a further sign of détente.

During all this time, presumably, intrigues were being spun inside Moscow against Khrushchev because of his unconventional and unorthodox policies, methods and style. In October 1964 he was removed from power (just at the moment when the Labour Government took office in Britain). He was replaced by men who turned out to be ultra-conventional and ultra-conservative, in Communist terms; Kosygin at first gave an impression of some intellectual flexibility, but Brezhnev emerged more and more as the holder of real power. He showed none.

In spite of this change in the Soviet leadership, the desire to keep up a dialogue with the United States continued, as did the Soviet-

Chinese quarrel. By the mid-1960s American involvement in the Vietnam war had become heavy and President Johnson was becoming violently unpopular with many people in Europe and the United States. However, the Soviet Government obviously had no intention of being drawn into the Vietnam war, beyond sending arms to Hanoi; in this, Moscow was determined not to be outbid by Peking.

The flare-up of the Arab–Israel crisis and the six-day war of June 1967 looked like producing a fresh and dangerous confrontation between the two superpowers. Moscow compelled all the Warsaw Pact countries, with the exception of Rumania, to break off relations with Israel, and launched bitter attacks on the United States. More Soviet warships entered the Mediterranean. But it soon became clear that the Soviet Union had no intention of going beyond political and propaganda support for the Arabs and the supply of arms to Egypt. Moreover, it wanted to maintain the dialogue with the United States. Kosygin went to New York, theoretically to support the Arab cause in the United Nations; what was more important was that he met Johnson at Glassboro, where presumably some sort of understanding was reached on the outside limits of the support which either superpower would give to its clients in the Middle East. The meeting also paved the way for the treaty to ban the spread of nuclear weapons which was signed in July 1968.

This in turn laid on the two superpowers the obligation – undertaken under considerable pressure from some of the non-nuclear powers – to seek agreement between themselves to halt their own private nuclear arms race. By this time, both probably wanted to do this. The economic waste of developing and manufacturing an interminable series of new weapons of attack and defence was too astronomical to be willingly accepted by either. When, within two months of the signing of the non-proliferation treaty, the Soviet Union and four of its Warsaw Pact partners invaded Czechoslovakia, the American Government's reaction was restrained, even though George Ball was allowed to conduct a verbal war with the Soviet delegate in the Security Council in New York. It seemed clear that the decision-makers in Washington felt that since Czechoslovakia lay within the Soviet sphere of control in Europe, its invasion could not become a cause of serious dispute between the two superpowers; nor should it put an end to prospects for talks between them on stopping the nuclear arms race.

However, when soon after there were rumours of a Soviet plan to invade Rumania, President Johnson, in a public speech, gave a discreet but clear warning to Moscow not to strike again. This was perhaps an illogical move since Rumania, however independent-minded, was still theoretically a member of the Warsaw Pact. But presumably Washington intended to convey to Moscow that if the Soviet Union, after invading Czechoslovakia, were to proceed to invade Rumania – or Yugoslavia – as well, it would become impossible to believe in the peaceful intentions of the Soviet leaders towards the West – or indeed in their rationality. However, the Soviet leaders were quite rational and did not attack either Rumania or Yugoslavia.

The storm over Czechoslovakia delayed the opening of the strategic arms limitation talks (SALT) between the two super-powers; but they began at last in Helsinki in November 1969. They proceeded at a leisurely pace, transferring to Vienna in the summer of 1970 and back to Helsinki in the autumn. The fact that these talks were going on did not of itself stop the nuclear race; in the summer of 1970 President Nixon urged the Congress to approve large-scale spending on defensive missiles so as to strengthen the American bargaining position in the SALT talks. Yet there seemed to be signs of a real desire on both sides for a nuclear understanding, or at the very least for a continuing dialogue.

One reason for Soviet interest in an understanding with the United States was of course the fact that China was itself a nuclear power in an early stage of development. Speculation about Chinese nuclear progress, appearing in the Soviet press in August 1970, was a sign of Soviet watchfulness. Yet another factor was probably China's re-emergence into world affairs after the years of isolation which resulted from Chairman Mao's cultural revolution. In the late summer of 1970, Peking re-appointed ambassadors to East European capitals, which some observers interpreted as the opening of a Chinese diplomatic offensive in Eastern Europe, where it was already on good terms with Rumania. This could obviously be worrying to Moscow, given the many discontents among its East European partners.

The Peking message was clear. As the Chinese Prime Minister, Chou En-lai, said on French television on 27 July 1970, it was that 'in the present world there are one or two superpowers which keep trying to oppress others by force, to maltreat the weak and the little, while disputing world hegemony between them'. Chou En-lai went on: 'the epoch when the great powers could decide the fate of the world is gone forever. We must break the myth of the great powers.'

During the 1960s, it was unlikely that either superpower ever thought in terms of a joint front with the other against the emerging third superpower, China. Moscow obviously at times suspected Washington of plotting an eventual deal with Peking. Nor could the Americans ever rule out the possibility of an eventual Moscow–Peking deal, perhaps after the departure of Chairman Mao. But towards the end of the 1960s the two superpowers clearly came to feel that they had a joint interest in preventing nuclear war, checking local conflicts before they could escalate and if possible checking expenditure on nuclear weapons. In an exchange of letters on the twenty-fifth anniversary of Potsdam, in August 1970, Nixon and Kosygin looked forward to future cooperation. Perhaps this was more than just an empty formality.

Britain on the Fringe of the Dialogue

In this dialogue of superpowers, there was little part for the West European (or East European) countries to play, except to applaud from the side-lines and to mutter occasionally among themselves. Britain had a rapidly shrinking claim to some sort of special status among the West Europeans. Exercising its continuing responsibility as one of the two co-chairmen of the 1954 conference on Indo-China, it reached agreement with the Soviet Union on calling the fourteen-nation Laos conference of 1961, which produced a settlement in 1962, based on an unstable balance between the three Laotian political groups. But when, soon after, fighting broke out again in Laos, Britain was unable to take a fresh initiative because by that time there was deadlock between the Soviet Union and the United States. The Soviet Union was pressing for a new international conference on Laos while the United States did not want one so long as fighting was going on. Britain went along with the United States. A Soviet note to Britain of July 1964 threatened that the Soviet Union would 'reconsider its position' as co-chairman of the Geneva conference unless Britain agreed to call an international conference in August. A visit to Moscow by the British Foreign Secretary (then R. A. Butler, later Lord Butler) failed to bring the Soviet Union and Britain together, though the Soviet Union did not carry out its threat about the co-chairmanship.

However, Britain's status as one of the two co-chairmen proved of very little use when the Vietnam war became a major conflict in the

I*

mid-1960s. Wilson would have won great popularity with a large section of the Labour Party and many West Europeans (to say nothing of most Commonwealth countries) if he had been ready to oppose American policy and actions in Vietnam. (De Gaulle was widely applauded for his direct challenge to the United States to name a date for unconditional withdrawal from Vietnam, made during his visit to Cambodia.) Wilson would not make any such gesture. He refused to send any form of material aid to the Americans in Vietnam, saying that Britain must keep itself aloof from the war so as to be able to exercise its role as co-chairman. But he also refused to dissociate himself from the United States. He was however driven by strong pressures either from some Commonwealth Prime Ministers or from inside the Labour Party to make repeated attempts at peace moves. All failed, and he was criticised for indulging in gimmicks. That did not prove that they were not sincerely meant.

The most dramatic was at the time of Kosygin's visit to London in February 1967. A good part of the Anglo-Soviet talks were taken up with Vietnam and Wilson told the House of Commons afterwards that he and the Foreign Secretary (George Brown) had striven unceasingly, 'almost without sleep', to get the United States and North Vietnam to the conference table. He said that he and Kosygin had created what he called 'an intricate mechanism leading to peace' during their talks. He did not describe it, but it was assumed that he had been in touch with President Johnson while Kosygin had been in touch with Hanoi in the hope of arranging reciprocal gestures, or actions, opening the way for peace talks.

The effort misfired, but according to Wilson, 'one gesture by North Vietnam . . . could have set in motion events which could have led to peace'. How far Kosygin had departed from the normal Soviet stand of leaving everything to the North Vietnamese was not altogether clear. But the joint communiqué on the Kosygin visit was friendlier than might have been expected, considering the usual Soviet line of all-out condemnation of American 'aggression'. It said that both governments 'deeply regretted the continuation of the Vietnam war'; they set forth their respective views on ways to bring about peace, would make every possible effort to achieve a settlement and would maintain contact to that end.

Nothing resulted. When Wilson visited Moscow and saw Brezhnev and Kosygin the following year, the Soviet line on Vietnam was obviously as harsh as it had ever been. The usual Soviet attitude towards Britain, over the Vietnam war, had been that the British were subservient to the Americans and therefore shared American guilt in some degree. On the other side the Americans, including Johnson, seemed to find British efforts at peace-making irritating and irrelevant, if not worse. Wilson's activities over Vietnam could therefore be criticised as futile and even harmful to Britain. But it could also be argued that peace in Vietnam was a British and West European interest, since the war distracted American energies from Europe, made the Americans unpopular in the other NATO countries, and weakened, both politically and economically, the powerful ally on which Western Europe depended for its security. Peace was therefore a legitimate aim to pursue, even if the methods chosen proved ineffective.

The real problem was that no European power, neither Britain nor France nor any other, had any serious chance of acting as peace-maker, mediator or go-between over Vietnam. West European influence in Washington, over Vietnam, was small; in Moscow it was even smaller; in Hanoi it did not count, even in the case of France.

There was a similar situation when the Arab–Israel conflict broke out in the summer of 1967. Twelve years before, Britain was still regarded as the dominant power in the Middle East, if a declining one. In 1967, the two superpowers dominated the area – in so far as it *could* be dominated. Britain could work actively, by diplomatic means and through the United Nations, to help in laying the foundations for a settlement; it could devise and sponsor the resolution of November 1967 which, because of its ambiguous wording, was – just – acceptable both to the Arabs and to Israel. But that did not stop further years of skirmishing across the Suez Canal, which remained closed. The French proposal for four-power talks on the Middle East was eventually put into practice, in New York; but the real work was done in two-power talks between the American State Department and the Soviet Ambassador in Washington. It was the two superpowers which agreed on the cease-fire proposal of 1970. Britain and France had little say and little influence in the matter.

In the disarmament field, Britain was able to play a rather larger part, as a minor nuclear power; France under de Gaulle opted out of all disarmament discussions. The British did useful though not decisive work in the long negotiations for a partial test ban treaty; British influence may have done something to strengthen the moderates and weaken the hard-liners in Washington; British ingenuity was fully stretched in trying to devise ways round technical difficulties. Yet if the United States and the Soviet Union had not both reached the point of wishing to sign a treaty, each in its own national interest, Britain could have done nothing. As things turned out, Britain was able to sign the treaty with the United States and the Soviet Union on a formal basis of equality.

This was a success for the Macmillan Government. The Labour Government, in turn, showed great activity in the negotiations for the non-proliferation treaty, making repeated efforts to overcome Soviet fears about the West Germans and their supposed determination to get their hands on nuclear weapons. This came up time and again – when Stewart, as Foreign Secretary, visited Moscow towards the end of 1965, when Wilson visited Moscow in February 1966, when George Brown, as Foreign Secretary, was in Moscow in the following November, and when Kosygin was in London in February 1967. By that time it was possible for the two governments publicly to 'note with satisfaction' the progress which was being made towards the treaty. Britain kept its special status as one of the three nuclear signatories when the treaty was concluded; but British assurances and pleas can only have had a small influence on the Soviet decision to do a deal with the United States on the treaty. In the SALT talks at the end of the 1960s, Britain had no part. Its nuclear armoury was far too small; the ABMs and MIRVs, about which the superpowers were bargaining, were beyond Britain's capacity.

At the disarmament committee in Geneva which met, under joint American-Soviet chairmanship, through most of the 1960s and into the 1970s, the two superpowers cooperated on a level above and somewhat apart from the other participants, drawn from NATO, Warsaw Pact and non-aligned countries. Cold war polemics were regarded as bad taste. Britain made suggestions and put forward draft proposals, for instance on biological warfare, and maintained good relations with both superpowers while remaining much closer to the United States. In so far as there was a confrontation between the two superpowers on the one side and the non-nuclear powers on the other, Britain, though retaining its nuclear status, seemed poised somewhere between the two.

Britain and the German Question
Over the reunification of Germany and Berlin, Britain and France retained at least theoretical equality of status with the superpowers,

because of the wartime agreements establishing joint four-power responsibility. So long as Adenauer remained Chancellor in Bonn, the official line of the three Western Powers had to be that progress towards German reunification was an essential condition for relaxation of tension in Europe; such was the strength of Adenauer's personality. The Macmillan Government had at times been suspected of straying from this narrow path, but had usually returned rapidly to it. Under the chancellorship of Erhard, there was a certain broadening of the Bonn line.

This was not immediately visible, because in the mid-1960s the Soviet Union and its allies were conducting an intensive campaign against the supposed Western plan to give nuclear weapons to the 'revanchist' West Germans, through the MLF or the ANF. On 12 June 1964 the Soviet Union signed a twenty-year treaty with East Germany of a fairly unprovocative character; the two parties undertook to work for the conclusion of a German peace treaty and 'the normalisation of the situation in Berlin' on this basis.

However, the three Western Powers thought it necessary, in consultation with Bonn, to make a joint declaration that the treaty could not affect the agreements and arrangements between the Soviet Union and themselves on Germany, 'including Berlin and access thereto'. They considered that the Soviet Government remained bound by them; and West Berlin was not an 'independent political unit' (as the Soviet Union and East Germany claimed). The Western Powers then said that while four-power responsibility could not be abrogated, they themselves had 'authorised the establishment of close ties' between West Berlin and West Germany, including the right of the West German Government to represent West Berlin in relations with the outside world. (Visits to West Berlin by members of the Bonn Government and meetings there of organs of the Bonn parliament were a constant source of friction and at times led to threats and harassment by the East Germans, backed by the Soviet Union. The Bonn Government's claim to represent West Berlin in the outside world repeatedly raised problems, especially in the conclusion of trade agreements with Warsaw Pact governments.)

Moscow took little notice of the Western declaration. At the beginning of September 1964, it was announced in Bonn that Khrushchev had accepted an invitation to visit West Germany. Perhaps he thought that having given limited satisfaction to the East German leader, Ulbricht, in the twenty-year treaty, he could turn to cultivating better relations with the West Germans, and satisfying his curiosity about them. The plan was probably unpopular with hardliners in Moscow. Six weeks later Khrushchev was removed from power; the visit never took place.

In March 1966, the Erhard Government made a new move: it put forward six-point 'peace proposals'. It offered to exchange declarations with the Soviet Union, Poland, Czechoslovakia and any other East European State banning the use of force in settlement of disputes, and to conclude bilateral agreements on an exchange of military observers to watch manoeuvres of armed forces; it would join any agreement for a gradual reduction of nuclear weapons in Germany, and proposed that all non-nuclear states in NATO or the Warsaw Pact should renounce the production of nuclear weapons and submit to international control. (West Germany had already done this under the Paris agreements of 1954.)

This West German move was supported by the Western Powers, but was rejected far more harshly than it deserved by the Soviet Union and the East European governments, on the grounds that Bonn had failed to recognise the existing frontiers in Europe or the legitimacy of the East German Government.

In December 1966, with the replacement of the Erhard Government by the 'grand coalition' of Christian Democrats and Social Democrats and the emergence of Willy Brandt as Foreign Minister, the move for better relations with the Soviet Union and the East European countries was speeded up and intensified. Czechoslovakia (under President Novotny) was very much interested, and would have liked to establish diplomatic relations with Bonn, because the stagnant Czechoslovak economy badly needed West German economic aid, in the form of trade, long-term credits and know-how. However, the legalists in Prague insisted that Bonn must declare that the Munich agreement of 1938 had been null and void from the start, a demand which raised legal complications for the West Germans. Moreover, Novotny did not want to upset Ulbricht by moving too fast, or by appearing to forget the East German demand for full recognition.

So contacts between Bonn and Prague were slow and difficult; Bonn took the easier path and established diplomatic relations with Rumania, which cared little about the approval of Ulbricht or even of Moscow. West German–Rumanian trade, already healthy, pushed quickly ahead. But Ulbricht and the Soviet Union were angry with

Bonn for meeting Rumanian approaches half-way and decided to put a stop to the whole policy of improving relations between West Germany and Eastern Europe. This was not difficult: they got the other East European governments to agree on strict conditions for any progress, including formal recognition by Bonn of the Oder–Neisse frontier between Poland and Germany, the frontier between the West German and East German states, full diplomatic recognition of the East German state and a declaration that the Munich agreement had been null and void from the start.

For the Coalition Government headed by the Christian Democrat Chancellor, Kiesinger, such demands were unacceptable, so that although West German trade with Eastern Europe prospered – much to the satisfaction of the East Europeans – there could be little progress on the political front. The Soviet invasion of Czechoslovakia raised new barriers. Moscow, on its side, accused the West Germans of plotting nefariously with the Czechoslovak reform movement identified with Dubček, and this was one of the pretexts for the invasion; on the other side, the West Germans were particularly deeply shocked by the invasion of their immediate neighbour, and showed great generosity to the thousands of refugees from Czechoslovakia.

When in the autumn of 1969 the Kiesinger Government was replaced by a Social Democrat–Free Democrat coalition, with the Social Democrats as the dominant partners, the Brandt *Ostpolitik* – the policy of conciliation with the East – got moving quickly. Willy Brandt's strategy was to move forward simultaneously on three fronts – negotiations with the Soviet Union, negotiations with Poland and an attempt to negotiate with the East German Government. Wisely, priority was given to the Soviet Union, as the key to progress on the other fronts. The outcome was the Soviet–West German treaty of friendship of 12 August 1970, signed amid smiles in the Kremlin by Brandt and Kosygin with Brezhnev looking over their shoulders and making jokes.

To achieve this remarkable result, Brandt had made considerable concessions, sensing that the German public as a whole was ready for them, even if some sections of the opposition Christian Democratic Party and the powerful press tycoon, Axel Springer, were not. Under the treaty West Germany said that it shared with the Soviet Union 'the realisation that peace can only be maintained in Europe if nobody disturbs the frontiers'. It undertook to 'respect without

259

restriction the territorial integrity of all States in Europe within their present frontiers' and declared that it had no territorial claims against anybody; it regarded the frontiers of all States in Europe as inviolable, including the Oder–Neisse line. 'Respect' for existing frontiers was in legal terms something different from formal recognition of them; so the position laid down by four-power agreement at Potsdam, that Germany's frontiers could only be finally settled in a German treaty, was theoretically safeguarded.

Moreover Brandt had not given full diplomatic recognition to the East German State; he had not renounced the ultimate goal of German reunification 'in free self-determination', which was specifically set out in a letter from his Foreign Minister, Walter Scheel, to the Soviet Foreign Minister. He had also preserved the principle of four-power responsibility for the German question and Berlin, through Article 4 of the treaty, which said that it 'shall not affect any bilateral or multilateral treaties or arrangements' previously concluded by either party. Finally, Brandt said that the West German parliament would not be asked to ratify the treaty until the four powers had reached an agreement improving the situation of West Berlin.

All this meant that Brandt had gone a considerable way towards meeting the Soviet demand for recognition of the existing position of divided Europe as permanent. But he had by no means gone the whole way; the Soviet Union had come some way to meet him. And even if the Poles were satisfied by the direct mention of the Oder–Neisse frontier, Ulbricht had little cause for pleasure.

Four months later – on 7 December – Brandt scored his second great achievement by signing a treaty with Poland, in Warsaw, on improving relations between the two countries. Since of all the European peoples, the Poles had the most cruel and bitter memories of German invasion and occupation, many people saw this as a vitally important act of reconciliation. In London, in the House of Commons on 9 December, Denis Healey, as Labour spokesman on foreign affairs, said that the influence of Brandt's *Ostpolitik* on the whole shape of European politics had been 'stupendous'; the whole situation in Europe had been transformed in the past twelve months by Brandt's courage and vision. The Conservative Government, if more cautious about future prospects, also gave the Brandt policy unreserved support.

The progress of the *Ostpolitik* had naturally been watched with very close interest by the other West European countries, in particular Britain and France, with their remaining responsibility for Germany and Berlin. In the late 1960s, their main role was to provide a secure and stable base for West German initiatives in East–West relations. For the British this was an easy and natural part to play. They were capable of understanding that the West Germans needed the feeling of security which NATO could give, before they could take up a more flexible and conciliatory position towards Eastern Europe. At the same time it was important that Bonn's *Ostpolitik* should not create fears or divisions among the West Europeans; West German membership of NATO and the process of political consultation inside NATO were some safeguard against this danger. In so far as Britain helped NATO to overcome the shock of de Gaulle's decision on withdrawal in 1966, it helped to create the conditions necessary for Brandt's *Ostpolitik*.

The British also had a great deal of sympathy for the *Ostpolitik*. They had, for a long time, wanted to move towards better East–West relations in Europe, and had worked actively for this from the mid-1960s onwards. But it was obvious that the key to worthwhile progress lay in Bonn. The Adenauer policy of giving top priority to German reunification had become sterile and ineffective, though loyalty to an allied government had prevented the British Government from saying so. Brandt personally inspired confidence; the British found it easy to understand him and trust him. In general, in spite of occasional fits of alarm and despondency in the British press about West German economic and financial strength, most people, at the end of the 1960s, were ready to accept West Germany as a leading West European power, with its own independent policy.

For the French, the situation was rather more complicated. De Gaulle was always a loyal ally to West Germany, especially on the Berlin question, though he was willing to say openly that he regarded the Oder–Neisse line as final, at a time when the British were still inhibited by respect for Bonn's feelings. De Gaulle, like the British, wanted détente in Europe, but he wished to be the main architect of this détente, acting as an indispensable mediator for the West Germans. He set out to convince Kiesinger that Bonn could do little without his help, and made it clear that he did not want Bonn to move too fast or too independently. When he championed the Adenauer hard line on German reunification, this may have been partly because this hard line effectively barred West Germany from taking useful initiatives to promote détente. His visit to Moscow in the summer of 1966 seemed designed partly to impress fellow-Europeans, especially West Germans, with the leading role of France in the field of East–West relations; so also perhaps was his visit to Bucharest in the summer of 1968.

After de Gaulle's departure, France gave open and probably sincere support to the Bonn *Ostpolitik*. Pompidou said with emphasis at his press conference on 4 July 1970 that he believed profoundly that this policy was in the general interest of Europe as a whole, both West and East. But there still seemed to be an undercurrent of uneasiness in France about West German success. Pompidou himself, at the same press conference, remarked that he was always reading that France dreaded German economic power. He said this was not true, but added that nations, like people, preferred to have neighbours less big than themselves, rather than too big.

When the distinguished French journalist and historian, André Fontaine, analysed Pompidou's foreign policy in February 1970, he suggested that although some sections of French political opinion were afraid of a West German-Soviet rapprochement, such as took place in the 1920s, Pompidou himself wisely did not take this attitude. France could not with good grace withhold support from the Bonn *Ostpolitik*, nor turn a cold shoulder on West Germany; after all, France, under de Gaulle, had actively pursued détente. At the same time, André Fontaine suggested, German size and strength could be held to impose the need to seek a counter-weight. For Pompidou, this meant that France should persevere in de Gaulle's policy of establishing good relations with the East, though it should not go so far as an 'exclusive alliance' with the Soviet Union.[24] When Pompidou visited the Soviet Union in October 1970, this appeared to be the policy he was pursuing. He made clear his displeasure that France had not been informed about the Soviet-West German negotiations and secured a promise of special arrangements for French-Soviet political consultations in future. The idea of a French–Russian understanding dated back to the early years of the century; de Gaulle had pursued it in 1944; it was hallowed by tradition, as a method of containing Germany. It was less certain that it was relevant to the 1970s, with Europe divided and the Soviet Union a superpower. The British would have been happy if France had sought a sense of security in the alternative solution, which was to bring Britain into the EEC and to give the Community a real political content. If this happened,

France need not feel 'alone' up against a more powerful West Germany; and it would be possible for Western Europe to work for détente on the basis of partnership, rather than a precarious system of weights and counter-weights.

Britain's Approach to the Soviet Union and the East Europeans in the 1960s

By the beginning of the 1960s, the Conservative Government had decided on a new approach to Eastern Europe. In the early post-war years, the British Government's attitude towards the Soviet-imposed Communist governments of Eastern Europe was one of strong disapproval. This however failed to bring these governments to better behaviour over basic human and political rights. Naturally, too, the Communist governments remained extremely unfriendly and mistrustful in their attitude towards Britain and other Western countries. As the 1960s opened, Britain was beginning to work for better relations with them. One argument was that this would indirectly benefit the East European peoples. So trade agreements were concluded and outstanding financial problems settled. With Rumania, for instance, a three-year trade agreement was concluded in 1960, together with a final settlement of British claims arising out of the Rumanian peace treaty and Rumanian post-war expropriation of British property. With Hungary, an air agreement was signed in 1960, a cultural agreement in 1962. Before the Conservative Government left office in 1964, Britain's relations with the Soviet Union and the East European governments had improved to such a point that all jamming of BBC broadcasts to all these countries had stopped, for the first time since the immediate post-war years.

The Labour Party, in opposition, was strongly in favour of better East–West relations. One of its complaints about the Conservative Government's effort to get Britain into the Common Market was that membership might restrict British freedom in the East–West field. In the debate in the House of Commons on 3 August 1961, Wilson said: 'we have a role to play in the world, perhaps a decisive role, at some historic moment, in building a bridge between East and West . . . and we must search our hearts and ask whether going in, or not going in, will best help in that role.' On 13 December 1962, he asked whether the Government was refusing to enter into long-term agreements with East European countries 'because of the fact that we should have to scrap and curtail all this trade if we entered the

European Economic Community'. After de Gaulle's veto, in the debate on 11 February 1963, he said that Britain had escaped from the danger that Common Market membership would have limited its freedom to make trade agreements with East European countries and would have forced it to place 'penal import levies' on agricultural imports from Eastern Europe.

When the Labour Government took office in 1964, it set out to speed up the improvement of relations both with the Soviet Union and with the East European countries. When in 1966 it decided to make its new approach to the Common Market, its spokesmen repeatedly declared that this would not interfere with Britain's policy in East–West relations, but would in fact help it; they did not explain exactly how. The Soviet Union and the East European governments took the opposite view; they had always been hostile to the Common Market on political grounds, regarding it as a sort of economic appendix to NATO (which cannot have pleased de Gaulle). They also claimed that it would harm East–West trade, increasing Western discrimination against them. They particularly disliked the provision in the Rome Treaty that the Common Market should eventually negotiate as a single unit in trade with outside countries: this would put an end to the bilateral trade agreements with individual West European countries which suited the East European countries and the Soviet Union.

When Kosygin visited London in February 1967, he made Soviet dislike of the prospect of British membership quite clear, conjuring up dream-like visions of a vast expansion of Anglo-Soviet trade as a better alternative for Britain. Although Wilson was eager for more trade and allowed part of Kosygin's vision to find its way into the joint communiqué, he did not accept the Soviet argument against British membership of the Common Market. He told the Parliamentary Labour Party on 27 April: 'our purpose is to make a reality of the unity of Western Europe. But we know this will be an empty achievement unless it leads first to an easing of tension and then to an honourable and lasting settlement of the outstanding problems that still divide Europe, Western Europe from Eastern Europe. This is something I have striven for for many years; and I am convinced that if Britain is a member of a united European community our chances of achieving this will be immeasurably greater.' In the House of Commons debate early in May 1967, George Brown, as Foreign Secretary, said that East–West relations were growing more flexible, because of changing attitudes, and the process of healing the division had started in the sphere of trade, commerce and culture; he went on: 'the success of this growing détente would be immeasurably greater if Britain were a member of a united European Economic Community.'

The Soviet Union and the East European governments were not convinced. The East Europeans, in particular, were already in a weak position in their dealings with the much richer and economically stronger West European countries; in dealings with a single West European economic unit, they could find themselves at a hopeless disadvantage. However the British Labour Government, partly perhaps as an assurance of good will, proceeded to conclude a series of technological agreements, providing for the exchange of specialists and information, facilities for study and research, and industrial cooperation, with all the East European governments and the Soviet Union, during 1967 and 1968. If Britain wanted to join the Common Market to help close the technological gap between the United States and Western Europe, it wanted to show that it was also ready to help close the gap between Western and Eastern Europe.

The Labour Government set out to develop relations with individual East European countries in both the economic and political fields. The Foreign Secretary, Stewart, in addition to visiting Yugoslavia, went to Czechoslovakia in April 1965 and Poland in the following September. In Prague, he was faced with the demand of the Czechoslovak Government that Britain should declare that the 1938 Munich agreement had been null and void from the start. This he refused to do; he declared it 'detestable and dead' and pointed out that Bonn had said categorically that it had no territorial claims on Czechoslovakia. But to say that the treaty had never been made would, Stewart said, be a dangerous precedent for other treaties. The Czechoslovak Foreign Minister, David, called Stewart's statement 'serious and important' but remained dissatisfied. The communiqué recorded the difference of view of the two sides on Munich; it also recorded that they had discussed various proposals on European security.

Stewart also discussed European security with the Polish Foreign Minister, Rapacki (author of the Rapacki Plan for nuclear arms limitation in central Europe). They agreed that – after careful preparation and in favourable circumstances – a conference on this issue 'would be useful'. In Poland, as in Czechoslovakia, Stewart was hampered by a political obstacle – his inability, because of loyalty to Bonn, to recognise the Oder–Neisse frontier between Poland and Germany as final. But Anglo-Polish trade increased rapidly; Britain was Poland's best customer in the West, though West Germany started pulling ahead at the end of the 1960s.

With Rumania, Britain's relations improved fast in the second half of the 1960s, as the Rumanian policy of independence, both political and economic, was developed. The Rumanian Government was eager to expand trade with the West, on terms which would get round the problem of its lack of hard currency and its small existing range of exports. At the beginning of 1968 a Rumanian Government delegation visited London to explore the expansion of bilateral economic relations, 'with special reference to methods of cooperation between the industrial enterprises between the two countries'. In the following September the Foreign Secretary, Stewart, visited Bucharest; the visit seemed to have more than usual significance since it came within three weeks of the invasion of Czechoslovakia, at a time when there were rumours of threatened Soviet action against Rumania. Apart from signing a consular convention, he had talks with the Rumanian Foreign Minister, Manescu, at which they were able, in the terms of the official statement, to 'take note of the outstanding growth of economic relations'. Trade between the two countries had grown eight-fold between 1960 and 1968. (The 1960 level was admittedly very low.)

The kind of economic cooperation which suited the Rumanians was ingenious. In 1968 Rumania placed an order worth £11 million for six British Aircraft Corporation 1–11 airliners. It had chosen British rather than Soviet airliners, partly no doubt to increase its economic independence, partly in order to encourage Western tourists to come to Rumania. Rumania's problem was how to pay for them. Another factor was Rumania's desire to start up an aircraft industry of its own. To do this it needed a reliable technological partner in the West to provide the necessary expert knowledge and skills. In the event, Rumanian ingenuity was matched by British ingenuity, with both the Board of Trade and the BAC playing a part. A complicated package deal was worked out. The BAC airliners were supplied to Rumania; in part-return, Rumanian goods such as cherry jam and wood products were marketed in the West through a Swiss firm; it suited BAC that a plant should be set up in Rumania for the assembly of several hundred Britten–Norman 'Norman Islanders', a very simple, cheap, twelve-passenger aircraft sold all over the world. This gave useful experience to Rumanian engineers and technicians; and the British also arranged facilities for their technical training. The plan worked to the considerable satisfaction of both sides.

Also in 1968, it was announced that Rumania had awarded Britain a £22 million contract for an automated irrigation system in the Danube Valley, payment to be made partly by the (eventual) products of the agricultural land reclaimed by the system. This was obviously a very long-term project, but one which might also have long-term consequences, for instance in British scientific and technical advice in agriculture.

In November 1969 the Rumanian Prime Minister, Maurer, visited London for talks with Wilson. Publicly, the two Prime Ministers welcomed 'the intensification of economic, technological, cultural and scientific cooperation', and agreed to expand it. On the political side, they jointly affirmed the principle on which Rumania took its stand in its relations with the Soviet Union, that relations between states must be based on the observance of the principle of national independence and sovereignty, equal rights, and non-interference in internal affairs. As for relations between Rumania and Britain, they said that these were based on 'trust and mutual respect'. These words for once seemed to have real meaning, although West Germany was Rumania's chief trade partner in the West, and although Rumania was wooed both by France and by the United States. (De Gaulle visited Rumania in 1968 and Nixon in 1969.)

With the Soviet Union itself, British relations during the 1960s were patchy. Purely bilateral relations progressed smoothly enough (though the invasion of Czechoslovakia in 1968 gave them a sharp jolt). The cultural agreement signed as a result of Macmillan's Moscow visit in 1959 led to a series of annual agreements for cultural exchanges, but – on the Soviet side – no real freedom of information or human contacts. In 1961 the BBC and Moscow Television undertook to exchange programmes. There was an agreement between the British and Soviet governments on the exchange of (non-secret) nuclear information and mutual visits of scientists.

A five-year trade agreement ran from 1959 to 1964, and was thereafter followed by further five-year agreements. The British Trade

Fair in Moscow in May 1961 attracted very many visitors; Khrushchev toured it and said (misleadingly): 'we shall buy everything the British want to sell.' Two months later there was a big Soviet Exhibition at Earls Court in London. In 1963 and 1964 the Soviet Union placed big orders in Britain for polythene, ethylene and terylene plants. Similar orders followed. A British Agricultural Show in the Soviet Union in 1964 led to an Anglo-Soviet agreement on co-operation in agricultural research, signed in January 1965. Wilson visited Moscow in February and again in July 1966; he called on the Soviet Union to buy more from Britain so as to get rid of the chronic British deficit in trade between the two countries. In July he toured a British Trade Fair in Moscow with Kosygin.

Kosygin's visit to London in February 1967 marked a high point in Anglo-Soviet relations. Differences over Vietnam were temporarily submerged in Wilson's effort to bring about a joint peace move. Kosygin was clearly determined to impress the British by his friendliness and reasonableness, and had considerable success, though his public attacks on West German 'neo-nazism' struck the wrong note. It was agreed that there should be a London–Moscow 'hot line', on the Washington–Moscow and Paris–Moscow models. Kosygin caught the British off balance by a surprise proposal for a new Anglo-Soviet treaty of friendship, cooperation and non-aggression. In the final communiqué, the British said they welcomed the proposal and looked forward to negotiations. But no treaty ever emerged. However, in the House of Commons in early May, Wilson said that relations between the Soviet Union and Britain were better 'than at any time in our history'.

Kosygin, with one eye on the new British approach to the Common Market, had particularly set out to flatter and allure Britain in the economic field. He told the Confederation of British Industry that the technological resources of the Soviet Union and Europe combined were greater than those of the United States; so there was no 'technological gap'. The communiqué on the Kosygin–Wilson talks spoke of the desirability of 'longer-term arrangements' for the 'forward planning' of the Soviet and British economies. This had little practical result, because the 'forward planning' of the British economy, in so far as it existed, was of a totally different kind from the highly-centralised State planning of the Soviet Union. However, at the time of the Kosygin visit, Courtaulds got a £9 million order to build an acrylic fibre plant in Byelorussia.

Following the Kosygin visit to London and the Wilson visit to Moscow in 1968, discussions took place between the British and Gosplan, the Soviet planning organisation. Gosplan's idea seemed to be that Britain should supply capital equipment, especially for the development of Siberia, on the basis of long-term contracts providing for the Soviet Union to pay for the equipment supplied in the form of a share of the eventual products. A British firm might be expected to build a lorry factory in the Soviet Union in the hope of being paid, one day, in lorries from the factory. But the terms suggested by the Soviet side did not seem attractive.

At the end of the 1960s Britain's trade with the East European countries and the Soviet Union was growing satisfactorily, within the very narrow limits set by the rigid and inflexible political and economic systems of these countries and by Soviet determination to keep a tight economic grip on its East European allies. (Rumania had achieved an exceptional position of independence.) Because of these limitations, the East European countries remained economically backward in comparison with the West Europeans; and their great difficulty in earning freely convertible currency forced them to use primitive and discriminatory trading methods.

These were the factors which most seriously hampered the growth of trade. There were also two lesser factors. One was Britain's membership of COCOM – the coordinating committee formed by the NATO countries, except for Iceland, together with Japan, which, since the beginning of the 1950s, had agreed on a long list of strategically important goods which were not to be exported to the Soviet Union and its allies (or China). This list was periodically reviewed; the United States always wanted to keep it as long as possible; there was, in the background, the threat of American trade reprisals against countries which violated the COCOM rules, or interpreted them in a different way from Washington. Britain on the other hand usually pressed for items to be taken off the embargo list. Soviet representatives often attacked it as a major obstacle to East–West trade, and to Anglo-Soviet trade in particular. Its real effect was much less than the Soviet Union suggested.

The other limiting factor was imposed by Britain itself, in the form of quantitative restrictions on the import of certain categories of goods from the Soviet Union or East European countries. This was a protectionist policy, held to be justified by the various disruptive and discriminatory trade measures used by the Soviet and East European governments in their dealings with the West. During the 1960s, however, Britain progressively liberalised its trade with the Soviet Union and Eastern Europe. In 1964, 1966 and 1969, restrictions were lifted from more and more categories of goods; Britain had little success in its attempts to bargain for counter-concessions from individual governments through the ending of discriminatory practices. By 1970 Britain had removed restrictions on the import of most goods from all East European countries (including East Germany) and the Soviet Union. But the National Farmers' Union was continuing to demand protection against agricultural imports from Eastern Europe. Britain was also carefully watching what the EEC was proposing to do about removing remaining quantitative restrictions on imports from Eastern Europe; the British aim would be to keep in step.

By 1970, Britain was alone among the West European countries in refusing to buy oil from the Soviet Union, which was anxious to step up its oil sales to the West as an easy way of earning hard currency needed for large-scale purchases of Western industrial equipment – partly for the more rapid development of Siberia. (The Soviet Union was curiously reluctant to use its gold to finance its imports, even after the 1967–68 speculation on a doubling of the gold price had faded away; however, by 1970, its exports of diamonds, through Britain, were earning useful hard currency.) One curious by-product of the Soviet drive to sell oil to the West was a Soviet warning to the East European countries that there would no longer be enough Soviet oil available for them, so that they had better look for oil elsewhere. In consequence Czechoslovakia and Bulgaria were trying at the end of the 1960s to buy Persian oil by means of barter deals. In so far as Soviet oil sales to the West led indirectly to a lessening of East European dependence on the Soviet Union, the development might have been welcomed in the West. However, in 1970 Britain was still standing out against Soviet oil. The official argument had always been that for Britain to become dependent on Soviet oil would give the Soviet Union a powerful strategic and political weapon. But there was little real question of British 'dependence'; the Soviet share in Britain's oil supplies was never likely to be more than small. The British oil companies' wish to exclude a new competitor may have weighed more heavily in the balance.

By 1970 Britain, like the EEC countries, had a network of five-year trade agreements with the East European countries and the Soviet Union. East Germany was the exception; there could be no agreement at government level because Britain did not recognise the East German regime. However, there was a three-year trade agreement between the Confederation of British Industry and the East Germans.

For all the East European states and the Soviet Union, Britain was a fairly important Western trade partner during the 1960s – for the Soviet Union and Poland, the biggest, though de Gaulle's Moscow visit led to a sharp rise in Soviet–French trade. West Germany, during the 1970s, could be expected to outstrip both Britain and France easily, as the Bonn *Ostpolitik* cleared away the political obstacles which had still hampered its trade with the Soviet Union and Eastern Europe (except for Rumania) during the 1960s.

This was a prospect which the British were ready to face with relative calm. Trade with the Soviet Union and Eastern Europe was not an important element in Britain's total foreign trade. In 1970 its share was around 4 per cent. Unless there were far-reaching changes inside the Soviet Union, in the relationship between the Soviet Union and the East European states, and in the economic systems of the East European countries, this trade was unlikely, during the 1970s, to form more than one-twentieth of the British total.

The Invasion of Czechoslovakia and British–Soviet relations
The sharpest shock to Anglo-Soviet relations during the 1960s was the invasion of Czechoslovakia in August 1968. This also marked the biggest crisis in relations between the Soviet Union and the East European Communist states since the Soviet suppression of the Hungarian uprising twelve years earlier. It showed that the Soviet Union, having turned its back on the new policy set out in its statement of 30 October 1956 (see pp. 130–3 above), during the Hungarian uprising, had failed to solve the fundamental problems of its relations with its allies.

In the mid-1960s, various changes were taking place in Eastern Europe. Rumania was displaying a surprisingly bold and independent front to the Soviet Union, while maintaining orthodox Communist rule internally. There were strong pressures for economic reform in Hungary, East Germany and above all, Czechoslovakia, where the economy, in pre-Communist days considerably ahead of other East European countries, had become stagnant, and was lagging behind its Communist neighbours, especially East Germany. One of the aims of the movements for economic reform – at least in Czechoslovakia and Hungary – was to be able to trade more efficiently and competitively with the West; this would make it possible to obtain from the West the industrial equipment and technical know-how which were needed for rapid industrial advance.

Until the middle of 1968, the Soviet Union seemed to be taking up a permissive attitude towards these new developments in Eastern Europe. It probably did not like them but did not seem to think it necessary to squash them. Brezhnev himself, through a visit to Prague, appeared to have given his personal backing to the changes in the Czechoslovak Communist Party leadership in January 1968, when Novotny was replaced by Dubček. There was talk, both in Western Europe and in Eastern Europe, about the theory of the eventual convergence of the two economic and political systems, as a bigger and bigger element of 'indicative' planning was introduced into the free enterprise system of the West, and a bigger and bigger element of 'autonomy' for individual enterprises was introduced into the state planning system of the East. The BBC Reith Lectures of 1966, by the American diplomat and economist, Professor J. K. Galbraith, had contributed to the discussion. After a time, Moscow frowned heavily on the 'convergence' theory. This was perhaps to be expected.

The 'Prague Spring' – the political reform movement which sprang out of the economic reform movement, and which came to be identified with Dubček – obviously shocked and alarmed Ulbricht, and thereafter the Soviet leaders. Such political freedom of speech was unheard of. It also worried the Hungarians, but in a different way; they thought that the only means of getting and keeping some small freedom to run their own affairs was to take the utmost care that nothing should irritate or arouse the Soviet overlord. Throughout Western Europe, on the other hand, the 'Prague Spring' was watched with great sympathy and even excitement, especially, perhaps, in West Germany and Britain. These feelings were all the stronger because the Czechoslovak authorities were allowing journalists from the West to enter the country freely and to report freely. Moscow naturally found this suspect and sinister.

As tension rose, with Soviet military manoeuvres in Czechoslovakia prolonged far beyond the date fixed for their end, leaders of five Warsaw Pact countries (all except Czechoslovakia and Rumania) met in Warsaw and sent a joint letter to the Czechoslovak Communist Party on 15 July, which stated their claim to the right to intervene in Czechoslovak internal affairs. This was the claim which later became known as the Brezhnev doctrine. The letter said: 'we cannot agree to have hostile forces push your country away from socialism and create a danger of Czechoslovakia being severed from the socialist community. This is something more than your own concern. It is the common concern of all the Communist and Workers' Parties and states united by alliance, cooperation and friendship. . . . The frontiers of the socialist world have moved to the centre of Europe, to the Elbe and the Bohemian Forest. We shall never agree to these historic gains of socialism . . . being put in danger.'

In spite of the threatening tone of the letter, the Czechoslovak party leaders found it hard to believe that the Soviet Union would depart so far from the principles of communism as to invade an allied country. There had been no talk in Czechoslovakia about leaving the Warsaw Pact and becoming neutral – or if there had, it had been very quickly suppressed. In their rather hurt reply of 18 July, the Czechoslovak leaders appealed specifically to the principle laid down in the Soviet Government's declaration of 30 October 1956, during the Hungarian uprising, that socialist nations could only build their mutual relations on the basis of complete equality, respect of territorial integrity, national independence and sovereignty and mutual non-interference in internal affairs.

The next step was the extraordinary three-day meeting of the entire Soviet Politburo and the Czechoslovak leaders at the frontier town of Cierna-nad-Tisou on 29 July. The only announced outcome was the decision to send a joint invitation to the Communist Parties of Bulgaria, East Germany, Hungary and Poland to a 'multilateral comradely meeting'. This meeting took place in Bratislava on 3 August. A long, turgid and confused statement emerged, amid public displays of amiability all round. What seemed, at the time, more important than all the words was the announcement that the last of the Soviet troops, who had lingered on after the closing-date for the manoeuvres, had left Czechoslovakia during the Bratislava meeting. On 4 August Dubček said in a broadcast that true internationalism must link the principles of mutual aid with those of respect for sovereignty and territorial integrity. He seemed to believe that the Soviet leaders had accepted this link. The crisis seemed to be over, or at least past the worst.

During August, however, there were signs that the Soviet leaders and Ulbricht disapproved of the way in which Dubček was interpreting the wordy, obscure Bratislava declaration. In particular, the Czechoslovak leadership was carrying out changes in the personnel of the Ministry of the Interior, affecting its Soviet 'advisers', and was preparing for a Party Congress early in September at which it was expected that the opponents of the reform movement would be voted out of office. Finally, the Soviet Ambassador in Prague was in contact with certain prominent hard-liners who were apparently ready to invite Soviet military intervention, assuming that they themselves would then be placed in power, thereby escaping dismissal or demotion at the coming Party Congress.

On the night of 21 August, Czechoslovakia was invaded by very large Soviet armed forces – estimates both above and below half a million men were given – and by very much smaller East German, Polish, Bulgarian and Hungarian forces. Whatever political planning there may have been on the Soviet side went badly wrong. The 'invitation' from the Czechoslovak Party leadership, or at least from a section of it, was not forthcoming, even though Dubček had his enemies. But the 'invitation' was the cover story which, at the start, Moscow used in its propaganda and its diplomatic handling of the whole affair. It then found itself unable to meet repeated challenges to name the Czechoslovak leaders who had issued the invitation. In any case, it was quite clear to the whole world that the invasion was nothing but the attempt of a superpower to impose its will by force on the legitimate leaders and the people of a small allied country. People in Britain, as elsewhere, had followed the sequence of events too closely to believe anything else.

In London (as in other Western capitals) the Soviet Ambassador communicated a message to the Government at 1.30 a.m. on 21 August, as the invasion was in progress, saying that the Government of Czechoslovakia had appealed to the Soviet Union and its allies for direct assistance, including the use of armed force. The message added that these forces would be withdrawn as 'the threat to security' was removed; the Soviet action was not directed against any European state nor against British interests, but was dictated by a concern to 'strengthen peace', in the face of a dangerous growth of tension. The Soviet Government, it went on, assumed that these developments would not harm Anglo-Soviet relations.

This message was interesting in that it showed that the Soviet Foreign Ministry, at least, was aware that the invasion would have widespread international repercussions, and might harm Soviet relations with West European countries in particular. (Britain, it was disclosed later, had given warning of this.) The Foreign Ministry was however probably powerless. It could only try to lessen the harm done. As things turned out, in the absence of any 'appeal from the Czechoslovak Government' (whose leading members were taken to Moscow as captives), this message had the worst possible effect.

The immediate reaction of the Foreign Office in London, on 21 August, was to state that the British Government regarded the Soviet action as a flagrant violation of all accepted standards of international behaviour. It was a tragedy not only for Czechoslovakia but for Europe and the whole world, and a serious blow to the efforts which so many countries had been making to improve relations between East and West.

The Government recalled Parliament from its summer recess and on 26 August the House of Commons debated Czechoslovakia. Wilson had a difficult job. On the one hand he wanted to express some of the horror and shock felt by many people in Britain; on the other hand, he felt he had to remind them that in the long run the process of trying to improve East–West relations would have to go on, simply because there was no other way forward. He spoke of the widespread feeling of 'impotent protest', and said that the Soviet Union had acted with 'the grim and cynical determination that no Communist country of Eastern Europe is to be allowed to decide for itself that it wished to turn away from uniformity and external control to new concepts of freedom and free expression'. The Russians, Wilson said, were concerned about the security of their 'buffer states to the West', but they feared still more that 'liberalisation, once rooted in a single country of Eastern Europe, would be impossible to contain'.

As for the future, Wilson said that it was necessary to maintain the defensive system of NATO, as an alliance determined on defence but equally determined on creating the conditions of détente: 'we all know that the only future for the world rests on continuing to work for détente between East and West.' 'Time will be needed, but I reject the view that the events of the past week leave us no choice except to relapse into the *immobilisme* of the cold war,' he went on. Wilson then said that governmental and parliamentary contacts with the invading countries would be reduced to a bare minimum 'for the immediate future'; there would not be a ban on cultural visits already

275

planned, though individual British citizens could decide for themselves whether or not to support them.

Wilson was also faced with the problem of explaining why Britain felt it had the right, or even the obligation, to object to the Soviet intervention in Czechoslovakia. This was not altogether easy. Although the Churchill–Stalin 'percentage agreement' of the war years had never applied to Czechoslovakia, and was in theory a temporary arrangement only, it had obviously encouraged the Soviet Union in regarding itself as entitled to a sharply defined 'sphere of influence' in Europe. Moreover, since the beginning of the 1960s the West European countries had been moving gradually towards acceptance of the division of Europe as the only practical foundation on which a détente could be based. This implied acquiescence in Soviet overlordship in Eastern Europe as a fact of life, if not a very pleasant one.

Wilson did not find a very satisfactory solution to the problem. He said that Britain must 'reject the assertion that a state, if it is powerful enough, has the right, within its own backyard, its own claimed sphere of influence, to extinguish the rights ... of any smaller nation which it thinks is standing in its way'. No one, Wilson said, was 'seeking to dictate to the Soviet Union and its allies any change in the relationships which have existed between them'. But 'what all of us in this House reject is that where these matters cannot be settled by discussion, one or more of the partners to that alliance have the right to impose a settlement by force ...'.

All this did not add up to a very coherent statement of Britain's right to object to the Soviet action against Czechoslovakia. By 31 August the American State Department had put forward a more concrete explanation for Western concern – that the *status quo* had been changed because there were larger Soviet forces now present in central Europe than at any time since the early post-war period. This, the State Department said, had changed the East–West military situation in Europe and was therefore of significance to the security of the United States and its allies.

The same argument was later taken up at the NATO meeting of ministers, which was held a month earlier than usual because of Czechoslovakia. The ministers said that 'the use of force and the stationing in Czechoslovakia of Soviet forces not hitherto deployed there have aroused grave uncertainty about the situation and about the calculations and intentions of the USSR. This uncertainty demands great vigilance on the part of the allies.' They decided in consequence to improve the 'quality, effectiveness and deployment of NATO's forces' both in manpower and equipment. The conventional capability of NATO's non-nuclear tactical air forces was to be increased, and certain additional units committed to the major NATO Commands. Britain offered a further infantry battalion, and additional Harrier aircraft, for the European command, and the 'almost continuous' stationing of an aircraft-carrier or other naval ship in the Mediterranean, in addition to forces already there. These military measures had been carefully calculated to demonstrate firmness but not to appear in any way provocative or alarmist.

The powerful outburst of feeling in Britain against the invasion of Czechoslovakia, together with the drastic curtailment by Britain of diplomatic and other official contacts, obviously did not leave Moscow cold. On 2 December 1968 the Soviet Union sent a note accusing the British Government of 'complicating and aggravating' Anglo-Soviet relations, 'using as a pretext the events in Czechoslovakia'. It said that a propaganda campaign hostile to the Soviet Union had been started in Britain, with the direct participation of British statesmen and politicians. The past few years had seen the beginning of favourable conditions for a fruitful development of contacts in science and technology; 'but the British Government has now taken a different road. . . . It has obviously decided to bring to nothing many positive gains which have been achieved . . .'. Britain, the note said, was 'driving to an end' contacts and exchanges; British officials were misrepresenting Soviet policy and making 'crude attacks' on the Soviet State. At the NATO meeting, Britain had been one of those 'who irresponsibly took a stand of direct confrontation with the Soviet Union . . .'. The Soviet note ended in a threatening tone: 'The course which the British Government has been pursuing recently . . . compels us to regard from a different angle not only the present state of Soviet-British relations but their prospects in various other spheres as well.'

Just over a week later a British reply was delivered. Britain, it said, wanted to pursue a policy of better understanding and deplored the fact that the progress so far made should have been halted by the invasion of Czechoslovakia. The note disclosed that before the invasion, 'it was clearly explained to the Soviet Government, through their ambassador in London, that action of this kind would inevitably affect our relations'. Britain firmly believed that the two countries must continue to do business together. But the Soviet action had inevitably caused a setback to mutual confidence. And the use of armed force 'against a European country' could not fail to be of concern to all members of NATO.

In this, the British note came near to saying that what happened to *any* European country, whether inside or outside the Soviet 'sphere of influence', was important for *all* other European countries. This was in line with the idea put forward by the British in NATO that there should be a 'code of good conduct' to be agreed among European countries of West and East. This would be one method of overcoming the East–West division and the 'Brezhnev doctrine' of the Soviet right of intervention in East European states. Unfortunately it was an idea which lacked dramatic appeal and was therefore slow in gaining support.

During 1969 Anglo-Soviet relations gradually moved back towards their earlier state of normality verging on amiability. Early in 1970 there were reports of an impending visit by Wilson to Moscow, which some people linked with the expectation of an early general election in Britain. Shortly before the election actually took place on 18 June, the Soviet Government, in a curiously clumsy piece of diplomacy, issued a public invitation to Wilson to visit Moscow. When Heath became Prime Minister, the idea was shelved for the time being. But there could be no doubt that the policy of détente, which had been started by the Macmillan Government, and which the Labour Government had not abandoned even when the shock of the Czechoslovak tragedy was greatest, would be carried forward by the Conservative Government under Heath.

22 The approach to a European security conference

During the second half of the 1960s, the NATO countries and the Warsaw Pact countries made a curious crab-wise advance towards each other; the ultimate meeting-point seemed destined to be a European security conference, or a series of European conferences or the setting up of some permanent European body to deal with East–West problems. The pressure for a conference came from the Warsaw Pact side; the motives of the various Warsaw Pact leaders for backing the idea were varied and mutually contradictory. The Western response was oblique and extremely cautious, partly because of the need to find out what the Eastern side was really up to.

The Soviet Union's motives were particularly obscure, and probably varied over the years according to circumstances. The idea of a European security conference could be traced back to Molotov's proposal, at the four-power Foreign Ministers' meeting in Berlin early in 1954, for a European security treaty, followed nine months later by the Soviet invitation to twenty-four European countries, and the United States, to a European security conference. At first, the Soviet purpose was obviously to block the rearmament of West Germany. Later, it seemed to be to get the West to accept the division of Europe – the *status quo* – as final, and legally and politically binding. In the 1950s, nothing came of the Soviet initiative.

Western proposals, in the early 1960s, for a NATO nuclear force including West Germany – the MLF or the ANF – provoked a hostile campaign by the Soviet Union, acting through the Warsaw Pact and other channels. The Warsaw Pact Political Consultative Committee – its council of ministers – met in January 1965 in Warsaw and issued a powerful blast against all such plans. The ministers added that the Warsaw Pact countries were ready to sign non-aggression pacts with NATO countries, and they called for the perpetuation of existing frontiers.

This could have been a move in the direction of a renewed proposal for a European security conference, designed mainly to block Western plans for a NATO nuclear force. However, at this point a fresh factor came into play – Rumania's policy of independence in external relations. On 7 May 1966 the Rumanian Communist Party leader, Ceausescu, called for the abolition of military blocs and of military bases and troops on the territory of other states. Military blocs, he said, were incompatible with the independence and national sovereignty of peoples, and with normal relations between states.

The Rumanian challenge displeased Moscow and Brezhnev paid an unannounced visit to Bucharest. But Ceausescu was not intimidated. A few days later it was reported that Rumania had sent notes to the Warsaw Pact Governments suggesting that Soviet troops and bases in Eastern Europe were no longer needed, seeing that the danger of conflict with the West had decreased; in any case the cost of maintaining troops should be borne by the state which sent them. The post of Warsaw Pact supreme commander, it was suggested, should rotate among member countries. The Rumanian Foreign Ministry confirmed that such a note had been sent, adding that Rumania would oppose any move to strengthen the Warsaw Pact by establishing a supranational authority over the member states.

The Soviet Union was apparently not ready to take the steps necessary to silence the irrepressible Rumanian leader. On the other hand, the Rumanians wanted to assert their independence of the Soviet Union without forcing things to an open break. Both seemed to have an interest in finding a face-saving arrangement for covering over their differences. A campaign for a European security conference seemed to fit the needs of both.

In the first week of July 1966 the Warsaw Pact Political Consultative Committee met in Bucharest and signed a 'Declaration on Europe', dated 5 July. This appeared to reflect some of Ceausescu's views. The Warsaw Pact countries called on all European states to develop good neighbourly relations, on the basis of the familiar principles of independence, national sovereignty, non-interference in internal affairs and peaceful co-existence. They called for the simultaneous dissolution of military alliances, and their replacement by a European security system. They then said: 'the convocation of a general European conference to discuss the question of ensuring security in Europe and organising general European cooperation would be of great positive importance.' They were ready to take part in such a conference with NATO countries and the European neutrals.

Nothing was said about the participation of the United States, though in 1954 it had been one of the countries invited by the Soviet Union to a conference. In 1966, it looked as though Moscow would like to exclude the United States, but was keeping the question open. It also seemed possible that the Soviet Union was in no hurry for the conference actually to take place, because of the difficulty of keeping the East European states, especially Rumania, under proper control if it did. But a propaganda campaign for a conference was harmless enough, and was a way of keeping the Rumanians out of mischief.

In the summer of 1966, the West European countries were more worried about de Gaulle's withdrawal from the NATO military structure than about a European security conference, and at their winter meeting, in December 1966, the NATO ministers carefully side-stepped any public statement on the idea. However, they went so far as to state cautiously that 'in the field of East–West relations, there are clearly different approaches which can be adopted, whether between individual countries or in a wider international framework.' They declared their willingness to explore ways of developing cooperation with the Soviet Union and the East European states.

During the following year, visits and diplomatic contacts between West and East European ministers and governments multiplied rapidly; the smaller countries, both West and East, were particularly active, and some of them formed a loose informal 'Group of Nine'. There seemed to be a general loosening up of political attitudes; the sharp dividing line between West European and East European countries became softer, even a little blurred; neutral Austria and non-aligned Yugoslavia helped to create an atmosphere of slightly muddled good will. Britain, preoccupied with its new approach to the Common Market, did not play an outstanding role, but believed that a multiplication of contacts between West and East European countries was very useful; as well as improving the European atmosphere, it might help to reveal what the East Europeans wanted out of a European security conference.

When the NATO ministers met in December 1967 they took official note of 'the extensive bilateral contacts made in recent months'. They also issued a 'Report on the Future Tasks of the Alliance' which declared that it had two main functions: first, to maintain adequate military strength to deter aggression; second, to 'pursue the search for progress towards a more stable relationship in which the underlying political issues can be solved.' The alliance could be used constructively in the interests of détente. Edging a step nearer to a direct mention of the proposal for a European security conference, it said that the participation of the Soviet Union and the United States would be necessary to achieve a settlement on the political problems in Europe – in other words, the United States would have to be invited before any conference could meet.

At their Reykjavik meeting in June 1968, the NATO ministers launched a new approach to the European security question, though still without mentioning a conference. This was a 'declaration on mutual and balanced force reductions', with which the British were very closely identified. France, because of de Gaulle's attitude to NATO, was not involved in it. The aim was to secure agreement between NATO and the Warsaw Pact on reductions which should be 'reciprocal and balanced in scope and timing', so as to maintain the existing degree of security at reduced cost, without 'de-stabilising' the situation in Europe. The NATO ministers said they were going to make preparations for discussions on this subject with the Soviet Union and the East European countries, and they called on them to join in the 'search for progress towards peace'.

This NATO proposal had some kinship with the 'Eden plans' of 1955. The idea behind it was that a certain military balance had been achieved in Europe between East and West, which seemed to have produced stability and the possibility of détente. All European countries could be assumed to want to cut their defence spending; certainly Britain did. With minimum good will on both sides, it should theoretically be possible to achieve the same balance and stability more cheaply. In the particular context of the Warsaw Pact proposal for a European security conference, the NATO proposal was also intended to reveal whether the Soviet Union was willing to allow any serious practical problems to be discussed, or whether it only wanted to use a conference to force the West to recognise the division of Europe.

The invasion of Czechoslovakia, two months later, was only a temporary obstacle. The NATO ministers, when they met in November 1968, said that although prospects for mutual balanced force reductions had suffered 'a severe setback', the allies intended to continue their studies, for a time when the atmosphere would be more favourable.

In the early spring of 1969, the Soviet Union was busily trying to make everyone forget Czechoslovakia; it also wanted to rally the shaken Warsaw Pact allies behind some non-controversial cause. The first meeting of the Warsaw Pact Political Consultative Committee after the invasion of Czechoslovakia was held in Budapest on 17 March and agreement was obtained for a new call for a European security conference, in a statement which was noticeably free from attacks on American imperialism or West German revanchism.

When the Atlantic alliance celebrated its twentieth birthday in Washington in April 1969, the ministers had to take some account of the Budapest statement. The British Foreign Secretary, Stewart, urged that the allies should not respond with a flat negative, though they must insist on the full representation of the United States and Canada at any conference. The ministers, in their joint statement, undertook to 'explore' with the Soviet Union and the East European countries 'which concrete issues best lend themselves to fruitful negotiation and an early resolution'.

By this time it had become clear that while none of the NATO allies had much enthusiasm for a European security conference, some, notably Britain, regarded it as ultimately inevitable, and therefore to be approached with good grace, if with caution, if only because it would be a mistake to leave it to the other side to make all the running. When Kosygin visited London in 1967, and again when Wilson visited Moscow in January 1968, the British and Soviet Prime Ministers had jointly stated that a European conference 'could be valuable'. (They also said that all the countries of Europe should be 'among the participants', a phrase which obliquely allowed for the British view that the United States should take part.) The Americans, however, were afraid that a conference would merely turn into a platform for anti-American and anti-West German propaganda, and were a good deal more negative. In 1969, the Americans may also have wanted to get the American-Soviet SALT talks going first, before embarking on a European conference of doubtful purpose.

In the autumn of 1969 the situation was changed by the formation of the new Social Democrat–Free Democrat Government in Bonn, which quickly launched a much more far-reaching *Ostpolitik* than its predecessor. It was clear that if this met a good response from the East, the atmosphere for a European security conference would be very much better; some of the more difficult obstacles might be removed in advance. The Warsaw Pact ministers, meeting in Prague at the end of October, made a further move: they proposed a European security conference in Helsinki in the first half of 1970 to discuss, first, the renunciation of the use or threat of force; next, the expansion of commercial, economic, scientific and technological relations between European countries, on a basis of equality of rights and in a spirit of cooperation. At the beginning of December, on the eve of the NATO ministers' meeting, there was a Warsaw Pact summit in Moscow which endorsed the Prague proposal and took up a relatively friendly attitude towards the new Bonn Government.

This renewed Warsaw Pact pressure for a conference was the main point of discussion at the NATO meeting on 4 and 5 December in Brussels. The American Secretary of State, William Rogers, gave the familiar warning that a large European conference would have an air of unreality. For Britain, Stewart suggested a study to show whether European security could best be dealt with in a conference or by some other method. Publicly, the ministers at last brought themselves to mention the proposal for a European conference directly. They said that 'careful advance preparation and prospects of concrete results' would be essential; and progress in bilateral and multilateral discussions already going on would 'improve the political atmosphere in Europe' and help to ensure the success of any eventual conference; the North American members of the alliance would of course take part.

The progress of Bonn's *Ostpolitik* during the early months of 1970 – and the fact that by this time Bonn had come to support the idea of a conference – made a further step seem possible when the NATO ministers met again in Rome on 26 May 1970. Yet another factor may have been the relatively good atmosphere at the American–Soviet SALT talks. For the first time, the American Secretary of State, Rogers, told the other NATO ministers that the time had come for a positive and favourable response to the idea of a European security conference. Stewart put forward a new British proposal, for a 'standing commission', perhaps in a neutral city, which would have the task of 'identifying' subjects for future negotiations, such as force reductions, freedom of movement, freedom of human relations, a code of conduct and cultural exchanges.

The British idea did not sound striking; but behind it was an effort to grapple in a sober practical way with the fundamental problem, for the West, of a European security conference. It was inevitable that, at such a conference, the West should go a long way towards meeting the Soviet demand for recognition of the *status quo* – a divided Europe – as lasting. But the West did not want the Soviet Union to use any Western concessions merely to tighten its grip on the East Europeans and rob them of all hope of a future in which they would have some degree of freedom, both national and individual. So the West wanted to get counter-concessions from the Soviet Union about greater freedom of movement, and of contacts of all kinds, between West and East in Europe. It also wanted to secure some assurance that acts such as the invasion of Czechoslovakia would never be repeated.

The Yalta agreement had shown the uselessness of documents which depended on the interpretation of such words as 'free' or 'democratic'. The practical problem of obtaining worthwhile concessions from the Soviet Union was therefore extremely difficult. One of the first essentials at any conference would be to get a clear and unambiguous definition of what it was going to discuss, as well as agreement on the range and scope of discussion. A 'standing commission' such as Stewart suggested could at least get on with this vital job, and could perhaps develop into a permanent body.

For the rest, the NATO ministers, at Rome, referred to Bonn's talks with the Soviet Union, Poland and East Germany, to the four-power talks on Berlin, and also to the SALT talks. They said that in so far as progress was recorded in all these various conversations, the allies 'would be ready to enter into multilateral contacts with all interested governments: one of the main purposes . . . would be to explore when it will be possible to convene a conference, or series of conferences, on European security and cooperation'. They also amplified their earlier proposals on mutual force reductions which, they said, had so far led to 'no meaningful reply'. (The Soviet line had been to suggest that these proposals belonged to the disarmament field, not a European security conference.)

The 'meaningful reply' soon came. Less than a month later the Warsaw Pact Foreign Ministers met in Budapest and took several steps forward. They specifically agreed that the United States and Canada should attend the European conference. They agreed that it would be useful to hold a number of European conferences; they accepted the British idea of setting up what they called 'an appropriate body of all interested countries on questions of security and cooperation in Europe'; this could be discussed at the conference. (The British had of course suggested a body which could have prepared for a conference as well as having a permanent job to do.) Finally, the Warsaw Pact ministers appeared to withdraw their earlier opposition to discussion of mutual force reductions: they would be ready to discuss the question of 'reducing foreign armed forces on the territory of European States'.

In the closing months of 1970, there seemed to be some cooling off on the Western side. This was because of doubts about Soviet willingness to make any real concessions. It was true that West Germany's treaties with the Soviet Union and Poland were very important steps forward. But in the four-power talks on improving the situation in Berlin, which had started in March, there had been very little progress; nor had there been any move forward in the contacts between West Germany and East Germany which had also begun earlier in the year. In both cases it seemed that Ulbricht's rigid inflexibility was the obstacle; Moscow seemed unable or unwilling to bend him, and the more isolated he became from his Warsaw Pact allies, the more he stiffened his attitudes. The Western powers had made the Berlin talks a test of Soviet good faith, and the Brandt Government had said it would not ask the West German Parliament to ratify the treaties with the Soviet Union and Poland until a Berlin settlement had been reached. So for the moment there was something of a deadlock.

The result was that when the Warsaw Pact leaders and the NATO ministers met simultaneously in the first week of December, there was a marked difference of approach to the proposed European security conference. The Warsaw Pact leaders declared that there was no reason to delay the summoning of a conference or to lay down advance conditions; however, they also said that they hoped for an outcome of the Berlin negotiations which would satisfy all parties. The NATO ministers welcomed the West German treaties with the Soviet Union and Poland but stressed the importance of reaching a Berlin settlement; as soon as the four-power talks had reached a satisfactory conclusion, they would be ready to start multilateral talks 'to explore when it would be possible to convene a conference, or a series of conferences, on security and cooperation in Europe'.

In Britain, there was no difference between the Conservative Government and the Labour Opposition over this insistence on the need for a Berlin agreement as a condition for a European security conference. In the foreign affairs debate of 9 December, Healey, for the Labour Party, said that only the readiness of the East Europeans to respond to the concrete evidence of good will offered by Bonn would justify the West in taking the risk of multilateral negotiations; if, as he hoped, there were progress on Berlin, then NATO should start talks with the Warsaw Pact and neutral countries with a view to holding a European security conference.

At the close of 1970, therefore, the main obstacle to a conference seemed to be Ulbricht's rigidity; progress depended on Brezhnev's readiness to soften him up. Brezhnev himself, in a speech at the end of November, sounded eager for a Berlin settlement which would satisfy all concerned, including the West Berliners. In spite of the rather cooler Western attitude, it looked as though the way was at last opening for a European security conference. There was no doubt that the East European governments wanted it: for most of them – particularly Rumania, but others too – it seemed to open up prospects for greater freedom in developing economic and other contacts with the West. Some degree of economic independence could lead in turn to some degree of political independence of the Soviet Union. This in turn might – whether the East European Communist leaders wanted it or not – lead to a little more freedom for the ordinary people of the East European countries.

The Soviet leaders of 1970 were most unlikely to relish such a prospect, even if, in return, they were to get some sort of Western recognition of the *status quo* in divided Europe. The best that could be hoped for was that they might come to admit to themselves that their existing relationship with their East European allies was unsatisfactory and precarious, and that a change would ultimately be necessary; they might then come to think that a European treaty, or series of agreements, or a 'standing commission' on security and cooperation between East and West, could provide a safer framework for an evolution of Soviet–East European relations than continued East–West tension and confrontation. If the Soviet leaders could not reach this level of maturity, then the conference would risk becoming an East–West diplomatic battle of the familiar kind.

For the West Europeans, a European security conference would provide the first serious test of their ability to merge their national policies in a joint policy which would be specifically European – independent of the United States though coordinated with American policy. If the West Europeans could do this, they could play a key role, collectively, at the conference. But their power to unite would depend greatly on the success or failure of the negotiations for expanding the Community of the Six to a Community of the Ten.

PART V

The balance-sheet of British
policy in Europe, 1945–70

23   The balance-sheet of British policy in Europe, 1945–70

The record of achievement and failure, in Britain's policy in a divided Europe, cannot be presented in the form of a simple balance-sheet. But certain items can be placed on one side or the other.

From 1942 onwards, responsible British politicians and officials identified two main tasks which they believed – correctly – that Britain must try to tackle. One was to halt the advance of Russian power westwards across Europe. The other was to build a West European alliance based on Anglo-French partnership, formed first with the immediate neighbours across the Channel, later on a wider basis. For both tasks, the British believed that American backing would be extremely important, but would not automatically be available; it would have to be sought with care and skill. In both tasks, British interests were – correctly – seen as identical with a wider European interest. In neither case could Britain act effectively alone. It could only act with close and willing partners.

Up to 1950 the British achievement, in carrying out both these tasks, was important. It was true that no means were found to reverse the fortunes of Hitler's war which had brought Soviet armies into the heart of Europe. But at least Churchill, Eden, Attlee and Bevin all understood the danger to the European peoples of Russia's instinct to expand – the almost unthinking instinct of a vast land power to stretch out in search of richer soil, warmer climates, sea outlets – or, in modern times, more highly-developed industrial areas. They at least tried to build some sort of emergency barriers which would set a limit to this expansion. As for the countries which were engulfed in the Soviet advance, the British at least bore witness to their historical and legal right to sovereign and independent statehood, and to the falsity of the myth of their spontaneous conversion to communism as a political creed. This could hardly be called a positive achievement, but in a longer-term perspective, it could prove to have had a real and lasting significance for their national survival.

Although the Dunkirk Treaty of 1947 turned out to be too fragile a basis for Anglo-French partnership, it promised well at the time.

Britain in a divided Europe

The West European alliance was achieved through the Brussels Treaty and the creation of Western Union in 1948; American backing was pledged in the following year through the Atlantic Pact. The British saw this West European alliance not just as an end in itself, but as a beginning of a deeper and wider union. Bevin told Acheson at the time of the signing of the Atlantic Pact that he hoped that arrangements under the Brussels Treaty could 'include a cabinet for Western Europe', and that he would like to see Germany brought in.[1] But in spite of Acheson's assurances to the contrary, the West European alliance created by Bevin was swallowed up in the American-led NATO and its chance of developing into a political union vanished too, as the initiative passed to the hands of the 'federalists' and 'supra-nationalists' of the Six. Bevin had also hoped that the OEEC, created as an emergency body to use American aid to stave off economic collapse, would develop into a permanent body for West European economic cooperation. This hope too was disappointed, again because the initiative passed to the Six.

Both the Western Union, created by the Brussels Treaty, and the OEEC would in fact have been capable of further development, and both had in fact done useful work before they were superseded. The British should perhaps have foreseen that they would be squeezed out. They always underestimated the enthusiasm and drive of the group of political leaders in Western Europe who, backed by many young people, wanted a much more closely welded and more formal West European Union than anything the British were themselves willing to join. The British could not share this enthusiasm, partly because their own experience of war had been less psychologically shattering than that of the mainland Europeans, partly because of their naturally slow-moving, cautious approach to novel political experiments (unless invented by themselves), and above all because of their sincere belief that the Commonwealth was a very valuable institution – valuable not just in terms of narrow British interest, but in terms of world peace and stability.

Although there were undoubtedly some nostalgic imperialists in Britain in the post-war era, the more general British idea of the Commonwealth was something bigger and better than a desire to cling on to power and prestige. It may have been unrealistic, it may have contained an element of emotional self-indulgence, but it was not narrowly selfish and it was certainly not anti-European. In any case the Commonwealth existed and continued to exist as more and more of its component parts achieved independent statehood and chose to remain inside it. In these circumstances it would have been a strangely irresponsible and destructive act for Britain to try to dissolve it. Britain would have to wait until it dissolved itself – if that time came.

The basic problem, in the long term, was the economic one. Britain was too small and weak, after the 1939–45 war, to supply the economic aid which the newly independent countries badly needed, and expected. On the other hand, for Britain, the traditional pattern of trade with the Commonwealth could not provide the basis for rapid economic growth and the prosperity which could have made it possible for Britain to help the developing Commonwealth countries more generously. Yet Britain could not destroy this traditional pattern of trade without harm to itself and without much more serious damage to some of the Commonwealth countries, especially such countries as New Zealand or Jamaica or Mauritius. The dilemma was a difficult one; and though the trade pattern changed a good deal during the 1960s, the problem was still there in 1970.

The Commonwealth was therefore a reality not a myth, a serious British responsibility and not just a relic of former grandeur. There was no real need why the Commonwealth should have formed a barrier between Britain and Western Europe. The difficulty was that both the supranationalists who created the Communities of the Six, and the Americans who backed them so strongly, refused to see the Commonwealth as anything but a British excuse for backsliding and reluctance to swallow the health-giving medicine of supranationalism. The Americans, too, were traditional believers in the bogey of British imperialism.

Perhaps if the British had tried rather harder to understand the genuine enthusiasm and idealism of the West European 'supranationalists', and if the 'supranationalists' had tried rather harder to understand the reality of the Commonwealth – and, perhaps, if the Americans had not backed the one side quite so hard against the other – the gulf between Britain and the 'supranationalists' need never have opened up. As things were, in the whole complex situation there was certainly a considerable element of British failure.

Yet if Britain failed to create the kind of West European political union of which Bevin had dreamed, the 'supranationalists' also failed to create the political union of which they had dreamed. Britain was sometimes also held responsible for this second failure. The argument was that, because of the shock of the war experience, there was a mood in Western Europe in the early post-war years which offered a unique chance of a great leap forward to a 'United States of Europe'; that this mood and chance might never come again; and that Britain's dead hand blighted the hope and warped and stunted the growth of the Community of the Six.

The main answer to this charge was that the 'supranationalists' seemed, in practice, to be toughened by the cold water Britain threw over their plans, rather than weakened by it. A more serious charge was that the British Conservative leaders, by the enthusiasm which they showed for the cause of a United States of Europe when they were in opposition, raised false hopes and created general confusion about the real British attitude. It was not surprising if the 'supranationalists' believed that things would change once the Conservatives came back to power. It was also unfortunate that the 'European' question became a matter of dispute between the British political parties; this, together with other unlucky circumstances, made the Labour Government even more unfriendly towards the first moves of the Six than they would otherwise have been.

One result of this confusion over Britain's position was that the 'supranationalists' never seem to have faced squarely the question whether they wanted Britain 'in' sufficiently to allow it some sort of special position which would make allowance for its Commonwealth connection and its national idiosyncrasies, on Churchill's 'with' but not 'of' formula (see above, p. 5). But admittedly it would have been very difficult for them to reach agreement among themselves on this important question of principle.

The British on their side never examined dispassionately exactly what it was they felt they could not swallow in the 'supranationalist' version of a West European union, as it was embodied in the Community of the Six. There were in fact three things: the system of (eventual) majority voting among member governments; a supranational bureaucracy, or civil service, over which the British Government and Parliament would have only very remote control; and a moral commitment to work for a West European federation as the final goal. A cynical political leader would perhaps have accepted these things at the start, confident that they could easily be evaded or blocked in practice. But many responsible people in Britain felt that, as Lord Strang said in 1960, this would be dishonest. It certainly would not have been possible to explain such a policy convincingly to Parliament or the general public, or to the Commonwealth – even though, during the 1960s, both Macmillan and Wilson came close to doing exactly that.

What had happened by then was that France, under de Gaulle, had begun to demonstrate that these obstacles were not to be taken seriously; whatever the provisions of the Rome Treaty, their ultimate interpretation rested with the member governments; if necessary, with a single member government. The apparent ease with which de Gaulle, and later Pompidou, disposed of 'supranationalism' raised the question of whether underneath Britain's honesty and scruples there might not have been a deeper and more instinctive fear of loss of freedom and submission to alien control. If so, then this fear existed in other countries than Britain. It was strong in France, and could be seen from time to time even in such 'European-minded' people as the Dutch and Belgians. The British might, however, have done more to take out this fear and examine it in the cold light of day, to see how far it was compatible with acceptance of military integration in NATO or Macmillan's theory of 'interdependence'.

As for the charge that Britain cast a blight on the development of the Community of the Six, de Gaulle should surely bear a bigger and more direct responsibility in the matter. If he had been willing to accept the supranational method, the Six would certainly have made progress towards political union without bothering about Britain. It was his rejection of supranationalism which made the Dutch and Belgians resist political advance without Britain, and gave substance to George Ball's remark that Britain, outside the Community, was a force for division, since it was like a great lodestone drawing with unequal degrees of force on each member state.

Another thing which did unquestionably stunt the growth of the European Community was the Anglo-French rivalry which reached foolish lengths during de Gaulle's time. The French, perhaps unconsciously, found it very hard to forgive the British for what they saw as the latter's good fortune in escaping conquest and occupation, and sitting in the councils of the highest war leaders in the 1939–45 war. Britain was still paying for this good fortune during the 1960s. Until the debt had been paid off and forgotten, there was not much Britain could do to end the rivalry, even if British psychological blunders or clumsiness were unhelpful. In itself, the Anglo-French rivalry had very little sense, unless it was assumed that within a West

European group, there had to be one single dominant power. In any case, by the end of the 1960s, neither Britain nor France was capable of dominating a West European community, whether of Six or of Ten. In economic terms, West Germany was more likely to play the dominant role if it so wished; luckily, it did not seem to have this wish.

As for Britain's 'special relationship' with the United States, this always seemed a rather artificial barrier between Britain and the Community of the Six. The British themselves were partly to blame in clinging to the idea of a privileged position among the West European allies when it was no longer acceptable to those allies. Yet the 'special relationship' was never entirely one-sided; the United States itself could never make up its mind whether it really wanted to end it once and for all. The idea of Britain as America's Trojan Horse inside the European citadel was fanciful. Most of the Six had just the same assessment as the British of the importance of their relationship with the United States; they did not want to reject this relationship, only to establish a better balance within it.

By the end of the 1960s, it looked as though the various West European problems, and the problem of the relationship between Western Europe and the United States, would solve themselves in time through a process of argument, negotiation and mutual adjustment. These methods would not necessarily solve the much more difficult problems of East–West relations in Europe, and of the relationship between the Soviet Union and its East European allies. A united Western Europe would not automatically find it easier to establish friendlier relations and easier contacts with Eastern Europe – whatever the optimistic but unsubstantiated forecasts of British political leaders in the 1960s. Economic and political unity in Western Europe could produce Soviet counter-moves aimed at creating even greater unity in the East. 'Unity' in that context could only mean a greater degree of Soviet political and economic control.

This was a real danger. On the other hand, the lesson of Hungary in 1956, of Czechoslovakia in 1968, of Tito's successful stand in 1948 and of the successful Rumanian assertion of partial independence in the 1960s was that the Soviet techniques of control were so crude and inefficient that in the last resort, only full-scale military force would work. Where, for one reason or another, the Soviet Union did not want to use armed force, the techniques of control failed. Therefore it would be a difficult problem for the Soviet Union, in practice, to establish tighter control over the East Europeans, short of new acts of military intervention which would put at risk the tentative Soviet–American understanding, at the superpower level, and the East–West détente in Europe, at a lower level, which Moscow seemed seriously to want – at least at the start of the 1970s.

There was therefore some chance of combining progress to West European unity with an easing of East–West tension and a lowering of East–West barriers in Europe. A particular weakness of the Soviet-East European relationship was its economic aspect. If West Europeans disliked some things in the American way of life and sometimes resented American economic penetration, at least, to them, America was the bringer of riches and prosperity. East Europeans found the Soviet way of life alien and unnatural; their belief in Communism, Soviet-style, was only skin-deep, if it existed at all; but above all, the Soviet Union was not the bringer of riches, but rather the overlord which barred the way to riches. This was something which the Soviet Union had literally done, when it stopped the East European states from taking up the American offer of Marshall aid in 1947. Since then, its various efforts to promote economic integration between itself and the East Europeans, through Comecon, had come against the hard fact that what the East Europeans really wanted, and needed, was greater economic contact with the West, not tighter links with the Soviet economy. The Rumanians had found the way towards contact with the West; the Hungarians were quietly and unobtrusively finding the way; the East Germans benefited from their special freedom to trade with West Germany. Czechoslovakia was moving in the same direction up until the 1968 invasion. For all of them, given their political and economic system and the post-war pattern of dependence on the Soviet Union, it was a slow, complicated and difficult process.

For the West Europeans, this situation offered an obvious opening. Even if their trade with Eastern Europe was unimportant in the context of their total trade with the outside world – somewhere around one-twentieth – nevertheless the benefits of expanding it, even modestly, were likely to be great. Quite apart from improving relations between the East and West European countries themselves, it would help to remove or lessen some of the tensions in relations between the Soviet Union and the East Europeans. There would be many pitfalls, because the leaders of the Soviet Union might at any moment take fright at their own boldness in allowing even small freedoms to the East Europeans. But a long process might be started which could in the long run be irreversible, undoing some of the harm done to Europe by the 1939–45 war, and restoring the East Europeans to a wider European community. Even if in 1970 the prospect seemed very remote, what the British had done between 1945 and 1970 could on the whole be seen as leading in the general direction of that far-off goal.

De Gaulle once described Britain as 'anxious and melancholy in the middle of the evolving universe', feeling its situation to be unjust and alarming. This was hardly the way in which the British themselves would have described their prevailing mood during the years between 1945 and 1970. But it was true that they felt that it was no longer possible for them to chart a precise course with reasonable certainty of reaching the hoped-for destination. Britain was too likely to be blown off course by political or economic squalls at home or by bigger international storms or contrary winds. There was no doubt that from the late 1950s onwards a remarkably persistent contrary wind was blowing from the France of de Gaulle.

But it was not only Britain which could not be sure of following a clear course to a planned goal. Other West European countries also found themselves in the middle of an evolving 'universe', exposed to economic and political uncertainties at home and uncontrollable outside events. The East Europeans were in varying degrees at the mercy of the whims of Moscow or palace revolutions inside the Kremlin. The pattern of European affairs in the post-war period was complicated and confusing and contained many random elements. All that any European country could do was to have a general will to move in a given general direction. The British could at least feel that within the limits of their heritage from the past and their human fallibility, they had tried to be good neighbours and to work for wider European interests than their own.

Notes

Part I

1 Konrad Adenauer, *Memoirs 1945–1953*, p. 388.
2 Sir Anthony Eden, *Memoirs: Full Circle*, p. 36.
3 Charles de Gaulle, *War Memoirs: Salvation 1944–1946*, documents, p. 99.
4 Adenauer, *Memoirs*, p. 388.
5 *The European Inheritance*, edited by Barker, Clark and Vaucher, vol. III, p. 18.
6 Charles de Gaulle, *Mémoires d'Espoir: Le Renouveau 1958–1962*, French edition, p. 179.
7 Lord Strang, *Britain in World Affairs: Henry VIII to Elizabeth II*, pp. 359–60.
8 De Gaulle, *Mémoires d'Espoir: Le Renouveau*, French edition, p. 198.
9 Francis Williams, *A Prime Minister Remembers*, pp. 42–3.
10 Sir Anthony Eden, *Memoirs: The Reckoning*, pp. 372 *et seq.*
11 ibid., pp. 397–8.
12 Winston Churchill, *The Second World War*, vol. VI, pp. 308–9.
13 Churchill, *The Second World War*, vol. VI, p. 222.
14 Strang, *Britain in World Affairs*, p. 325.
15 W. N. Medlicott, *British Foreign Policy since Versailles*, p. 239.
16 Eden, *The Reckoning*, pp. 289–99.
17 ibid., p. 318.
18 ibid., pp. 323–4.
19 ibid., pp. 404–5.
20 ibid., p. 439.
21 ibid., p. 459.
22 Churchill, *The Second World War*, vol. VI, p. 131.
23 ibid., p. 439.
24 ibid., pp. 498–9.
25 ibid., p. 522.
26 US Department of State, *Foreign Relations of the United States: Diplomatic Papers, 1945*, vol. IV, p. 483, pp. 496–7, p. 509, quoted in *International Affairs*, London, July 1970, p. 531.
27 Churchill, *The Second World War*, vol. VI, p. 414.
28 Eden, *The Reckoning*, p. 374.
29 Williams, *A Prime Minister Remembers*, pp. 51–2.

Part II

1 Williams, *A Prime Minister Remembers*, pp. 70 *et seq.*
2 Milovan Djilas, *Conversations with Stalin*, pp. 22–3.
3 Churchill, *The Second World War*, vol. VI, p. 488.
4 Dean Acheson, *Present at the Creation*, p. 122.

Notes

5 Francis Williams, *Ernest Bevin*, p. 251.
6 Williams, *A Prime Minister Remembers*, p. 160.
7 Sir Ivone Kirkpatrick, *The Inner Circle*, p. 205.
8 Williams, *A Prime Minister Remembers*, p. 155.
9 Acheson, *Present at the Creation*, p. 341.
10 Adenauer, *Memoirs 1945–1953*, pp. 267 et seq.
11 Kirkpatrick, *The Inner Circle*, pp. 238 et seq.
12 Adenauer, *Memoirs 1945–1953*, pp. 272–3.
13 Acheson, *Present at the Creation*, p. 440.
14 Michael R. Gordon, *Conflict and Consensus in Labour's Foreign Policy 1944–1965*, p. 182.
15 Williams, *Ernest Bevin*, pp. 262–3.
16 Acheson, *Present at the Creation*, p. 217.
17 ibid., p. 266.
18 ibid,. p. 284.
19 ibid., p. 493.
20 Political and Economic Planning, *European Unity – A Survey of the European Organisations*, pp. 83–4.
21 Adenauer, *Memoirs 1945–1953*, p. 384.
22 Eden, *Memoirs: Full Circle*, p. 30.
23 George Ball, *The Discipline of Power*, p. 73.
24 Lord Gladwyn, *De Gaulle's Europe, or Why the General Says No*, pp. 10–11.
25 Adenauer, *Memoirs 1945–1953*, p. 338.
26 Acheson, *Present at the Creation*, p. 387.
27 Medlicott, *British Foreign Policy since Versailles 1919–1963*, p. 273.
28 Williams, *A Prime Minister Remembers*, p. 236.
29 Acheson, *Present at the Creation*, p. 484.
30 ibid., p. 323.
31 Williams, *A Prime Minister Remembers*. p. 171.

Part III

1 Piers Dixon, *Double Diploma, The Life of Sir Pierson Dixon, Don and Diplomat*, p. 278.
2 Acheson, *Present at the Creation*, pp. 458–9.
3 Harold Macmillan, *Tides of Fortune 1945–1955*, p. 220.
4 Acheson, *Present at the Creation*, pp. 598–9.
5 Kirkpatrick, *The Inner Circle*, p. 261.
6 Eden, *Memoirs: Full Circle*, p. 358.
7 Sir William Hayter, *The Kremlin and the Embassy*, p. 139.
8 Eden, *Memoirs: Full Circle*, p. 443.
9 ibid., p. 452.
10 ibid., pp. 541–2.
11 Hayter, *The Kremlin and the Embassy*, p. 143.
12 ibid., p. 152–3.
13 De Gaulle, *Mémoires d'Espoir: Le Renouveau 1958–1962*, French edition, p. 234.

14 Political and Economic Planning, *Growth in the British Economy*, p. 150.
15 ibid., p. 168.
16 Eden, *Memoirs: Full Circle*, p. 174.
17 Miriam Camps, *Britain and the European Community 1955–63*, p. 28.
18 ibid., pp. 43–5.
19 T. S. Hutchison, *Economics and Economic Policy in Britain 1946–1966*, p. 170.
20 Camps, *Britain and the European Community 1955–1963*, pp. 49–50.
21 Macmillan, *Tides of Fortune 1945–1955*, p. 466 and elsewhere.
22 Harold Macmillan, *Riding the Storm 1955–1959*, p. 437.
23 ibid., p. 444.
24 Acheson, *Present at the Creation*, p. 552.
25 De Gaulle, *Mémoires d'Espoir: Le Renouveau 1958–1962*, French edition, pp. 214–5.
26 De Gaulle, *Mémoires d'Espoir: Le Renouveau 1958–1962*, French edition, p. 199.
27 Macmillan, *Riding the Storm 1955–1959*, pp. 449–50.
28 De Gaulle, *Mémoires d'Espoir: Le Renouveau 1958–1962*, French edition, pp. 188–9.
29 Macmillan, *Riding the Storm 1955–1959*, p. 453.
30 ibid., p. 455.
31 ibid., p. 455.
32 De Gaulle, *Mémoires d'Espoir: Le Renouveau 1958–1962*, French edition, p. 190.

Part IV

1 Ball, *The Discipline of Power*, pp. 78–81.
2 William Pickles, *Not with Europe, – the Political Case for Staying Out*, Fabian International Bureau, p. 35.
3 Dixon, *Double Diploma*, p. 287.
4 Harold Wilson, *Purpose in Politics*, p. 113.
5 Ball, *The Discipline of Power*, p. 85.
6 Dixon, *Double Diploma*, p. 295, p. 300.
7 ibid., p. 287.
8 Gladwyn, *De Gaulle's Europe or Why the General says No*, pp. 76–77.
9 ibid., p. 72.
10 Dixon, *Double Diploma*, pp. 279 et seq.
11 De Gaulle, *Mémoires d'Espoir: Le Renouveau 1958–1962*, French edition, pp. 230–32.
12 Wolf Mendel, *Deterrence and Persuasion*, pp. 29–30.
13 Kirkpatrick, *The Inner Circle*, p. 261.
14 *International Affairs*, London, July 1965, p. 412.
15 Ball, *The Discipline of Power*, p. 103.
16 ibid., p. 105.
17 ibid., p. 106.

Notes

18 *International Affairs*, London, April 1965, p. 202.
19 *Le Monde*, 25 June 1970.
20 *Le Monde*, 30 June 1970.
21 *Le Monde*, 13 March 1970.
22 *Le Monde*, 27 May 1970.
23 *Le Monde*, 27 June 1970.
24 *Le Monde*, 3 February 1970.

Part V

1 Acheson, *Present at the Creation*, p. 287.

Select bibliography

Part I

Winston Churchill, *The Second World War*, especially vol. VI, Cassell, 1954.

Sir Anthony Eden, *Memoirs: The Reckoning*, Cassell, 1965.

Charles de Gaulle, *War Memoirs: Salvation 1944–46*, Weidenfeld & Nicolson, 1960.

W. N. Medlicott, *British Foreign Policy since Versailles 1919–1963*, 2nd edition, Methuen, 1968. (Also for Parts II and III.)

W. N. Medlicott, *Contemporary England 1914–1962*, Longmans, 1967.

Survey of International Affairs 1939–1946: Hitler's Europe, edited by Arnold Toynbee and Veronica M. Toynbee, OUP, 1954.

The European Inheritance, vol. III, edited by Barker, Clark and Vaucher, OUP, 1954.

David Thomson, *Europe since Napoleon*, Penguin, 1966.

Part II

Dean Acheson, *Present at the Creation*, Hamish Hamilton, 1970. (Also for Part III.)

Konrad Adenauer, *Memoirs 1945–1953*, Weidenfeld & Nicolson, 1966.

Alan Bullock, *The Life and Times of Ernest Bevin*, vol. II: *Minister of Labour 1940–1945*, Heinemann, 1967.

Michael R. Gordon, *Conflict and Consensus in Labour's Foreign Policy 1945–1965*, Stanford University Press, 1969. (Also for Part III.)

Sir Ivone Kirkpatrick, *The Inner Circle*, Macmillan, 1959. (Also for Part III.)

Harold Macmillan, *Tides of Fortune 1945–1955*, Macmillan, 1969. (Also for Part III.)

F. S. Northedge, *British Foreign Policy – the Process of Readjustment 1945–1961*, Allen & Unwin, 1962. (Also for Part III.)

Political and Economic Planning, *European Unity – a Survey of the European Organisations*, Allen & Unwin, 1968. (Also for Part III.)

Francis Williams, *A Prime Minister Remembers*, Heinemann, 1961.

Francis Williams, *Ernest Bevin*, Hutchinson, 1952.

Part III

Miriam Camps, *Britain and the European Community 1955–1963*, OUP, 1964. (Also essential for Part IV.)

Sir Anthony Eden, *Memoirs: Full Circle*, Cassell, 1960.

Charles de Gaulle, *Mémoires d'Espoir: Le Renouveau 1958–1962*, French edition: Plon, 1970. (Also for Part IV.)

Select bibliography

Sir William Hayter, *The Kremlin and the Embassy*, Hodder & Stoughton, 1966.

Harold Macmillan, *Riding the Storm 1955-1959*, Macmillan, 1971.

Political and Economic Planning, *Growth in the British Economy*, Allen & Unwin, 1960.

C. M. Woodhouse, *Post-War Britain*, The Bodley Head, 1966. (Also for Part IV.)

Part IV

George Ball, *The Discipline of Power*, Little, Brown & Company, 1968.

Piers Dixon, *Double Diploma, the Life of Sir Pierson Dixon, Don and Diplomat*, Hutchinson, 1968.

Lord Gladwyn, *De Gaulle's Europe, or Why the General Says No*, Secker & Warburg, 1969.

Wolf Mendel, *French Nuclear Armament in the Context of National Policy 1945-1969*, Faber, 1970.

Dorothy Pickles, *The Fifth French Republic*, Methuen, 1960.

Dorothy Pickles, *The Uneasy Entente*, OUP, 1966.

Harold Wilson, *Purpose in Politics*, Weidenfeld & Nicolson, 1964.

Note: for most of the period and most aspects of it, very useful articles are to be found in *International Affairs* (Royal Institute of International Affairs, Quarterly).

Index

(*Note: only those biographical facts are recorded which are relevant to the book*)

Index

Index

Morrison, Herbert (Baron) (Foreign Secretary 1951), 4, 5, 19, 101, 109
Munich agreement, 12–13, 25–80, 265
Mussolini, Benito, 12

Nagy, Imre (Hungarian Prime Minister 1956), 130
Napoleon, 3, 10, 154, 158, 169
Nasser, Gamal Abdel, 129, 134
NATO (North Atlantic Treaty Organisation), and Germany, 57, 62; and Western Union, 68, 292; Truman on, 70; Atlantic Pact signed, 71, 292; and EDC plan 106–7, 109–11, 114; and Western European Union, 116–7; Soviet Union proposes joining, 125; non-aggression treaty with Warsaw Pact mooted, 125; Khrushchev on, 127; and atomic weapons, 136; British spending on, 146–7; and European political union, 180–1; dependence on US, 186, 193, 195, 201–2, 204, 210; British nuclear force committed to, 196, 206; French naval units withdrawn from, 197; and 'flexible response' doctrine, 198, 214; and MLF project, 195, 197, 199–200; and ANF project, 200, 206; and Nuclear Planning Group, 201; French partial withdrawal from, 201, 213, 222, 281; and 'European' or 'Anglo-French' deterrent, 203–10; and 'European defence identity', 212–6; and British 'East of Suez' policy, 212–3, 215; Nixon's pledge on US troops for, 216; de Gaulle's view of, 234; and West German *Ostpolitik*, 261; and invasion of Czechoslovakia, 275–8; and European security conference, 279–87
Nehru, Pandit Jawarhalal, 137
New Zealand, and British approach to EEC, 175, 177, 183, 228, 293
Nigeria, 178
Nixon, Richard (US Vice-President 1953–61; President 1969–), 130, 201–2, 214, 253, 267
Norway, and Soviet-Finnish war, 26; Soviet pressure on, 70; joins NATO, 71; American bases in, 108; joins EFTA, 160–1; and EEC, 225, 229, 244
Novotny, Antonin (Czechoslovak President 1957–68), 258, 272
Nuclear deterrent, British, *see* H-bomb
Nuclear non-proliferation treaty, 165, 206–7, 251, 256
Nuclear test ban treaty, 165, 255–6

Organisation for Economic Co-operation and Development (OECD), formed, 161
Organisation for European Economic Cooperation (OEEC), 3, 74, 77, 103; set up, 79; working of, 80; disappears, 80; British hopes of, 152, 292; and negotiations for European Free Trade Area, 153–60
Ormsby-Gore, David (Lord Harlech) (British Ambassador to US 1961–5), 194
Ottawa conference 1932, 149
Ottoman empire, 11

Pakistan, 177
Paul, Prince Regent of Yugoslavia, 23
Peter, King of Yugoslavia, 23–4
Petkov, Nikola (Bulgarian Agrarian leader 1945–7), 45–6
Pickles, William, 174
Pleven, René (French Prime Minister 1950–1, 1951–2, Foreign Minister 1958), 84, 106–7, 158
Poher, Alain, 239
Poland, Anglo-French pledge to, 13; in Battle of Britain, 18; British obligations to, 22; con-

Index

Soviet Union, treaty with Britain, 21, 26–7, 108; denounced, 117; 1939 negotiations with Britain, 25; war with Finland, 26; British fears of, 27, 29, 291; 'percentage agreement' with Britain, 29, 276; Churchill on, 40; aims in Eastern Europe, 42, 44; British post-war policy towards, 53–5, 291; and Marshall aid, 77, 297; sets up Cominform and Comecon, 77; aims in Mediterranean, 97, 129, 212, 251; anti-Western propaganda, 98; differences with West over Germany, 56–60, 103–15, 117–8; forms Warsaw Pact, 117–8; and British 'summitry', 119–23, 128, 135–6, 143–4; and European security conference, 123–5, 279–87; Soviet leaders in London, 128–9, 254–5, 264, 268; and Suez crisis, 129–34; and Hungarian uprising, 130–4; in Berlin crisis, 137–44; Macmillan visit to, 139–41; nuclear threat from, 193; concludes non-proliferation treaty, 207; dialogue with US, 249–53; in SALT talks, 8, 202, 211, 252; signs treaty with West Germany, 259–60, 286; dislikes EEC, 264–5; improved British relations with, 267–9; London–Moscow 'hot line', 268; British trade policy towards, 269–71; Czechoslovakia, invasion of, see Czechoslovakia

Spaak, Paul-Henri (President of Consultative Assembly of Council of Europe 1949–51, Belgian Foreign Minister 1954–7), 85, 151–4

Spain, 78

Springer, Axel, 259

Stalin, Josef Vissarionovich, 7, 10, 14, 21–2, 26–30, 32, 40–5, 50, 71–2, 77, 98, 113, 119, 132, 143–4, 276

Sterling balances, 53, 228–9, 247

Stewart, Michael (Foreign Secretary 1965–6, 1968–70), 174, 218, 232–3, 256, 265–6, 283–5

Strang, Lord (William) (Permanent Under-Secretary Foreign Office 1949–53), 14, 25, 119, 169, 294

Strauss, Franz Josef (West German Defence Minister 1956–62, Finance Minister 1966–9), 204, 235

Suez, British base, 97, 100; crisis, 97, 102, 129–35; and Hungarian uprising, 130–4; impact on Commonwealth, 165; Canal closed, 224

Summitry, Churchill initiates, 120–4: Geneva meeting, 124–8, 138; Anglo-Soviet summit 1956, 128–9; Macmillan revives, 141–2; Paris meeting 1960, 142

Sweden, and Soviet-Finnish war, 26; and EFTA, 160–1; and EEC, 225

Switzerland, British trade with, 149; and EFTA, 160–1; and EEC, 225

Syria, 22, 24

Teheran conference 1943, 30

Thomson, George (Minister of State Foreign Office 1964–6, Chancellor of Duchy of Lancaster 1966–7, 1969–70), 220, 243

Tito, Marshal, 24, 42, 49–50, 98, 132, 296

Trieste, 31; post-war dispute and settlement, 50

Truman, Harry S. (US President 1945–53), 31–2, 51, 53, 62, 69, 89–91, 106, 148, 188

Truman doctrine, 69, 71

Turkey, British aid ended, 69; Truman doctrine on, 69; Soviet pressure on, 70; joins NATO, 71

Ulbricht, Walter (East German Communist leader), 140, 250,

Index